Bridge and Lagoon, Glen Oak Park, Peoria, Ill.

Flower Beds in Bradley

...er, Landing at Dock, Peoria, Ill.

POST CARD

THIS SPACE FOR WRITING

THIS SPACE FOR THE ADDRESS

PEORIA, ILL.
JUN 4
5 30 PM
1909

U.S. POSTAGE
ONE CENT

Miss Mable Powell.
Mendota
Ill.

Germany

PEORIA!

To Kay
with Best wishes for Christmas
From Peoria!

Jerry Klein, Dec. 1985

Published by Visual Communications, Inc. in cooperation with the Peoria Historical Society.

Written by

Jerry Klein

2

"My history has been composed to be an everlasting possession, not the showpiece of an hour." — Thucydides

"If men could learn from history, what lessons it might teach us! But passion and party blind our eyes, and the light which experience gives is a lantern on the stern, which shines only on the waves behind us!" — Samuel Taylor Coleridge

History, whether it deals with a nation, a civilization, a war or a city, must by its nature be selective and subjective. The alternative is a bewildering and unreadable compilation of names and dates, minutes of meetings, details and minutiae which is both undigestible and unreadable.

The major purpose of this new history, "Peoria", is to rekindle an interest in a city whose rich and colorful past has largely been obliterated, forgotten or dismissed as unimportant.

It is intended to create a sense of pride in this very old and very typical and yet very unique American urban center, and to inspire further investigation into a past that is as colorful and illuminating as that of almost any city in the New World.

This Peoria has existed in one form or another for over 300 years. Its story deserves another, hopefully fascinating telling.

I wish to dedicate this book to my children - Jerry, Jeff, Lisa, Marilou, Jim, Jeanne and Barb - to my parents and to my wife for giving me a special awareness of the past, an appreciation-for the present and a hope for the future.

Visual Communications, Inc.
Publisher

Andrew L. McDonald
E. Lawrence McDonald
Project Coordinators

Jeffery P. Van Echaute
Margaret A. Cordell
Designers

Regina Nagle
Production

Nancy M. Buckrop
Business Manager

ISBN 0-9615759-0-5

VISUAL COMMUNICATIONS, INC.
423 - FIRST NATIONAL BANK BLDG.
PEORIA, ILLINOIS 61206

PRINTED IN THE UNITED STATES OF AMERICA.

FIRST PRINTING: NOVEMBER 1985

The author wishes first of all to express his appreciation for the work and patience of his wife, Mary, whose exhaustive research, inspiration and computer expertise has been invaluable. Further thanks are due to the members of the Reference Department of the Peoria Public Library, notably Carolann Purcell; and to the personnel of the Special Collections Center at Bradley University's Cullom-Davis Library, expecially to Chuck Frey and Sherri Schneider. To Lee Roten, photographer and historian, a special thanks is tendered for his skill, promptness, and counsel. Also a debt of gratitude is due to the F-Stop Society for its generosity in lending its valuable historical collection.

And to the Peoria Historical Society special appreciation is extended for making this volume possible. Unless otherwise specified, all photographs are from the Historical Society's extensive collection.

A book of this nature cannot be produced without the support of local businesses, and a very special thanks is extended to Heidi Klingelhofer, who represented this book to those businessmen when the volume itself was little more than a concept.

James Daken, Peoria City Manager, and John T. McConnell of the PEORIA JOURNAL STAR were most supportive of the project in its earliest days, and additional thanks are due to the Journal Star's Howard Alexander, David Auer, Colette Colgan and Liz Baum for their help in typesetting the text. Robert Long and Cindy Bruhn of Typefaces, Inc., made considerable contributions as well.

The publisher expresses gratitude as well to Marilyn Walker and Aldene Becker for their assistance during the project; to Ann Hunzeker who served as an invaluable consultant in this computer age, and to Martha Burkart who provided invaluable editorial advice.

Many of these were among the first people to catch the vision of what this book might be.

The publisher and author as well gratefully acknowledge the assistance of the Peoria Historical Society's Research Board - Robert A. Jones, chairman, John Austin, E. James Bambrick, Glenn M. Belcke, William Bowers, L. Sidney Eslinger, Charles Frey, Merle Glick, Robert K. Middleton, Russell Peters, Sherri Hinton Schneider, Georganna Tucker and Karl Wheatley.

These and many others, living or dead, former or present Peorians are also present in these pages in a very special way.

4

It is no accident that many of the world's most historic, romantic, and beautiful cities are located on rivers. Mention Paris, London, Rome, Vienna, Budapest, Prague, or Cologne and there are the rivers - the Seine, the Thames, the Tiber, the Danube, the Moldau, the Rhine.

There are quite logical reasons, of course, such as transportation or even mere scenic splendor and accessibility. People have always been drawn to rivers even though they may flood in the springtime and, these days, carry unbearable amounts of pollution, chemicals and sediment.

It does not matter. The old men still fish in the Seine at Paris. And in Vienna, the strains of "The Beautiful Blue Danube" still echo along the Prater, even though that river's color may be no more than a myth.

These rivers have served as ancient transmission lines for settlers, invaders, commerce.

As men have always been attracted to rivers, so did they come to the site of Peoria. The Illinois River with its two lakes and surrounding dramatic bluffs is perhaps one of the loveliest of all the world's river valleys. "We have seen nothing like this in all our travels," wrote Father Marquette of his 1673 passage through here.

A SIDEWHEELER CHURNS NORTHWARD PAST THE UPPER FREE BRIDGE AND INTO THE NARROWS, THE "DETROIT" OF THE FRENCH.

Over two hundred years later, Theodore Roosevelt looked across the river valley from what is now Grand View Drive and called it "The World's Most Beautiful Drive." It remains a magnificent spectacle, astonishing people who have travelled throughout the world and have seen nothing more beautiful in all their journeys.

The gaze falls across wide, fertile bottomlands, thickly wooded bluffs and the endless prairie beyond. Here is Peoria, nestled at the south end of the Peoria lakes, the "fond du lac" of the French, and the northern shore remains almost unchanged from the days when Father Marquette paddled into this "Pimiteoui," this "fat lake."

First, of course, the lower orders arrived. That great chain of natural events unfolded slowly: from fish to birds to animals to men, with water as the catalyst. The civilization that grew on this spot was almost inevitable.

For the Indians, the magnet was water. Water to drink. Water abounding with fish. Water which attracted animals of all varieties and birds of amazing diversity. There was sustenance and life in the river. It was and is an artery, vital and surging, life-giving and endlessly fascinating.

Then came the French in their Indian-paddled canoes, spreading a civilization and a faith along these watery arteries, leaving lost forts and forgotten martyrs in their wake.

Finally, the Americans. Their flatboats gave way to steamboats, the steamboats to tugboats, throbbing diesels, pleasure yachts and sailboats, all drawing sustenance from the river and nourishing what has become this city of Peoria.

There is romance, mystery, wonder here. What follows is an attempt to celebrate this incredibly rich and vital history of Peoria.

History too often is regarded as a series of names and dates that have little bearing on the present, something that happened at Plymouth Rock, Lexington or Valley Forge. So we are taught.

No. History happened at Peoria, too, in yesterday's headlines....in a strange, lost fort that was built over 300 years ago....in a river that was carved in a time we can only dimly comprehend....in a city that grew from a brawling river town and wild vaudeville stopover to a surging industrial center, such a complex mingling of the real American culture that it has become a microcosm of America itself.

Listen....

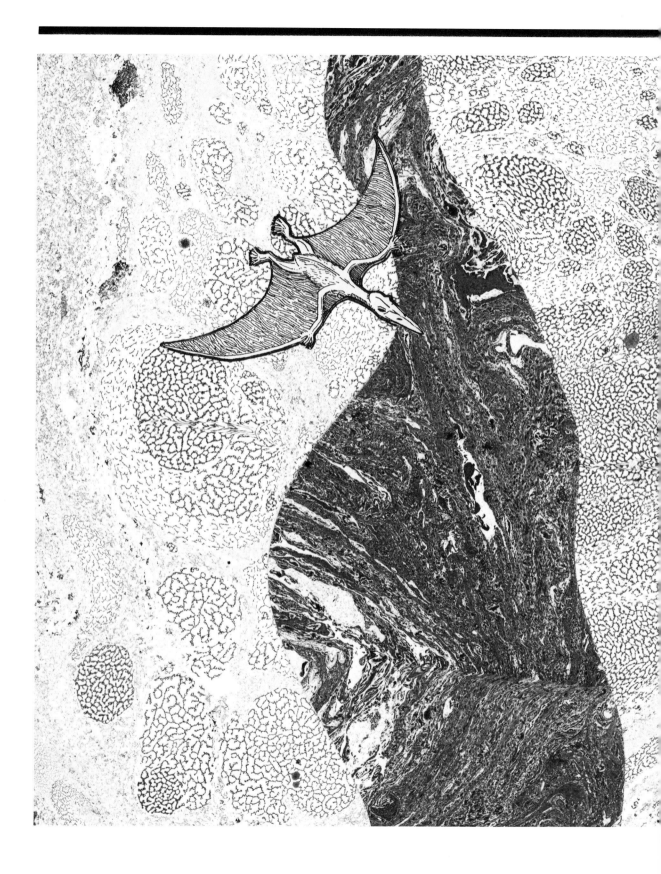

CHAPTER ONE

THE BEGINNINGS: PREHISTORIC PEORIA

How, in the broad, flat plains of Illinois, did this scenic area come to be? From Grand View Drive and the bluffs of the city to the Illinois River bottom. The passage of the glaciers and the great runoff to siltation and the threatened demise of the Illinois River as we know it. A geological overview.

PTERODACTYL EYE-VIEW—
PREHISTORIC PEORIA AREA.
(AMY MULCAHY, ILLUSTRATOR)

8

Whenever the earth was formed and whatever one might believe about the manner of its creation or development, the site of Peoria was always here. Not, of course, in its present form. The geological development of this state and this area has been painstakingly traced, and none of us can ever quite know, or even imagine what this area must have looked like in its formative period.

Some measure this slow progress over millions of years. The story recounted in Genesis applies here as well as in the Holy Land or at Mount Ararat. The awesome forces that shaped this fair and fertile land are worth contemplating and recounting, even in a speculative fashion.

This is glaciated country here, sanded smooth by repeated incursions of immense layers of ice. These first acted like a carpenter's plane and later like a fine-toothed file, leveling the primordial peaks, squashing the tropical rain forests into muck, eventually forming coal, and finally leaving in their wake a land with the richest and most productive topsoil on earth.

Imagine what this Peoria area must have looked like at one time! The mind can scarcely picture a Peoria where dinosaurs roamed, where vast forests of unknown species of trees, where plants, and ferns proliferated in fetid, bog-like swamplands, or where extinct mastodons tramped through an endlessly frozen wasteland.

But it must have been so. The evidence is clear. There are incredibly rich seams of coal, made of decayed and compressed vegetable matter; the underlay of limestone; the bones and teeth of extinct mammals; the sand pits with their sea shells; the layers of hardpan, or clay, beneath the surface; and that rich and abundant covering of fine loam, so filled with organic and mineral riches as to make this the real land of plenty.

The river came later. As the walls of ice, some say two miles thick, over 10,000 feet high - as high as a World War I airplane could fly - receded, the melting waters created our inland rivers, as well as the Great Lakes. The sheer force that carved the valleys and fashioned the bluffs of what is now Lake Peoria must have been staggering, relentless in power, and obviously astonishing in results.

To anyone casually aware of the process of erosion or the shaping action of running water, it must be evident that the river at one time extended from bluff to bluff, from Grand View Drive to the top of Germantown Hill. Then, little by little, century by century, the flow was channeled and the narrowing valley was gouged deeper and deeper until this Illinois River reached what are roughly its present limits.

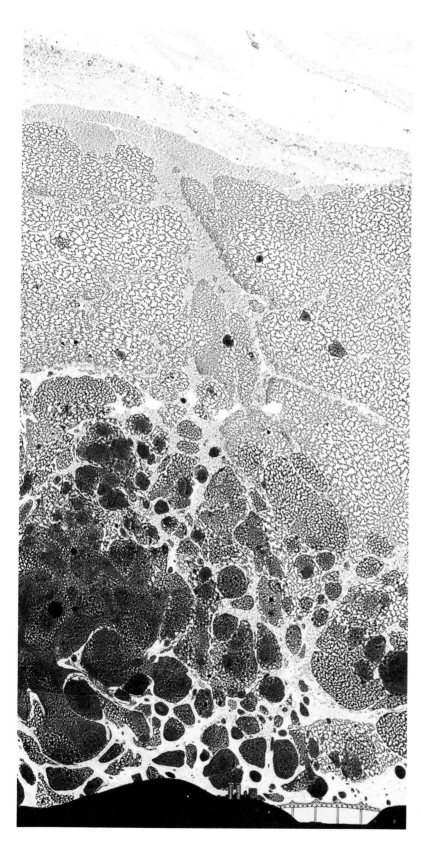

SILHOUETTE OF PEORIA
SKYLINE UNDER TWO MILES
OF ICE. (AMY MULCAHY,
ILLUSTRATOR)

Even before this, the earth in what is now this river valley underwent cataclysmic changes. It was repeatedly inundated by shallow seas that left layers of shells, some of which, in their original form, can be found even today in the sandy areas along the bluffs. In other areas, fossils were compacted into firm rock to form thick areas of limestone. Interior forces pushed the ground upwards to form a dry and rocky landscape like that of the moon. Summers and winters beyond numbering came and went. The shallow seas retreated, bringing the kind of tropical vegetation and climate so conducive to prehistoric and now extinct forms of animal and marine life. One can perhaps envision a kind of primordial ooze here, a rain forest populated by awesome, slithery creatures and gigantic cockroaches.

The story is recorded only in the remains of the marine life that comprise the immense deposits of limestone, some of them over 400 feet thick. These are separated by layers of sandstone and shale, formed during the dry land periods when rain and the forces of freezing and thawing split and broke the rocks, and by eons of blowing dust and sand. Finally, relatively close to the surface as geological measurements go, came the vast beds of coal that underlie the area. These were formed over thousands of generations when the middle of Illinois was a vast marsh in which the branches, leaves and trunks of massive trees rotted and decayed to form ooze, peat, and finally, coal.

These seams of coal were later covered by an inflow of water, then by a sediment of mud and sand and gravel. The land was washed by rain and blown by wind over centuries when the earth was presumably warm and tropical.

Then came the dawn of the awesome glacial era, when the climate changed so radically that more snow fell each winter than melted in the summer. The resulting accumulation became so immense that it lowered the temperature of the atmosphere, bringing even more snow. Eventually, the snow packed into ice, in much the same way that one makes an ice ball out of slush, and the sheer weight of the snow mass caused it to spread in all directions.

The glaciers that slid across Illinois apparently came from Canada's Labrador region, a thousand and more miles to the north, grinding slowly to the southwest and scouring the earth's surface with their accumulated baggage of sand, pebbles, rocks and boulders, and leaving here and there immense chunks of otherwise immovable pieces of rock and stone.

Illinois was virtually rubbed flat in this process, except for the area round Galena, and that in the southern portion of the state. When the climate changed and the great glacial melt finally began, this Illinois River valley was pretty much carved and filled to its present shape.

The pre-glacial river was considerably lower than it is now. Today, the uplands of Peoria rise about 175 feet above the river, whereas they were once 259 feet above the rocky floor of the pre-glacial river. And the present shape of the river with its Peoria Lakes has been further defined by the pinching off caused by the deposits carried by Farm Creek at the south and Ten Mile Creek at the point of the narrows the "Detroit" of the French.

One of the results of this virtual lake has been a very wide river with a very slow current. It might be noted that when the French first passed here in 1673, they were paddling upstream, because the Indians told them the Illinois was not only the more direct route back, but far easier to paddle against than the Mississippi with its much stronger current. Even the state song celebrates this river, this "gently flowing Illinois."

But slow-moving rivers, unfortunately, do not possess the ability to wash themselves clean. The Illinois became even more placid when the U. S. Army Corps of Engineers installed the locks in the 1920's that formed a series of pools. And slowly, gradually, the two, great scenic Peoria Lakes have continued to fill up with a mucky sediment that has choked off the gravel bed and reduced the depth in many areas to a few feet.

The worst predictions are that the river will become a massive swamp or marsh by the year 2000, bisected by a barge canal, and otherwise lost to the sailors, fishermen and others for whom it is now a scenic and recreational treasure.

But it remains, at this moment, the "fat lake," the "Pimiteoui," where valley, bluff and river combine to form a location of such spectacular beauty and natural abundance as to make the location of Peoria, from the beginning of time, quite inevitable.

CHAPTER TWO

PEORIA'S INDIANS: THE RISE AND FALL OF A CIVILIZATION

Who were these Indians? How did they get here? From the mound-builders to the seed-gatherers and farmers. The myth of the "noble savage", and the good Indian, Black Partridge. The Peoria tribe today and the decline of this simple, doomed civilization in its dealing with the new settlers.

LASALLE AND DE TONTI FEASTING AT THE PEORIA VILLAGE, JANUARY 5TH, 1680, IN PAINTING BY AMERICAN ARTIST GEORGE CATLIN, 1796-1872. (COURTESY NATIONAL GALLERY OF ART, AND ILLINIWEK)

14

A HOPEWELLIAN PRIEST.
(ILLINOIS HISTORY DIGEST).

A POTAWATOMI CHIEF WITH
CALUMET. (ILLINOIS HISTORY
DIGEST).

When the last of the great crushing ice sheets began its slow retreat somewhere between 10,000 and 20,000 years ago, when the rivers ran full and the summertimes became alive again with the grasses of the tundra and the songs of the birds, man followed.

No one has yet pinpointed the date when the first men moved into this western hemisphere or this Illinois valley, but archeological evidence suggested he must have hunted along the edge of the ice for the great mammoths, mastodons and giant sloths. He then remained when the woods that eventually grew up nurtured the smaller animals - the deer, the otter, the beaver, and up on the prairies, the buffalo, elk, wolves and coyotes.

These native Americans, or Amerindians, surely came across from Siberia, across the Bering Straits when there was still a land route between Asia and the tip of Alaska. It was believed to be no massive migration, but rather small bands of people heading south to flee the ice that had covered Europe and Asia, as well as America. They spread slowly over the New World throughout misty eons that no one remembers, or can chart, increased in numbers, developed their own languages and cultures, and eventually populated both North and South America.

They have been called "children of the dawn" and they are among the oldest of all men.

They were here in America long before the pyramids arose in Egypt, long before the Babylonians recorded their history on clay tablets, long before the Phoenicians followed their trade routes along the shores of the Mediterranean, and very long before the Greeks and Romans provided the cradle of what has become Western Civilization.

But they left no language, no written words, no oral history -only legends and mounds, bones and artifacts.

Not until the French arrived in this river valley in the 17th century was anything written about these Indians. Then they became almost invariably misinterpreted, misunderstood, misapprehended. To Rousseau, they were idealized as "the noble savage," members of a society so perfectly attuned to nature and to one another, so admirably governed without police, laws, aristocracy or social convention that their very freedom and lack of restraint helped form some of the philosophies that ultimately led to the French Revolution. To those who observed them closely, however, they were often vain and licentious, handsome in appearance, but simple, cowardly and brutal.

The truth, of course, lies somewhere in between.

16

More modern research, such as that undertaken by Stuart Struever and his workers at Kampsville's Koster Site, suggests that the Amerindians who once occupied this area were members of a highly developed society. Seed gathering, farming and hunting were highly organized pursuits that in some instances resulted in a single society that existed for a thousand years or more. It has been proposed, in fact, that some of these early Indians enjoyed far more leisure and lived lives far less hectic and stressful than we live today. There was also a highly developed sense of ritual. Burials of 5000 and more years ago indicate that these people believed in an afterlife to which their elaborate mounds and burial customs testify.

And yet they remain an enduring enigma. They neither owned the land nor did they change it. Their villages were temporary abodes and their hunting grounds seasonal. It was this very lack of the concept of ownership as held by Europeans that brought the Indians into such inevitable conflict with the white settlers who surged into the area in the early 19th century, staking their claims, carving out their homesteads, erecting their fences, all of which was to make the Indian way of life impossible. These were two cultures bent on a collision course. They could not coexist, and the European, with his greater technology and more highly developed culture, was bound to win.

It was not an equal struggle. And yet one is still tempted to wonder which was the better way. The Indian civilization, with all its primitive simplicity, lasted at least 10,000 years and left the land virtually intact. Ours has existed here about 300 years and there are already serious questions as to how long it can continue.

Our short reign has brought artifacts beyond comprehension. Huge cities. Junkyards. Highways. Silted rivers. Polluted skies. An environmental impact that is irreversible. The Indians, in contrast, changed virtually nothing and left very little. Arrowheads. Spear points. Burial mounds.

And who, happening upon an arrowhead or spear point, has not been struck by its implications. Who loosed it? What was its target? Who made it? And what incredible adventures did the hunter experience?

Unfortunately, we have little to go on. These Indians at Peoria must have hunted everything from prehistoric, extinct animals to deer, pheasant, buffalo and wild turkeys in these same hills and woods we now cross with our automobiles. For this was "Pimiteoui," the "fat lake," a place abounding since the dawn of man with fish, turtles, clams, birds and mammals.

It was a favorite hunting ground, a natural larder. But even such abundance was subject to depletion. It is popular these days to depict the native American Indian as a wise conservationist, but this does not seem to have been the case, at least in the historic times. Some early French observers, for instance, were appalled at the waste the Indians displayed, killing far more animals than they could possibly use. Neither were their villages particularly tidy, nor their garbage disposal habits necessarily praiseworthy.

If there is an inconsistency to the view of the Indian, there is also an enigma to the changing patterns of his society. For some unknown reasons, the ancient, cultured civilizations died out, leaving behind only bits of elaborate pottery, arrowheads and spearpoints and those carefully formed burial mounds. There is little more we have to detail the lives of these pre-Columban inhabitants of Peoria, but surely the area must have been either inhabited by or used as a rich hunting grounds for unknown numbers of years.

When the French first passed through in 1673, there was no mention made of a permanent settlement here. Most of the Peoria Indians at the time were on the other side of the Mississippi and only bands of hunters were here, which suggests that this was a game preserve utilized during the fall and winter by the Illini tribes who were concentrated in what is now Utica.

Later, however, whole tribes gathered here in that loose federation of villages made up of Kaskaskias, Peorias, Moingwenas, Tamaroas and others. And at one time, this Peoria Lake was surrounded by a number of villages stretching from Chillicothe to Bartonville.

18

And of these, nothing remains but the arrowheads, the shards of pottery, a few mounds and bones.

But these, remember, were not people who believed in the ownership of the land or the possession of property. It was a piece of wisdom and naivete that ultimately was to deprive them of all these lands through which they once roamed so freely.

It is remarkable that they managed their simple way of life for thousands of years, sharing the land in a common bond and living in a society that, for all its lack of structure and organization, probably lasted longer than any other society in all of history.

There was, of course, a rise and fall to the Indian condition. Whole societies came and went, cultures developed and then faded, tribes evolved and then died out, and even the names we assign to these pre-historic people are arbitrary. We have traced them more or less from what we call Paleo-Indians who arrived as the glaciers retreated and perhaps remained in scattered bands, to Archaic man, the Initial Woodland period, the Hopewellian civilization, the final Woodland on up to the Iliniwek, who first saw the white man arrive as their own history was coming to an end.

WAR DANCE OF THE SAUK AND FOX INDIANS. FROM A PAINTING BY GEORGE CATLIN.

For these Iliniwek already were in decline when Father Marquette passed here in 1673 and supposedly baptized an infant of the Peoria tribe. Recurring wars with the fierce Iroquois, the Fox, the Osage, and many other tribes, had either scattered many of them beyond the Mississippi or sent them fleeing from their ancestral lands.

When LaSalle and Tonti built Fort Crevecoeur in the late winter of 1680, there was an Illini village of about 80 cabins at the southern end of Lake Peoria. When Tonti returned a dozen years later to build the new Fort St. Louis on this lake, there were more than 260 cabins here. Tonti's cousin, Pierre de Liette, noted at the time that there were six villages of Illini at Peoria.

This Peoria formed the major tribe of the Illini confederation, whose territory and power at one time were formidable. Their hunting grounds stretched from the Wisconsin River on the north, the Mississippi on the west, to the Ohio on the east. But the tribe was never large. The entire confederation of Illinois at one time numbered 100,000 inhabitants in 60 villages and were one of the most powerful tribes in all of New France.

But under pressure from the Iroquois and others, they gradually moved to the south. A hundred years after the building of Fort Crevecoeur, the Kickapoos and Potawatomies had moved into the old Illini villages surrounding Lake Peoria, and the Peorias settled near Ste. Genevieve, or St. Louis, and slowly drifted westward. By 1827, some of them had reached the shores of the Marais des Cygnes in Kansas. Finally, the remnants of this once mighty Illini nation became known as the Confederated Peoria Indians in Kansas and later, the Peoria Tribe of Indians in Oklahoma, where the last survivors still live today.

This was virtually a local version of that tragic Trail of Tears in which thousands of Indians were uprooted and sent away from their ancestral lands under increasing pressure from white settlers, comparable in scope almost to the awesome refugee movements that followed World War II.

These Illinois Indians lived their hunting, gathering, semi-agricultural life for countless generations. They preferred their nomadic, drifting life, forever seeking the best hunting ground. They did not accumulate the benefit of permanent cities, nor did they gather wealth as we know it or any fixed written knowledge from generation to generation. They were satisfied with the challenge of day-to-day living and showed no interest in abstraction, preferring to live from harvest to harvest, from hunt to hunt. What we have come to know as

(TOP)
ROBERT CAVALIER SIEUR DE LA SALLE. (ILLINOIS HISTORY DIGEST).

(BOTTOM)
HENRI DE TONTI, FROM AN 1685 PAINTING. (ILLINOIS HISTORY DIGEST).

20

progress was hardly noticeable in their long reign over this land. It was, therefore, inevitable that there should be a clash between this simple, native culture and that of the white settlers. Who would win was almost a foregone conclusion.

Despite the claims of the idealists, the Indians were not precisely the noble savages of myth. Some practiced cannibalism, and some tortured their prisoners with the most exquisite and excruciating methods of killing imaginable. Others were lazy, thieving, lustful, vain, cowardly and deceitful. In victory they were awesome, in defeat pitiful. And yet there was something to their naturalness that inevitably was destroyed in their encounters with the Europeans. The white man gave the Indians trinkets for their furs, empty promises for their land, and nothing for their culture, their beliefs, their self-respect or their freedom.

It has been noted that the Spanish crushed the Indian, the English scorned and neglected him, and the French embraced and cherished him.

Too simple, perhaps, but somehow true. And the American settler, it might be added, finally got rid of him.

By 1818, when Illinois was admitted to the Union, the white population was largely confined to the American bottoms. The vast area north of the confluence of the Illinois River with the Mississippi was still the domain of Indian hunting parties and fur traders. By this time, the survivors of the once mighty Illinois nation were far reduced. Small bands of the Peoria Indians still roamed the shores of the lower Illinois River, but the Potawatomies, the Foxes, and the Kickapoos had already moved in.

In a treaty concluded at Edwardsville on September 25, 1818, between Governor Ninian Edwards and August Chouteau, the members of the Illinois tribes received $2000 and the Peoria Indians an additional figure for the almost seven million acres of land they once controlled. They also received 694 acres in Blackwater River in the Missouri Territory.

As early as 1764, some of the remnants of the Peoria tribe had settled near the new city of St. Louis. There already was a permanent settlement of Peorias at Ste. Genevieve and these Indians were described as "indolent, drunkards and thieves."

One of the first acts of the administration of Andrew Jackson in 1830 was the Indian Removal Act. Jackson was an old Indian fighter who was convinced the new settlers had to move westward. And this awesome resettlement of the eastern and southern tribes onto barren and inhospitable land west of the Mississippi was said to match the pathos from the cargo holds of slave ships. These people, sunk in despondency, were herded from place to place, matching almost any death march in history, as they were expelled from the land of their fathers.

But these treaties concluded with the United States were invariably worded to last "as long as the grass grows and the water runs." Hardly. The grass stopped growing and the water stopped running every winter. John Reynolds, who became governor of Illinois in 1830, wrote with obvious anguish..."Not only had the aborigines of Illinois had an undoubted right to the country they occupied, but the climate, fertility of soil and other advantages, made them happy in their mode of life....The whites discovered the Indians peaceable and happy in Illinois, and at this day all are torn from their own country and whole tribes have been destroyed. Attempts have been made for ages to improve the Northern Indians, and they obstinately refused to accept this boon. It seems it is a decree of heaven that they cannot become civilized men. It seems the progress of the country must make the aborigines yield to the onward march of civilization and Christianity. Although it may seem hard to force the Indians from their own country to accommodate the white population, yet it is the only wise and humane policy that can be adopted. It is a heart-rending sight to see the poor natives driven from their own country. Their tears and lamentations on leaving Illinois would pierce a heart of stone. We must submit to the decrees of Providence. Nevertheless, it is difficult to find good reason for the expulsion of the Indians from their own country. But with or without reason, the Indians must emigrate, leaving Illinois, the finest country on earth, for the peaceable occupation of the white man."

VIEW OF PEORIA—1832.
(SIMEON DEWITT DROWN).

22

In his Reminiscences of Early Peoria, Odillon B. Slane, great-uncle of Henry Slane, the present Chairman of the Board of the Peoria Journal Star, recounts a story of an Indian and a baby girl, which gives a particular insight into the character of the Indians who lived here shortly after the Americans arrived. Odillon Slane was the son of Benjamin Slane, who came to Fort Clark, Peoria, from Virginia in November, 1831, and later worked as a laborer at Jubilee College. The Slane cabin stood between the site of the later Rock Island depot and the edge of Peoria Lake. Slane wrote that his father saw deer running up Main Street and watched wolves slink about the area where the courthouse now stands. The remains of Fort Clark were still here at the time of his story:

"All boys love to hear Indian stories and they love to play Indian, too. Why this is so I do not know, unless it is that the child mind trends to primitive conditions. Many an Indian story have I heard my father tell as I sat by the old home fireside. This one in particular always thrilled me. The Indians never knocked at the door of the white settler's home. They had not been taught such a custom. One day when the rest of the family was away, a sick woman lay in one of the little cabins on the river bank, and suddenly an Indian entered. He seemed to be partially intoxicated, and he demanded whiskey. The sick woman told him there was no whiskey in the house, but he still demanded whiskey and approached the bed in a threatening manner, reaching for the knife in his belt. The woman turned back the covers of the bed and showed him a tiny new baby only a few days old, sleeping by her side. The Indian looked down in wonder; "white papoose!" he exclaimed, and motioning to her to cover it up again, he tiptoed to the door and was gone. I know that this story is true, because that woman was my grandmother and the babe was my Aunt Jane Root, who died in Nebraska some years ago."

CHIEF PATH-OF-STORM, LAST OF THE PEORIA CHIEFS. (F-STOP SOCIETY).

24

PEORIA INDIAN. (F-STOP
SOCIETY).

Reynolds' incredible decree reveals some of the anguish that
afflicted men of conscience in his day, and our own, regarding
the Indian problem. It remains even now as a subject for
gnawing and unrelenting guilt.

History writes a quick coda to this once mighty Illinois nation
and its predominate Peoria tribe. The survivors signed
treaties with the United States on October 27, 1832, in Castor
Hill, St. Louis County, ceding all their lands in Illinois and
Missouri. In exchange, they received 150 sections of land on
the Osage River (Marais des Cygnes) in territory yet
unorganized. There were about 200 Peorias involved in this
move.

But the Trail of Tears had not ended. When Kansas was
organized in 1854, the influx of more white men called for the
removal of as many Indians as possible. The leader of the
Peoria Indians was a famous man known as Baptiste Peoria.
He and his confederated tribe again gave up their land, 92,000
acres. Each member of the tribe was given 160 acres in return.
Their reservation disintegrated and many of the individuals
were unable to manage their shares. They were further
humiliated by government harassment and the ravages of
cheap whiskey. They finally sought another tract of land in
the northeast corner of Oklahoma, the Ouapaw reservation.

In 1867, 55 members of the Confederated Peoria Tribe
remained in Kansas. The rest, 163, moved into Indian
territory in what is now Oklahoma. Their descendants still
live there, in Ottawa County, and they are buried in the
Peoria Cemetery there, the last remnants of a once mighty
nation.

This nation was not initially destroyed by the white men, but
by the Fox, Sioux, Chippewas, Ottawas, Potawatomies,
Cherokees, Chicksaws and others. Oddly, the French were
their best allies, shielding them from vicious attacks by the
Iroquois, the Fox and the Kickapoos. When the Peoria
Indians ceded their hunting grounds in Illinois, they had none
left. They had already been restricted to the vicinity of the
French villages by their hostile and belligerent neighbors.
They finally ceded lands they no longer controlled.

The others who moved into Illinois in their wake had very
little time left. The settlers were arriving after the War of
1812, pouring out of the east, through Kentucky and Indiana
and into Illinois and its incredibly rich and fertile prairies.
The Indians were swept away like tall grass before the scythe.

By 1956, the tribal roll of Peoria Indians in Oklahoma
numbered 640 members. By 1971, payment roll of the tribe
listed 2328 names, a number swollen by new births and more
memberships by intermarriage. But these Peoria Indians are

the same as people without a country. No racial characteristics are identifiable. Their culture is dead. Not even the oldest members of the tribe remember the folklore, songs, or ceremonials of their ancestors. Culturally, they are identical with the white society in which they live. They hardly know their history, but are rather aware of themselves as the Peorias who came from Kansas, not the last survivors of this once great Illinois nation which fought off the Iroquois, welcomed the French, and once, for a very long time, held sway over this blessed land.

These are Indians who have "been scattered like dust and leaves when the mighty mists of October seize them and whirl them aloft."

And all that remains here now is the name they have left....Peoria.

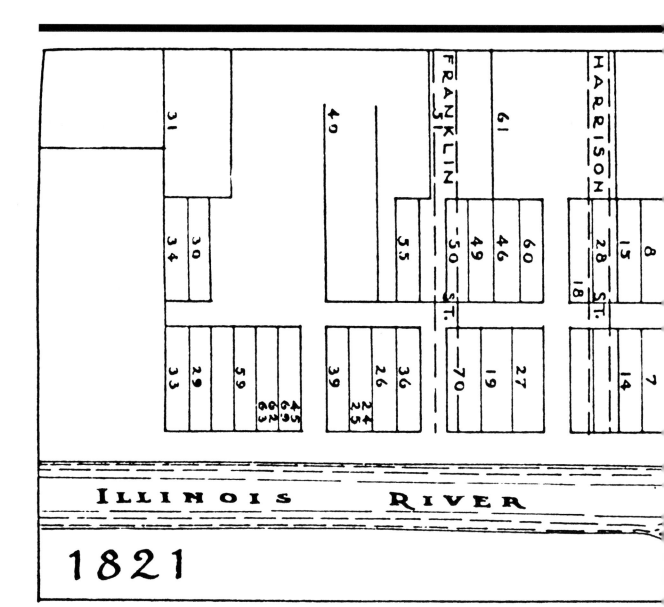

1821

ILLINOIS RIVER

CLAIMS TO LOTS
—◦—

CHARLES LA BELLE
OUT-LOT OR FIELD OF
TEN ARPENS. CLAIM No. 61
HYPOLITE MAILLET
OUT-LOT OR FIELD OF
SIX ARPENS. CLAIM No. 51
FRANCIS RACINE, JR.
OUT-LOT OR FIELD OF
THREE OR FOUR ARPENS · 40
SIMON ROI. OUT-LOT OR
FIELD OF SIX ARPENS No. 31

FRANCIS RACINE, SEN.
FIELD OF ABOUT TWENTY
ARPENS.
A. BURBONNE · · · · 66
A. DESCHAMPS
LOUIS P. PILETTE · · 12
THOMAS FORSYTHE
300 FEET SQUARE · 8
JACQUES METTE · · 15
SIMON ROI · · · · · 28
PIERRE LAVASSIEUR
DIT CHAMBERLAIN · 18
CHARLES LA BELLE · 60

JOSEPH COUDIER · · 46
HYPOLITE MAILLET · 49
HYPOLITE MAILLET · 50
MICHAEL LE CLAIRE · 55
SIMON ROI · · · · · · 30
ANTOINE ROI · · · · 34
R BELONGE
A. GRAND BOIS · 54
LOUIS PENNENNEAU 68
ANTOINE BURBONNE · 65
HYPOLITE MAILLET · · 47
FELIX FONTAINE · · · 42
LOUIS P. PILETTE · · · II

THOMAS F
300 FEET
JACQUES M
FRANCIS BUC
LOUIS BISSO
MICHAEL LA
PIERRE LAV
DIT CHAMB
LOUIS PENN
FRANCIS RA
ANTOINE L
THOMAS L
ANTOINE L

Where are the evidences of over 120 years of French history here today? The chapter traces the French of Peoria from Pere Marquette and LaSalle to their expulsion in 1812. The Fort Crevecoeur mystery, Fort St. Louis. The Ville de Maillet and its inhabitants and the French claims. Almost no signs of French Peoria remain, save for a few names.

LIBERTY ST.

12

66

42 47 54

41 65

PORT CLARK

LAKE PEORIA

·· 7
·· 14
MED)
MED)
· 27

· 19
· 70
N· 36
· 26
· 24
· 25

FELIX FONTAINE ··· 41
FRANCIS RACINE, JR. · 39
BAPTISTE RABOIN · 45
LOUIS PENNENNEAU · 69
SIMON BERTRAND · 62
ANTOINE LEPANNIE · 63
JOHN B BLONDEAU · 59
FRANCIS DUPRE (NOT CLAIMED)
SIMON ROI ······ 29
ANTOINE ROI ···· 33

CITY MAP DRAWN BY
E. BERNARD HULSEBUS.

28

BEAVER AT WORK. (PEORIA PUBLIC LIBRARY).

Hardly anyone arriving in Peoria these days would have the least reason to suspect that this was one of the most important centers of French civilization in the entire west, that this location was French for 131 years, almost as long as it has been American, 171 years. The French era ended with an episode so disgraceful and so cowardly that it ranks with Longfellow's story of "Evangeline" and has been almost systematically covered up.

Almost nothing remains of French Peoria. A few place names. A fort which almost everyone recognizes has been perpetuated in the wrong location. Old, mostly unread accounts. And a series of lawsuits over the French claims that dragged on for years.

Not a trace is to be found of the village that once stood here. It has been obliterated by modern Peoria, dissolving slowly over the years beneath railroad tracks, brick streets, houses and commercial development. Its churches, blacksmith shops, wine presses, stores and homes have all been lost beneath the vital, teeming river town that grew along the shores of the Illinois River. The new inhabitants of this growing town had little inclination to celebrate the past history of the area they were so quickly developing into a thriving and profitable commercial center.

From here beaver pelts by the thousands poured out to the hatmakers of France, an enterprise nourished by the king's minister, Colbert. Documents bearing the green and white ribbons of Louis XIV arrived here from the lavish Palace of Versailles, and this was, in fact, a part of one of the most glorious, overwrought and splendid empires that has ever existed.

Had history taken a slightly different course, French might still be the official language here, or Moliere our Shakespeare.

Peoria has a rich and incredibly colorful past and it fully deserves its place in the sun.

Peoria's modern history has its beginning in the epic voyages of Father Jacques Marquette and Louis Jolliet, who, in 1673, were ordered by Comte de Frontenac, the Governor of Canada, to seek "the river as far as the sea." This was to be the passage to China, an idea which had fired the imagination of explorers since the time of Columbus. And on May 17, 1673, Marquette and Jolliet, along with five men, pushed off in two canoes from the Mission of St. Ignace, at the Michigan Straits of Mackinac, on what was to be a journey as significant in its way as Marco Polo's venture to China.

The adventurers carried Indian corn and smoked meat. Three of the rowers were Pierre Porteret, Jacques Largilliers, and Pierre Moreau. Their route carried them across the Great Lakes to the vicinity of what is now Green Bay, from where they paddled along the Fox River to a portage, crossed over to the Wisconsin River and entered the Mississippi near the present-day Prairie du Chien.

FACSIMILE OF FATHER HENNEPIN'S MAP OF 1685. (FROM BESS'S HISTORY OF PEORIA).

30

A DRAWING OF FATHER MARQUETTE FROM THE FRONTISPIECE OF "PERE MARQUETTE, PRIEST, PIONEER AND ADVENTURER" BY AGNES REPPLIER, DOUBLEDAY, DORAN & CO.

If Father Marquette did not precisely discover the Mississippi - that achievement historically belongs to De Soto - he was the first to recognize its scope and its importance. Guided by information furnished by friendly Indians, Marquette and his party descended the river to near what is now Memphis; and there, warned that the Spanish might be present if they went farther, turned back and began the long, arduous journey upstream, against the current.

Indians along the way had told Marquette and Jolliet the best way back to the Great Lakes. It proved to be good advice, for the route followed the far more placid Illinois River to the Des Plaines, with a portage to the Chicago River and into Lake Michigan.

And so, while Father Marquette and Jolliet may not have been the real discoverers of the Mississippi, they were apparently the first white men to traverse the Illinois and to pass the site of the future Peoria.

It is not certain the two French canoes stopped here at all, although Father Marquette spent at least three days among the Peoria Indians somewhere on the Illinois River. He writes in his journal that he had the satisfaction of saving one soul, that of a child he baptized just before it died.

Father Marquette had first found the Peoria Indians on his way down the Mississippi in June of 1673. They were camped at the mouth of a tributary stream historians believe was the Des Moines River. On June 25, the explorers noticed footprints leading inland. Marquette and Jolliet followed the prints to an Indian village, where they cried out to attract attention. The Indians, luckily, recognized them as Frenchmen by reason of their travels and their trading, and welcomed them with typical hospitality. They were given a calumet to smoke, and an old man honored them with a surprising ceremonial.

"This man stood erect," wrote Father Marquette, "and stark naked, with his hands extended and lifted toward the sun, as if he wished to protect himself from its rays, which nevertheless shone upon his face through his fingers. When we came near him, he paid us this compliment: 'How beautiful the sun is, O Frenchman, when thou comest to visit us! All our village awaits thee and thou shalt enter our cabins in peace.' "

It was an incident and a quotation that was to reappear many years later almost word for word in Longfellow's "The Song of Hiawatha."

Marquette also relates in his journal that he and Jolliet were hand-fed by the Indians, as if they were infants, and that the meal consisted of fish, boiled corn meal, a freshly killed dog (which they declined) and buffalo meat.

They left the next morning and continued their journey down the Mississippi, which Marquette had labeled the "Conception" in honor of the December eighth feast honoring Mary, the mother of Jesus. Just below the site of Alton, they discovered a pair of monsters painted on the rocky cliffs, supposedly ogres or images of the Piasa Bird, which have long since vanished. By the time they arrived at the mouth of the Missouri, the explorers already suspected that the Mississippi emptied into the Gulf of Mexico and was not, after all, a route to the Orient. But they pressed on, besieged by heat and mosquitoes, past the Ohio and on to the mouth of the Arkansas River. Here friendly Indians warned them there were hostile tribes farther on - and also the Spaniards.

So they turned back, heading for Canada again with all the information they had gathered. They departed from Arkansas on July 17; and Marquette, nearly exhausted, contracted dysentery, an illness that would cause his death in less than two years.

The Illinois proved far less arduous than the Mississippi on the return trip. Even for the weary priest, it must have appeared almost a paradise. He wrote, in what is believed to be the first description recorded of the Peoria area and its lakes, "We have seen nothing like this river that we enter as regards its fertility of soil, its prairies and woods, its cattle, elk, deer, wildcats, bustards, swans, ducks, parroquets and even beaver. There are many small lakes and rivers. That on which we sailed is wide, deep and still for 65 leagues."

In addition to visiting the Peoria tribe, the Frenchmen stopped at the Indian village known as Kaskaskia, where Utica now stands. This was the principal village of the Illinois tribe, where as many as 10,000 Indians lived. After promising to return and instruct the Indians in the faith, the explorers continued to Lake Michigan and north to Green Bay, which they reached late in September. Theirs had been a trip of nearly 2500 miles in a little more than four months.

Jolliet left for Quebec to report on the journey, but Marquette remained hoping to regain his strength. He spent the winter and the following summer at the Jesuit Mission of St. Francis, and in October, 1674, he began his return trip to the Illinois country to make good his pledge to preach the

32

ROBERT CAVALIER SIEUR DE LA SALLE. (FROM "ILINIWEK").

faith to these people. It was an arduous, debilitating journey. Near the site of Chicago, his illness returned and he spent most of the winter there. By April, he reached the Illinois village of Kaskaskia and was received, as his superior wrote, "as an angel from heaven."

He was there for Holy Week, celebrating Mass and instructing the Indians. But a few days after Easter, he turned north again, hoping to die among his fellow Jesuits. He did not make it. He and his companions, paddling north along the shore of Lake Michigan, got as far as Ludington, Michigan, on their way to St. Ignace. It was here that Father Marquette died on April 18, 1674. He was not yet 38 years old.

He died with a crucifix in front of his eyes. And as his superior wrote, he was happy to have died "in a wretched cabin in the midst of the forests and bereft of all human succor....as he had always prayed."

His companions buried him there. Two years later, a band of Indians, who had been taught by the priest, came upon his grave, exhumed the body, and enclosed the bones in a bark casket. This they took to St. Ignace and the remains of the famous explorer-priest were buried there before the altar in the little chapel.

In 1706, the St. Ignace Mission was abandoned. It was not until 200 years later that archeologists attempted to find Marquette's remains. They found the grave, but it had been despoiled. Only 27 pieces of bone remained, the largest about an inch and a half long. A few of these were buried under the monument that has been erected at St. Ignace. The rest were put into a vault at Marquette University in Milwaukee, in case Father Marquette is ever canonized as a saint of the Catholic Church.

But if the efforts of Father Marquette raise visions of sanctity, those of LaSalle, who followed him, give cause for sorrow. There is almost the feeling of the "beau geste," the noble gesture, in the exploits of LaSalle, whose record is almost one of continuous failure. The forts he built were abandoned or destroyed, his men deserted him, he lost his fortune, and, eventually, his life in his bold adventures along the Mississippi and Illinois Rivers.

LASALLE TAKES POSSESSION OF THE MISSISSIPPI VALLEY IN THE NAME OF KING LOUIS XIV. (FROM BESS'S HISTORY OF PEORIA).

Robert Cavalier, Sieur de LaSalle, who had been ennobled by Louis XIV and was perhaps as much at home in the glittering salons of Versailles as in the trackless wilderness of Illinois, strikes an unlikely picture as one of the pioneering explorers. He is invariably depicted dressed for some courtly

RICHARD PHILLIPS AT THE PEORIA HISTORICAL SOCIETY DESIGNATED SITE OF FORT CREVECOEUR. (JACK BRADLEY PHOTO).

function in an elegantly plumed hat and an elaborate coat festooned with ornate buttons. And yet he must have hacked his way through miles of underbrush and thorns, slogged through swamps, been drenched by rain and buffeted by blizzards.

The fort he built at Peoria in the late winter of 1680, the first such structure in the entire Illinois country, was not only the subject of heartbreak at the time, but of continuous mystery ever since.

It was named Fort Crevecoeur - broken heart - and some suggest it reflected his mood at the time. What seems more likely is that the name commemorates a battle fought in Flanders some nine years earlier by Louis XIV and only in retrospect did the meaning of the name seem applicable.

LaSalle was an adventurer, convinced that his fortune did not lie in a France that had become the most powerful nation on earth at the time, but in this New World, where he hoped to find the mouth of the Mississippi and establish a series of forts. He was also attracted by the immensely lucrative fur trade, particularly that in beaver pelts, which were utilized in Europe for highly fashionable (and very warm) hats.

34

MAP OF FORT CREVECOEUR.
(FROM "ILINIWEK").

With these goals in mind, LaSalle first arrived in Canada in 1666, and spent more than a decade in the wilderness. He sailed back to France in 1677 in order to convince Louis XIV of the value of setting up a chain of forts in the Mississippi Valley to keep out the Spanish and English. The king agreed and gave LaSalle the authority to explore the "western parts of New France," to build and maintain whatever forts he thought necessary, and to have a monopoly in the buffalo hide trade.

The following year, LaSalle returned to Canada. He began his journeys at Fort Frontenac, at the present sight of Kingston at the northeast tip of Lake Ontario. He and his men paddled across the lake to Niagara Falls, and here paused to build the "Griffin," the first sailing ship on the Great Lakes, and then filled it with supplies.

With his new ship, LaSalle headed across Lake Erie, up through Lake St. Clair and into Lake Huron, then to the top of the Michigan peninsula, stopping at the Jesuit mission of St. Ignace.

At Green Bay, LaSalle loaded the "Griffin" with furs collected by some of his men who had gone on before him. He sent the ship back to Niagara to deliver the furs to pay some of his debts. It was later to return to Lake Michigan with provisions for his future journeys. The "Griffin," however, was never seen again. It became the first of those mysterious disappearances which are sprinkled throughout the maritime history of the Great Lakes.

Meanwhile, LaSalle and his men headed south in four canoes, traversing the western shore of Lake Michigan, past the present sites of Milwaukee and Chicago, and circled eastward at the southern end of the lake to land at the St. Joseph River, near the present Benton Harbor. They arrived in November, 1679.

Here, LaSalle was to meet his famous lieutenant, Henri de Tonti. Tonti belonged to a distinguished Italian family which had devised a famous lottery, known as "The Tontine." He had long served in the French army and had lost a hand in combat. It had been replaced by an artificial one made of iron. It was an attribute which made him feared and respected among the Indians.

While waiting for Tonti to arrive, LaSalle built a fort on the St. Joseph. When Tonti arrived, he brought news that nothing had been heard of the "Griffin." LaSalle sent two men back to Mackinac to watch for the ship and the rest of the party - 33 men in eight canoes - set off for the Illinois country.

They followed the St. Joseph across the corner of Michigan and into Indiana near South Bend. Here they portaged to the Kankakee River, which joins the Des Plaines south of Chicago to form the Illinois. On January 5, 1680, they reached the present site of Peoria.

Here LaSalle found several hundred Indians, members of the Peoria tribe, and he decided to winter among them. These were generally peaceable Indians. There were, however, rabble-rousers present who stirred up some hostility against the Frenchmen and it is reported that six of LaSalle's men, including two carpenters, promptly deserted, fleeing into the woods and disappearing. In order to prevent further problems and to achieve a safe base of operation, LaSalle took his men a few miles downstream from the Indian village and began the building of Fort Crevecoeur.

FORT ST. LOUIS, FORMERLY CREVECOEUR. (FROM "ILINIWEK").

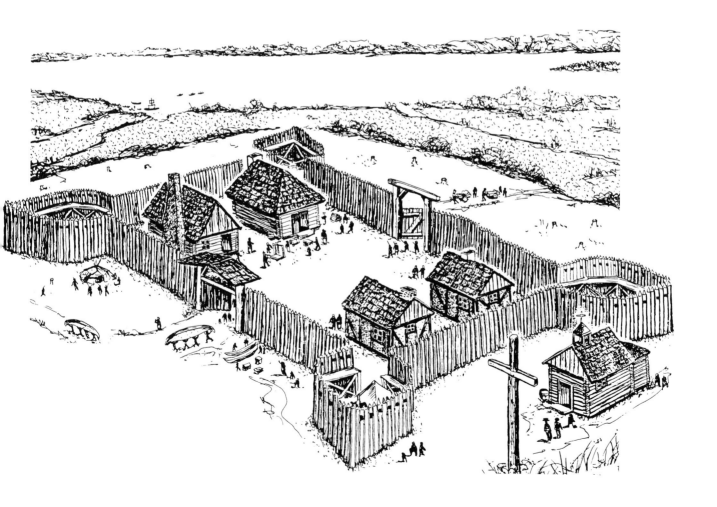

36

This was not only to be the first permanent structure erected by white men in the entire Mississippi Valley, but a source of enduring conflict and dispute. Where was it located? How was it destroyed? How long did it exist? What did it look like?

French fortifications from the time of LaSalle through Verdun in World War I and the ill-fated Maginot Line of a generation later, have always been singular for their ingenuity and location. The reigning military expert of LaSalle's time was Sebastian Vauban, who was the fortification expert under Louis XIV and whose traditions and precepts were followed for centuries. It is safe to assume that LaSalle and Tonti, being educated men, were aware of his doctrines and that any fort they would erect along the river would provide ready access to the water, would provide defense on the remaining three sides, would have a commanding view of the surrounding area and would not be built, as it were, on sand.

Out of the dozen or more sites suggested today as being the location of this fort, only three seem to be logical choices. One is that extensively researched by Captain Arthur Lagron, former French Army civil engineer, whose suggested location

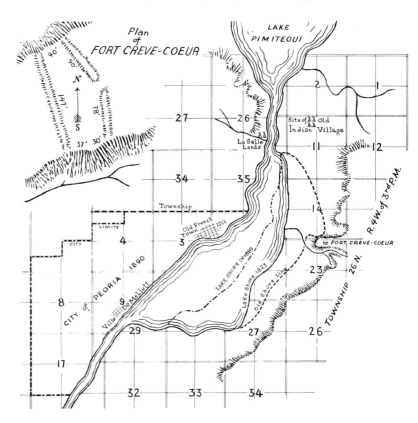

MAP OF FORT CREVECOEUR LOCATION, COMPILED FROM MAPS AND SURVEYS BY GEORGE F. WIGHTMAN, 1890. (FROM "ILINIWEK").

has long vanished beneath the tracks of the Peoria and Pekin Union railway yard, roughly below the bluff where Fort Crevecoeur Park now stands. Since nothing remains, the claim remains forever unprovable.

A second site is that selected earlier in this century by Peoria attorney, Dan R. Sheen, who located it in East Peoria at a point opposite Fayette Street in Peoria. According to the writings of those who saw Fort Crevecoeur, Sheen alleged, it was a league from Pimiteoui, a half league from Omaha's camp, defended on one side by a river, with a marsh in front of it and the main bank of the river being 200 paces distant. The river, he said, spread to it in rainy seasons, it was near the Indian village where LaSalle landed and located on a "little mound," "knoll," "hillock" or "eminence," that it adjoined the woods, had wide, deep ravines on two sides and near water that did not freeze in the winter.

The area here, too, has changed considerably over the years, although Sheen claimed to have found blackened timbers on the site that could well have remained from the fort, which was supposedly pillaged on April 16, 1680.

The third likely location is that selected by the Peoria Historical Society, known as the upper hill site and marked, in 1902, with a small obelisk that still stands today. This location was the focus of extensive research by historian Richard Phillips until his death in 1982. Using dozens of maps and accounts, he attempted to prove that Fort Crevecoeur was on (and not below) the lower lake known as Pimiteoui, that the Indian village where LaSalle landed was at the narrows, later called "Little Detroit," and that the league of which LaSalle writes would place the fort precisely on the spot where the Historical Society erected its marker.

The description of Father Hennepin, who accompanied LaSalle, places the fort half a league - a mile and a half -below the narrows. It was at this same point that city engineers Simeon De Witt Drown in 1846, and George F. Wightman in 1890, located the ruins of Fort St. Louis, which Phillips maintains was built at the site of the abondoned Fort Crevecouer.

The CHICAGO TRIBUNE in November, 1889, sent Charles Lambert, a special correspondent, to Peoria, to write a story on the site of Fort Crevecoeur, which Wightman had surveyed. Wightman had exposed certain areas where the postholes of the palisade were visible. Lambert also visited Jack Shepard's Fort Crevecoeur Museum, located below the hill. For years, Shepard maintained a collection of several thousand Indian and French artifacts which he had picked up on the site of the fort.

There are questions that will perhaps remain forever unanswered. It is generally accepted that the original Fort Crevecoeur was destroyed. Although LaSalle, Tonti, and 33 men left on their journey to Peoria, there must have been very few of these remaining at the fort by April, 1680. Six had deserted. At the end of February, LaSalle sent Father Louis Hennepin and two other Frenchmen to explore the Illinois farther south. On March 1, LaSalle himself left Fort Crevecoeur with six Frenchmen and an Indian for the long journey to Fort Frontenac. When he reached what is now Starved Rock, LaSalle sent two members of his party back to Tonti with word for him to return with them to build a new fort atop this rock. After Tonti left to carry out this charge, there could have been no more than a handful of men remaining at Fort Crevecoeur. While they may have attempted to burn and destroy the fort, it seems a difficult task. Newly cut Illinois hardwood will not readily burn. Neither could a few men dismantle a fort constructed of such heavy tree trunks, nor would they have had any real reason to do so. LaSalle also had started construction on a forty-ton sailing vessel at Fort Crevecoeur, which he planned to use to explore the Illinois and Mississippi. Old woodcuts show the abandoned fort and the remains of the boat, with a grim reminder left behind by the deserters, saying "Nous sommes tous les sauvages" - we are all savages.

In the meantime, Tonti had built his Fort St. Louis atop the rock - "le rocher" - near Utica. And when it proved to be indefensible, largely because of the difficulty of supplying it with water, Tonti deserted it, returned to Pimiteoui and named the new fort here "St. Louis." Several old maps locate it on the Richard Phillips site with the notation "Fort St. Louis, devant Creve Coeur," "devant" meaning "previously."

This was the winter of 1691-92, and according to the historian Clarence Walworth Alvord, the fort "was surrounded by 1800 pickets, had two large log houses, one for lodging and one for a warehouse, and, to shelter soldiers, two other houses built of uprights. Around the new fort there soon collected French settlers, who thus formed the first permanent village in Illinois."

John Reynolds, fourth governor of Illinois, in his autobiography written in 1879, documented Fort Crevecoeur and Fort St. Louis II as being on the same location:

> **❝** On this lake, east of the present city of Peoria, LaSalle with his party made a small fort in 1680 and from its hardship, called it Crevecoeur...Indian traders and others mostly employed in that commerce resided at the Old Fort, as it was called, from the time LaSalle erected the fort in 1680 down

to the year 1781, when John Baptiste
Maillet made a new location and village
about one mile and a half west of the old
village at the outlet of the lake. This was
called La Ville de Maillet, that is Maillet
City. I think at the Old Fort, as it was
called, there was not much cultivation of the
earth achieved; but the inhabitants
depended mostly on the Indian trade and
cheese for support. At the new settlement,
gardens and small fields of grain were
cultivated by the inhabitants."

Reynolds later wrote in his "Pioneer History of Illinois," that
the site of Fort Crevecoeur "has been uniformly recognized by
the old French inhabitants down to the present time. And it
may be said with equal truth that some continuous
settlement has existed at or near Fort Crevecoeur since its
first establishment to the present time."

Phillips maintained that the site is one of the most sacred
places in North America. The first Mass in all of Louisiana
was celebrated here and five priests who walked back and
forth daily between the village and the fort all met violent
deaths. It is a site, he claimed, worthy of a basilica.

When Tonti's new Fort St. Louis was finished here in 1692,
there were about 3000 Indians in the area, a population equal
to that of New York. This was 200 years after Columbus
discovered America. Johann Sebastian Bach was only seven
years old. The American Revolution was 84 years in the
future. Yet from that time to the present, there has been an
almost continuous settlement at Peoria, and for 120 years it
was exclusively French.

It was for some few years apparently abandoned, but it
continued as a mission, trading post, and town, and was until
1812 one of the most enduring of all settlements in New
France.

Much of the history and heroism of these years can be
gleaned from THE JESUIT RELATIONS, a record of the
reports and letters sent to the headquarters in Quebec or
Paris by the missionaries who labored here. It might strike us
as odd that these French priests were bringing an alien
culture to the Indians but something very similar still occurs
today among the Cree Indians of Canada, who pray the
rosary and sing Marian hymns in their own tongue. Father
Claude Allouez wrote of the French priests chanting the
"Vexilla Regis" among the savage Indians, "who sometimes
listened with great respect to the story of the Crucifixion."

40

The northern end of Peoria Lake—"Pimiteoui"—was the scene of one of those Indian massacres that seem, in modern times, to be almost beyond belief. What is also surprising, perhaps, is the fact that it is so little known, as if history had conspired to bury the episode in shame and silence. The only reminder is a small plaque set in stones just off Spring Bay Road across from a small tavern known as the "Duck Inn."

It reads, with eloquent simplicity: "Here in October, 1812, 300 Rangers under Gov. Ninian Edwards, Col. William Russell and Capt. Samuel Judy, massacred thirty defenseless Potawatomie Indians, old men, women and children, and completely destroyed their village while the hunters were absent and their chief, Muck-et-ep-koe-kee, Black Partridge, hero of the Fort Dearborn Massacre, was on a mission of mercy to rescue Lt. Helm from the Indians on the Au Sable River. This monument erected by William L. Zeller, Spring Bay, and Harry L. Spooner, Peoria Historical Society, 1954."

Edwards had marched out of Fort Russell near Edwardsville on October 14, 1812, determined to crush the hostile Indians north of Peoria and to avenge the Fort Dearborn massacre. But in settling upon Black Partridge's village, he was about to unleash a tragic mistake and a senseless slaughter.

When the troopers attacked the sleeping village, there was no resistance. According to one account, the Indians made a stand in the woods, pouring out a galling fire that killed Patrick White of Belleville and John Shur of Edwardsville. About thirty Indians were killed, most of them old men, women and some children.

The village was burned to the ground, the food and ponies taken away, and the survivors fled to the mouth of Crow Creek, where they forded the river to Gomo's camp, at the site of the present-day Chillicothe. The troops, fearing reprisal from the thousands of Indians in the area, marched all day and camped on the prairie near Cruger that night.

But it was a futile and senseless assault, largely because Black Partridge remained friendly to the Americans during the War of 1812 and did not succumb to the English attempts to get him to participate in an Indian uprising. He was, in fact, supposedly near Chicago, trying to arrange a ransom for Lt. Helm, who was being held prisoner on the Kankakee River. Black Partridge was known as the hero of the Fort

Dearborn massacre, having saved the wife of Lt. Helm from scalping by a young Indian, an incident commemorated by a statue in the foyer of the Chicago Historical Society.

When he returned from the ransom attempt, Black Partridge found his village destroyed and among the half-consumed remains was his favorite daughter and her infant child. He vowed vengeance and eventually led a force of 300 men against settlements in Randolph, St. Clair, and Madison Counties. But peace was restored and Black Partridge retired to his former village beside the Big Spring to spend the rest of his days.

Eventually the Potawatomies were cleared from the area and resettled across the Mississippi after signing away their rights to the land here, often by fraudulent means. At the treaty signed in St. Louis in 1816, the Potawatomies were allowed to remain on their land "so long as the land continued to be the property of the United States." As soon as it was sold, however, it was no longer U.S. property.

Black Partridge died in 1819 or 1820. According to Spencer Ellsworth in the History of Marshall County, "He was an old man. His wife and children were dead, his people grown few in number. The buffalo had fled the country and the land was passing into the hands of the palefaces. There was little left to live for. With no desire to longer live, he looked his last upon the green grass and blue sky, turned his face to the wall, and died.

"There was a deep sorrow among his people. He was laid in a rough box, clad in his richest robes with his ornaments, arms, pipe and tobacco beside him and when securely bound with thongs was hoisted into the forks of a big ash tree growing a few rods distant, where it stood after the Indians had departed and was cut down by an old man named 'Fields'."

According to the Illinois State Museum Scientific Papers, "The Edwards campaign in the War of 1812 stole a march on the Indians. Since Gomo, Shequenbec and Black Partridge were going to attack the whites, he destroyed Black Partridge's village and broke the back of the Indian War."

That view seems to be a minority opinion. The more accepted, perhaps less popular view, is that this was a brutal and cowardly attack, the massacre of innocents at the village of one of the "good Indians."

CHIEF BLACK PARTRIDGE (CENTER) IN THIS SCULPTURE AT THE CHICAGO HISTORICAL SOCIETY. (JERRY KLEIN PHOTO).

42

LASALLE BEGINS HIS
JOURNEY ON THE ILLINOIS.
(FROM BESS'S HISTORY OF
PEORIA).

LASALLE'S CANOES ENTERING
LAKE PEORIA. (FROM BESS'S
HISTORY OF PEORIA).

"The men are libertines," wrote Father Julien Binneteau in 1699. But "there are also women married to some of our Frenchmen who would be a good example to the best regulated household in France."

He also wrote that Father Marest is "somewhat too zealous...he works excessively during the day and he sits up at night to improve himself in the language; he would like to learn the whole vocabulary in five or six months. There is another missionary...here from the Province of Guyenne and his name is Father Pinet. He has had the happiness of sending to heaven the soul of the famous Chief Peouris."

In one of his reports that same year, Father Marest noted: "Every day before sunrise we say Mass for the convenience of our Christians, who go from it to their work. The savages chant the prayers or recite them together during the Mass. In the afternoon, three time a week, there is general catechism for the people. Saturdays and Sundays are completely occupied in hearing confessions."

Father Gravier, who was regarded as the founder of the Illinois missions, wrote an eloquent plea for supplies for the Illinois missions in 1702. "Father Binet," he said, "died there from exhaustion; but if he had had a few drops of Spanish wine, for which he asked us during his last illness....and some little dainties such as sugar, or other things, or had we been able to provide some fresh food for him, he would perhaps still be alive."

FUR TRAPPERS ON THE RIVER. (PHOTO COURTESY LAKEVIEW MUSEUM).

Among the list of goods he requested were winter and summer cassocks, breeches, hats, hoods, mittens, shoes, thread, pins, sugar, vinegar, nails, wire, bullets, knives, soap, awls, and tobacco.

The lives of these missionaries were apparently a frustrating combination of rewards and disappointments. The women and children responded to their teachings, but the Indian men, like those of some nationalities since, seemed quite impervious to the attractions of organized religion. "Nothing is more difficult than the conversion of these savages," wrote Father Gabriel Marest in 1712. "As they are absolute masters of themselves, without being subject to any law, the independence in which they live enslaves them to the most brutal passions - the worst among these being gluttony and the love of pleasure."

"There would have been less difficulty converting the Illinois if the prayer (or the Catholic laws) had permitted polygamy among them," noted Father Sebastian Rale. But he continued that "there are none, even the medicine men, of course the worst enemies of religion, who do not send their children to be instructed and baptized."

While the siege by the Fox Indians around 1722 may have driven both the Peoria Indians and the French from Peoria, they were back after the defeat of the Fox in 1730. A memorial to Congress in 1807 claimed that the village of Peoria had been established about 1730 and that some of the signers had been born here and inherited land from their fathers. How large, how active, and how permanent Peoria was throughout much of the early 18th century remains largely speculative. The French, much like the Indians whose habits they adopted, tended to come and go since they were traders, trappers and "couriers de bois" rather than farmers or settlers.

Peoria could certainly be found in some sort of organized village form since shortly after 1730. In 1759, after the successful British assault on the Plains of Abraham near Quebec and the subsequent defeat at Quebec, French rule ceased here. The Illinois territory was ceded to England in 1763, and in December of that year, the French military

44

BRITISH UNION JACK. (PEORIA PUBLIC LIBRARY).

commander, Neyon de Villiers, reported from Fort de Chartres: "I recalled from Peoria M. Toulon and his garrison."

The British influence here was almost negligible. They occupied the land in 1765, but there was little evidence of any occupation in Peoria. That same year there are records that Antoine Saint Francois sowed his corn at Peoria. For the French here, life went on the same as usual.

This brief and apparently uneventful British rule ended during the Revolutionary War when the Americans captured Kaskaskia in 1778, and Vincennes in Indiana in 1779.

By this time, Jean Baptiste Maillet, whom many regard as the founder of modern Peoria and the major presence here in its early history, was already living and working at Peoria. He was a French Canadian by birth who apparently settled here around 1766. There is documented evidence that Maillet sold

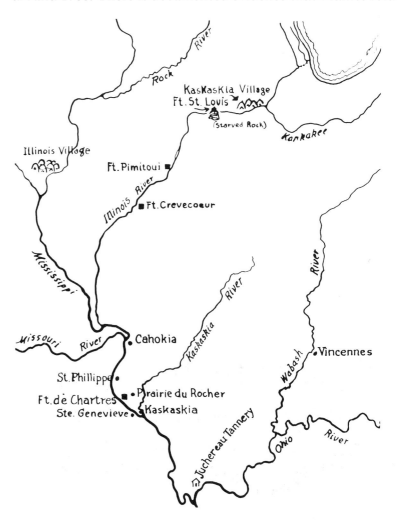

THE ILLINOIS COUNTRY IN THE DAYS OF THE FRENCH.

some land to Jean Baptiste Point du Sable on March 13, 1773. Du Sable, who lived here about ten years and then moved to Chicago, was one of that city's first permanent settlers in 1790, which means that Chicago was founded by a former Peorian.

Maillet's original settlement was located in the vicinity of what many believe was old Fort St. Louis, along the river at Caroline Street on the north side. It seems to have been an unhealthy spot and around 1778, Maillet moved a mile and a half to the south, to what is now downtown Peoria. Many of the French settlers followed him and the town that grew here was widely known as La Ville de Maillet.

For a time, at least until 1797, there were two French villages here, but by that year, the original site was abandoned and roughly 100 people clustered around Maillet's new village. Maillet had apparently received some kind of commission from the United States during the Revolutionary War and was named commandant of the village. He might even have led an expedition against the British at St. Joseph. He was definitely favorable to the American cause once he discovered the French were heavily involved with us against the British.

The French today regard the later victories of the Revolutionary War as their own as well as ours. Among the famous battles celebrated in historic paintings still on display at Versailles is Yorktown.

By 1790, Maillet was captain of the Illinois Militia and a process server for the court in Cahokia. According to some, he was almost a feudal lord, presiding over his little village with a mixture of arrogance and condescension, granting concessions on one hand and restricting the use of meadowlands on the other. He was killed in a dispute in 1801, and Thomas Forsyth, originally a British subject, emerged as the major figure in Peoria. He, along with his half-brother John Kinzie (also one of the earlier settlers of Chicago), opened a trading post here about 1806.

A ledger from that year shows Forsyth providing Hippolyte Maillet - son of Jean - with calico, whiskey, candles, gunpowder, and corn and giving him credit for 28 pounds of beef and one cow's hide. A Margaret Courselle bought two snuff boxes and a pack of cards from Forsyth the same year and was credited with 76 pounds of beef in the barter system apparently in use then.

Forsyth's records show that the pelts of 2680 raccoons and other raw furs - including deerskins, beaver, otter, muskrat, mink, badger, wildcat, fox, wolf, lynx and bear - were shipped from Peoria to Chicago on January 14, 1812.

46

CHARLES BALLANCE,
(DECEASED)
PEORIA.

There are two almost wildly divergent views of the French for whom Peoria, or the "Ville de Maillet," was for so long home. It is perhaps unfortunate that the one expounded by the early Peoria settler and attorney, Charles Ballance, has largely prevailed and helps account for the fact that French history here has been virtually obliterated.

The view of Ballance was undoubtedly that of a lawyer who for many years fought the land claims of the French after they were expelled from Peoria during the War of 1812. To suggest that they were

highly colored, if not prejudiced, is hardly overstating the case.

In his own history of Peoria, Ballance states, "Nor should we allow ourselves to be deceived as to the amount of civilization that existed here before the French village was broken up in 1812. Attempts have been made to convince men that there was a fine, flourishing settlement here, of civilized, enterprising, intelligent people.

"I apprehend that the men LaSalle and others brought here were of the lower class and most ignorant of the French population.

"If not, they had woefully deteriorated between the time they were brought here and the destruction of their village.

"These were fishermen and hunters, not farmers. All the fields they pretended ever to have in cultivation amounted to less than 300 acres, even if none of the fields had been deserted before they left.

"When the village was burnt, I think they had less than 200 acres in cultivation. They sometimes acted as voyageurs for the Indian traders, but of manufacturing they had none. They had not a schoolhouse or church, nor a dwelling house that deserved the name. I saw and examined the ground on which their homes had stood, before the ground was disturbed, and I am able to state that there was not a stone nor brick wall in the village for any purpose, nor was there a cellar."

Although others had observed vineyards, wine presses, and churches here, Ballance dismissed the evidence.

"That they had no gardens, in the common acceptance of the term, is manifest from this: many of the cultivated plants, when once introduced to a place, if deserted by man, will never cease to grow there. Yet when the present population commenced to settle here about forty years ago, there was not to be found in this neighborhood, a vestige of a tree, shrub or plant belonging to Europe.

"I have seen many affidavits and other papers signed by these men, but signed with a mark. I remember as exceptions to this rule that Thomas Forsyth, Michael Le Croix, and Antoine la Pance wrote their names. There were probably others that could write, but I do not remember them. I remember no case where a French woman could write."

Historian Percival Rennick concedes that these were largely unlettered men, as were many of the early pioneers and settlers, both English and American. But his view of French Peoria is somewhat more idyllic.

He wrote, "They received little or no mail and very few, if any, could have read a letter had one been received. Yet through the traders and voyageurs they heard of the doings in Quebec and Paris. They had many blessings. The streams were full of fish and the forests and prairies abounded in game.

"All their personal disputes were settled by the parish priest and all their business disputes were settled in a meeting called by the 'Syndic.' They understood the Indians, and the Indians believed the French to be their friends."

The acceptance and understanding of the Indians on the part of the French seems to be agreed upon by most historians. It remains in sharp contrast to the treatment accorded the Indians by the British, and later by the Americans. While the French lived with the Indians and often intermarried with these native Americans, the view of the British was far less tolerant and that of the American settlers came to be typified by the remark of General Philip Henry Sheridan that "the only good Indian is a dead Indian."

When the British began occupying the Illinois territory after it was ceded to them by the French in 1763, they used almost any means possible to dominate the Indians and take over their land. Traders from the British colonies in many instances were suspected of murder and robbery, of corrupting the Indians with rum, of cheating and overcharging them, and even of spreading smallpox among the tribes.

Sir Geoffrey Amherst, leader of the English armies in America, wrote to General Bouquet, "I wish there was not an Indian settlement within a thousand miles of our country, for they are only fit to live with the inhabitants of the woods (wild beasts), being more allied to the brute than to human creation. Could it not be contrived to send the smallpox among those disaffected tribes of Indians. We must on this occasion use every stratagem in our power to reduce them."

Bouquet responded that he would try to inoculate the Indians with some blankets that might fall into their hands "and take care not to get the disease myself."

Whether the plan was ever carried out was never proved, but an Indian chief confessed to a French officer in 1864, "The French, our brothers, have never given us any disease, but the English have scarcely arrived and they have caused nearly all our children to die by the smallpox they have brought."

Edward Coles, in his 1820 account, noted that the Peoria French lived in peace with the Indians. "From that happy facility of adapting themselves to their situation and associates, for which the French are so remarkable, the inhabitants of Peoria lived generally in harmony with their savage neighbors."

In a time when the genocidal crimes against the Indians of this country have at last become recognized for what they are, the record of the early French who lived here deserves to be suitably recognized.

48

NINIAN EDWARDS, FROM AN ORIGINAL PAINTING OWNED BY THE CHICAGO HISTORICAL SOCIETY.

By that time, the second war with England in less than a generation had started and French Peoria was in its final, tragic days. The British were busy inciting the Indians in the Illinois territory to take up arms against the United States. They were somewhat successful with the Kickapoos and Piankeshaws, but the Potawatomies around Peoria were unwilling to join them. Nevertheless, Governor Ninian Edwards had received reports that Peoria was a hotbed of Indian troubles and in October, 1812, he dispatched an expedition against the Indians here that was to be one of the most senseless and brutal tragedies of the entire U.S.-Indian relations. (See the accompanying story on Black Partridge).

At the same time, Peoria itself was to become the target of a useless and brutal attack. Edwards' expedition against the Indians here was to be two-pronged campaign, by land and by water; but Captain Thomas Craig, who had been sent with his troops in two boats, did not arrive until after Black Partridge's village had been destroyed.

Craig neverthless stopped at Peoria, where he and his men reportedly broke into Forsyth's warehouse and the store of Felix la Fontaine, where they helped themselves to two kegs of wine.

No one knows whether they were inflamed by drink or frustrated at having missed the "fun" of an Indian massacre, but while anchored off Peoria, they were apparently fired on by someone - probably Indians. Craig's men wasted no time. They stormed ashore to loot and burn the village. While the British were guilty of burning Washington, D. C., it was the Americans who burned Peoria. Even worse, Craig took the men of Peoria as prisoners. Leaving the women and children behind in the cold of November, 1812, he took the men downstream and dropped them in the vicinity of Savage's ferry, near Alton.

Despite a later defense by lawyer Ballance, and Craig's own protestations, it was an act widely condemned. Peoria historian Ernest East labeled it the revenge of a "ruffian."

"Like the village of Grand Pre in Longfellow's 'Evangeline,'" East wrote, "La Ville de Maillet on the site of Peoria was given to the torch by a ruthless military commander."

It was November 8, 1812, for better or for worse, which marked the end of French Peoria.

Eventually the French families who had lived here were reunited in the St. Louis area. Among those who had lived here at what is now the foot of Libery Street were Forsyth, Jacques Mette, Francis Buche, Louis Bisson, Michael la Croix, P. Lavassieur, L. Pennenneau, Francis Racine, Charles LaBelle, Baptiste Raboin, John Blondeau, Francis Dupre, and a family name Roi.

None, with the possible exception of Bisson, who, in later chronicles turns up as a fur trader known in an anglicized spelling as Beesaw, ever returned to Peoria. The old streets and lanes of La Ville de Maillet - called a "French cowpath" by Ballance - became Liberty and Water Streets. And despite years of the French trying to regain their lands in a court battle that dragged on for nearly half a century, Peoria was to be no longer French. The tangle that resulted eventually found its way to the U. S. Supreme Court and involved such legal talent as Abraham Lincoln. Some of the French did gain monetary satisfaction, but Attorney Ballance was credited with blocking most of the French claims.

Except for a French-run trading post at Opa, near the bottom of Creve Coeur hill, the French were gone with the wind, leaving only the memories of missionaries and traders, trappers and explorers.

Today, little is left except for a few names. There is a one-block street on Peoria's East Bluff named LaSalle. There is the Hotel Pere Marquette. There is a Tonti Circle and a Creve Coeur, with its reconstructed fort. There is, on the Illinois River navigation charts, a Lake Beesaw - named unquestionably after the fur trader Bisson. Otherwise, those 131 years when Peoria was French have been so successfully erased that they might never have been. But they were. They were!

CHAPTER FOUR

THE AMERICANS ARRIVE: PEORIA TAKES SHAPE

From the remains of Fort Clark and the arrival of the first American settlers in 1819 to the life of Josiah Fulton, Charles Ballance and Hamilton, the surveyor. Early growth and progress. The immigrants arrive and Peoria grows to become a city.

A PAINTING FROM 1833 SAID TO BE AT FORT CLARK. (COURTESY LAKEVIEW MUSEUM).

Once the French village of La Ville de Maillet had been burned and sacked and the inhabitants scattered, the site that was to become Peoria remained virtually uninhabited for over a half dozen years.

Following the Battle of New Orleans and the conclusion of the War of 1812, the great westward emigration began in earnest. One easterner, who resided near the Allegheny River, which lay along one of the major paths, counted 260 wagons passing westward in a single day. But the tide did not reach here until the spring of 1819; and aside from the erection of Fort Clark by Brigadier General Benjamin Howard in 1813, Peoria was unoccupied, save for an occasional trapper or Indian.

General Harrison's fort was almost as unused and shortlived as LaSalle's Fort Crevecoeur had been 133 years earlier. Howard had marched here with an army of 1400 men to attack the hostile Indian villages around Peoria Lake, many of whose warriors were led by the formerly friendly Black Partridge. The destruction of his village at the Big Spring, across from Chillicothe, had left him bitter and hostile and understandably so. When Howard arrived, the Indians were gone and the general returned to the foot of Peoria Lake and erected his 100-square foot stockade at what is now Liberty and Water streets.

It apparently was occupied for a very short time. When Gurdon S. Hubbard, an employee of John Jacob Astor's American Fur Company, arrived here in 1818, he found Fort Clark burned and Indians present. Presumably, they had set fire to the deserted structure, although for what reason it is hard to imagine. It also seems rather odd that Fort Clark, although abandoned and burned, was still identifiable as a fort several years later, while Fort Crevecoeur seems to have vanished almost without a trace, and very quickly at that.

When the first settlers came to Fort Clark in April, 1819, they reportedly found two deserted log cabins, presumably a part of the fort, and sufficient remains of Fort Clark to determine that it had indeed been a fort.

These first settlers were Abner Eads, Josiah Fulton, his brother Seth, all from Virginia; Joseph Hersey of New York; and S. Daugherty, J. Davis and T. Russell of Kentucky. Eads and Hersey arrived with pack horses and the rest arrived on a keel boat, apparently poled upriver.

It appears that Fort Clark, as Peoria was originally known, was as primitive, or perhaps more so, than the French village it replaced. These first American residents, most of them of English stock, lived in rude log cabins through some very unpleasant winters. They were not particularly friendly to the Indians, as the French had been, and so they received little aid from that quarter. There were, in fact, early conflicts between those French who remained in the area and the new American settlers over the treatment of Indians. The French contended the Indians should be allowed to roam free, but the Americans felt that this was unsafe.

If the beginning of Fort Clark/Peoria was not particularly auspicious, these first tough and determined Americans were, nevertheless, destined to bring a formidable change to the area. The one who remained the longest and saw the most change was Josiah Fulton, who lived out his long and productive life here.

JOSIAH FULTON. (PEORIA PUBLIC LIBRARY).

Shortly after arriving in 1819, Fulton bought eighty acres (in the very heart of the present city) from the United States Government at $1.25 per acre. Part of his original land later became the site of the courthouse and another that of Rouse's Hall, where the First National Bank now stands. Since Fulton was primarily a farmer, he sold this land and in 1828 acquired eighty acres in the area that is now Glen Oak Avenue. In 1832, Fulton married Augusta P. Hughes, whose parents had arrived here from Georgia seven years earlier. The Fultons had ten children and Josiah remained in such good health that at the age of ninety, he walked two miles from his son's home on Knoxville to the PEORIA JOURNAL office downtown, and then to the Grand Opera House to pay for his tickets for the new season.

Abner Eads, another first settler, had the distinction in 1819 of bringing his wife to Peoria as the first American woman to reside in the community. He lived here fourteen years, moved to Galena where he became well-known, and in 1854 struck out for California. While returning home to get his wife, he died and Mrs. Eads eventually moved on, alone, to California.

Most of the others who came to Fort Clark in that April of 1819 went onward, although Seth Fulton opened a hotel on Water Street, near Eaton, in 1827 and then moved to Galena. The honor of Peoria's very first hotel, such as it was, belongs, however, to John Bogardus, who opened the doors to his "Travellers' Rest" in a log cabin on the riverbank in 1826.

54

While the early settlers in the Peoria area found a lush, verdant, and unspoiled land, there were, nevertheless, great hazards to be found—among them diseases such as malaria, diphtheria, and consumption. In cemeteries throughout the area, tombstones from this period of history tell a tragic story of the hardships of pioneer life—the deaths of young mothers in childbirth and the menace to children of diphtheria and scarlet fever. There is the family in 1864 which lost three children in one week's time and two more later in the year; the family that lost three children in four months; or the family whose three children died at Christmastime in 1879. Eleven of the thirteen children of one family died in infancy or early childhood, six of these within three weeks time during the "Black Diphtheria" epidemic of 1880.

According to the Journal of the Illinois State Historical Society:

"The prairies were quagged with bogs, swamps, and stagnant bodies of water, admirable incubators for noxious insects and malarial disease and fevers, to say nothing of the intestinal epidemics due to imperfect means and improper methods of food preservation during the hot seasons. . .What was the menace for one was the menace for all, and the doctor had to fight to keep himself well. . .

. . .The year 1833 is memorable in the annals of Illinois for the terrible visitation of Asiatic Cholera, brought the summer before with the regular troops. . .who came to assist our militia in their Indian war. Its most distinguished victim in the state was Gov. Ninian Edwards, who died of the scourge at his home in Belleville on the 20th day of July, 1833, in his 58th year of age. . .

. . .Cholera generally followed the course of rivers. . .and usually attacked coast or river towns first, probably not because of any particular affinity of its germs for water . . .but more likely because our rivers were the principal routes of travel in the pioneer period."

The Bloomington, Illinois Western Whig reported on May 12, 1849:

"What is the exact nature of the malignant agent in the atmosphere which causes this disease has not been discovered . . .but it is undoubtedly a miasma arising from the decay of vegetable matter about the mouth of the Ganges in Asia where it takes its periodical rise and spreads on westward through Europe and America."

And the Bloomington, Illinois Pantagraph on August 1, 1855 said:

"There has been manifested some little disposition to censure us for publishing three or four deaths last week as by cholera—fearing that it might keep people away from Bloomington and injure business men. . .We are not unaware that it is the custom with many editors to conceal the truth in such diseases for fear that it might injure the character or the business of their places, but in such rascality we will not participate."

While nothing conclusive can be determined regarding the effects on Peoria of the cholera epidemics of 1833, 1849, and 1854, the city seems to have been spared the ravages of most of these outbreaks. There are no listings of the deaths in Peoria before 1843, and there is no public record of the number of deaths from 1847 through 1849, a time-span that covers the period of the reputedly worst epidemic—1849-1850. In 1938, Fayette B. Shaw wrote, in an article recorded in the Journal of the Illinois State Historical Society, Volume 30: "Peoria was checked in its growth by the cholera epidemic of 1849-1850, yet the population increased from 3014 in 1847 to 6202 at the close of 1850."

In areas close to Peoria— LaSalle and Lourdes (the present-day Germantown Hills), the percentage of deaths in 1854-1855 in relation to the overall population was greater than at any other time in their history. This percentage figure for Peoria nearly doubled from 1854 to 1855, indicating that perhaps, locally, this was the worst epidemic in our early history.

This early Peoria was hardly a boom town. By the early 1830's, the settlement consisted of a mere twenty-one log cabins and seven frame houses. The first of these modern framed structures apparently was raised by John Hamlin in 1825. It measured eighteen by twenty-four feet, was constructed of split and shaved logs and stood at the corner of what is now Main and Perry streets.

The same year that Hamlin built his home, Peoria County was laid out and at the time it included both Galena and Chicago. Hamlin was a member of the first grand jury to be summoned here. The jury brought an indictment against the Indian, Nomaque, who was accused of killing Pierre Landry, a Frenchman. Nomaque's attorney was William S. Hamilton, the son of Alexander Hamilton, who remained here to lay out the town of Peoria the following year. Hamilton carried the case to the U. S. Supreme Court but Nomaque's conviction was upheld. The Indian eventually escaped from jail and fought with Black Hawk in the war that bears his name.

Hamlin has other distinctions. He owned the first flour mill in Peoria, built in 1831 along the banks of the Kickapoo. He had the steamboat "Peoria" built in Pittsburgh in 1830 and pressed it into service between here and St. Louis. In September, 1854, he signed a letter inviting Abraham Lincoln here to debate Douglas. He also was one of the founders of the Peoria National Bank. He lived for several years at 111 North Jefferson, adjacent to Rouse's Hall on one side and the home of Robert Ingersoll on the other.

WILLIAM S. HAMILTON.

AN EARLY HORSE-POWERED CULTIVATOR. (F-STOP SOCIETY).

A FARMER IDENTIFIED AS SIEBOLD THE GARDENER AT THE OLD CITY MARKET WHERE THE PEORIA CITY HALL NOW STANDS. (PEORIA PUBLIC LIBRARY).

PEORIA, AUGUST 29TH, 1831,
IN A LITHOGRAPH BY
J.M. ROBERTS.

58

AN EARLY ETCHING OF
PEORIA'S FIRST COURTHOUSE.

PEORIA'S COURTHOUSE
IN THE EARLY 1900'S.

By 1825, the population had grown to 1236 and a new fourteen by sixteen foot log courthouse was built near old Fort Clark. Before the second courthouse was completed ten years later, at a cost of $15,000, the grand jury frequently held its sessions underneath a crab apple tree.

Even then, there were varying reactions to Peoria. When Aquilla Moffatt, son of Captain Joseph Moffatt, arrived here with his family in June, 1822, he recalled later: "When I stepped from the boat and looked out over the prairie and to the bluffs and trees beyond, I thought it was the grandest scene of beauty my eyes ever beheld, and I never expect to look upon a grander range of beauty until my spiritual eyes are opened in the Eden of Eternity beyond the end of mortality."

Somewhat less enthusiastic was Patrick Shirreff, a Scottish farmer who passed here in 1833 during a tour of the United States to determine if his younger brother should emigrate. The village of Peoria, he observed, "exhibits marks of considerable age, but none of prosperity. I found the dinner hour past and fared indifferently. There being nothing to attract attention at Peoria, I recrossed the ferry where the horse was still standing, and bent my way to Pekin, which I reached a little before sunset."

A somewhat happier view was offered in 1840 by Eliza R. Steel whose travel accounts bear a certain flowery ring appropriate to the times: "We bade adieu to sweet Peoria with regret," she wrote. "The remembrances of it will long 'perfume our minds' as old Izaak Walton says. Its situation, its excellent society, and religious privileges and its good schools most certainly make it a desirable place of residence or trade."

Seven years later, J. H. Buckingham of the BOSTON COURIER passed here on the steamboat "Dial" and found Peoria "beautifully situated" and "already the seat of a great business with one of the most grand and interesting views in the world." But he reports spending little time here and finding almost everybody asleep.

One of the first residents of Peoria was a black, Jean Baptiste Point du Sable, who arrived here about 1773, lived in Peoria on and off for several years, and left around 1779 to become the first permanent settler of Chicago.

What became of du Sable, a French-speaking native of San Domingo, is uncertain. The Journal of the Illinois State Historical Society reports that he lived at Chicago for sixteen years and then disappeared, supposedly dying at Peoria near Fort Clark. Peoria historian, Ernest East, claims that du Sable was driven out of Chicago by the English for supposedly aiding the Americans and that he died on August 28, 1818, and is buried at St. Borromeo Catholic Church in St. Charles, Missouri.

Thomas Forsyth, who lived here when the French were expelled in 1812, reportedly had a black indentured servant in his custody named Jeffrey Nash, and Simeon De Witt Drown's 1844 Peoria City Directory lists Alex Labadier as a "colored" barber.

Peoria also was the scene of considerable pro- and anti-slavery agitation before the Civil War. The home of Moses Pettengill was an important depot on the underground railroad.

The first black school was founded in Peoria in 1856, and there were special schools for blacks until they were integrated into the public schools in 1871. Peoria's first black church was the Ward A.M.E. Chapel, founded in 1846, and the first black constable and notary public in the city was Henry Gibson who, in 1904, won an early civil rights suit when he was denied a seat on the main floor of the Main Street Theatre. He won the suit and $25 in damages.

PEORIA AS DRAWN BY H. BROSIUS IN 1872.

THE OLD LOWRY CHURCH,
BUILT 1835 ON JACKSON
BELOW ADAMS.

It may be impossible to assign a precise turning point to Peoria's early history, but sometime in the early 1830's the impetus that turned this from a frontier, log-cabin settlement into a progressive town and city began to be felt. By 1834, the first newspaper, THE ILLINOIS CHAMPION AND PEORIA HERALD, was being published. By 1838, a stage and mail coach had started regular service between Peoria and Oquawka.

By 1834, also, the first churches were founded. These included the First Methodist, St. John's Episcopal, First Presbyterian and First Congregational. Within the next two years, the Lowry Presbyterian Church building arose at Adams and Jackson and the Main Street Presbyterian congregation built a twenty-eight by fifty foot building at what is now 420 Main Street. The First Baptist Church was organized in 1836. Three years later, one of the area's first Catholic churches -and the only church from this period still standing today -was built at Kickapoo under the direction of Father Joseph Raho. It was known as St. Patrick's and may be seen today in the little cemetery just north of the town of Kickapoo. The same year, the First Methodist Episcopal Church arose at South Madison and Fulton streets.

The early 1830's also brought some of Peoria's more prominent early citizens. One was Charles Ballance, who arrived in 1831 from Madison County, Kentucky. There were only two other attorneys here at the time, John L. Bogardus and Lewis Bigelow. This was a time when legal education and expertise was hardly as well honed as it is today. Ballance, in fact, lacked experience to such an extent that he once travelled to Chicago to ascertain the proceedings of an actual court in session. He also built the first school house here, on Walnut Street between Washington and Adams, and like Hamilton before him, was a surveyor as well.

Some of the early property Ballance acquired was located between Adams Street and the river in a stretch running from Franklin to Pecan. This was part of old French Peoria and Ballance spent thirty years fighting the French claims over this piece of land.

Ballance also served as mayor of Peoria in 1855, and in 1862 organized the 77th regiment of Illinois Volunteers for the Civil War and became its colonel. He published his ambitious history of Peoria in 1870 and died here on August 10, 1872. Among the other early arrivals were Benjamin Slane, who came on the steamboat "Don Juan" in 1831 and built a cabin near Fort Clark; Moses Pettengill, who became the first hardware merchant after he arrived in 1833 and later built a home on Moss Avenue that is today operated by the Peoria Historical Society; and Dr. Rudolphus Rouse, who came on

THE PETTENGILL-MORRON HOUSE, 1212 W. MOSS, BUILT 1868 BY MOSES PETTENGILL AND GIVEN TO THE PEORIA HISTORICAL SOCIETY FOLLOWING THE DEATH OF ITS LAST OWNER-OCCUPANT, MISS JEAN MCLEAN MORRON.

62

horseback from New York in 1833. At the time, the only other doctor was Augustus Langsworthy, whose practice extended from Springfield to Chicago. Once he arrived here, Dr. Rouse wrote enthusiastically to his wife in New York:

> Let us haste to Illinois, Bonny Lady,
>
> Far from the city's pomp and noise,
>
> Where the wild flower in its pride,
>
> Decks the prairie far and wide,
>
> Content and happy we'll reside, Bonny Lady.

Dr. Rouse is understandably not remembered for his poetry as much as for his founding of Rouse's Opera House, which opened in 1837 and provided perhaps the first high class entertainment to be seen in the growing city. The Opera House was located on the site of the present First National Bank Building and for years was a scene for touring opera and theatre productions. Rouse also organized the Peoria Medical Society in 1848 and was an adventuresome businessman and real estate dealer. He remained in practice as "Physicians and Surgeons" with Dr. Edward Dickinson at the corner of Main and Jefferson until his death in 1873.

MAIN STREET FROM THE TOP OF THE HILL, ABOUT 1888. (COURTESY LEE ROTEN).

In 1844, Simeon De Witt Drown had published Peoria's first directory in which he noted: "The rapid growth of our town since 1840, and particularly during the last year, in which upwards of fifty buildings were erected, and nearly all of a permanent material - brick or stone - seems to warrant the publication of such a work as is here presented." Peoria's future seemed secured.

Drown, whose work is dated April 1, 1844, claimed that Peoria's natural advantages surpass those of any other interior point in the state and are excelled by few, if any, in the great west. He wrote:

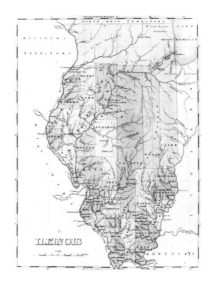

MAP OF ILLINOIS, ABOUT 1840.

❝❝ Situated on the best navigable stream (of its size) in our vast union, with a back country of unequaled fertility, what can prevent its becoming a great commercial metropolis? Add to this the advantage to be derived from the Illinois and Michigan Canal, which it must share in greater degree than any other river point, not even excepting Peru, the termination of that work, and who can realize our ultimate greatness? We are already the center of the most extensive mail region in this state and the great thoroughfare for the travel from every point of the compass. We have daily lines of stages to Springfield (at the south) and Chicago (at the northeast); tri-weekly to Burlington, Iowa (at the west), Galena (at the north) and Danville (at the east); and a semi-weekly line to Rushville and Quincy (at the southwest). Our facilities for communication by water are even greater than these. For the past four years we have had a daily mail packet to Peru and regular semi-weekly and weekly packets to St. Louis, besides numerous transient arrivals and departures, sometimes affording a passage to either of the points named at almost any hour of the day....Other statistics will be seen throughout its pages, from which it will be acknowledged that the view here taken is by no means exaggerated."

Drown was perhaps more of a prophet than he realized. As he published this first directory, Peoria was poised for a period of growth that perhaps exceeded anything the worthy surveyor and chronicler ever imagined.

64

Peoria has long been known as a heavily German city. During the 1983 tricentennial celebrating the arrival of the first German immigrants in the country, it was claimed that forty per cent of all Peorians were of German heritage.

However, the ethnic makeup of the city is far more complex. It has become, in fact, the almost-idealized melting pot with its German and Irish-English majorities and large pockets of Lebanese, Italian, Swedes, and smaller groups of Orientals, Hungarians, Czechs and Slovaks, Dutch, French, Danes, Hispanics, Polish, Greeks, Norwegians, and Swiss.

While most of the early settlers following the French expulsion were of English descent, the Germans were not far behind. One of the first Germans to settle here was Jacob Koch, who arrived in 1834, when the city was composed of seven frame houses and twenty-one log cabins. He lived for several weeks in a tent. The second German settler was Valentine Schlinck, who had helped to build the Catholic Church in Kickapoo and who became active in the dry goods, hotel, and real estate business here.

The first German inn in the city, the Union Hotel, was run by "Mutter" Slough in the early 1800's. It was located at 210 South Washington. She was a true pioneer who arrived here in 1832 and later sent for her family in Pennsylvania.

Following the 1848 revolution in Germany, the Germans poured by the thousands into the Midwest with its rich farmlands. Many were hardworking, frugal farmers, but there also were doctors, brewers, businessmen, and intellectuals. In 1844, there were forty German homes here; by 1856, the German population numbered 576. It swelled to 2000 by 1876; and by 1900, 10,000 Germans lived in Peoria.

Some of these sought to create a new Germany in America. Another group were known disdainfully as the "German Yankees" who had little interest in their heritage; but the largest percentage were German-Americans, who wanted to be Americans while retaining their language, hoping to blend the best characteristics of German life with that of American life. They attempted to preserve their culture through schools, newspapers, churches, and clubs. At times their enthusiasm for singing and celebration (inevitably accompanied by beer) ran counter to a strain of native Puritanism; and the Continental Sunday of the Germans versus the Puritan Sabbath erupted into a stone-throwing episode on July 4, 1869, at a typically exuberant German-American picnic at which Robert Ingersoll spoke.

By 1905, there were seven German schools in Peoria and a proliferation of newspapers, among them the Banner, the Deutsche Zeitung, Die Sohne, and Die Peoria Volksfreund. With their "Turnverein," "Schutzenverein," "Liederkranz Society," "Steuben Club," and their great "Sangerfests" at the Academy of Music, the Germans added immeasurably to the cultural life of the city. They celebrated gleefully the 100th anniversary of Schiller's birth and death, the winning of the Franco-Prussian War in 1871, and the dedication of the War Memorial executed by the Peoria German-American sculptor, Fritz Triebel, in 1899.

The German language, which had been treasured by generations, was severely curtailed by World War I and virtually eliminated by World War II, but the German influence, if Anglicized, remains a major factor in the past and present of the city.

Many of the Irish came to this part of the country as railroad workers and members of construction crews on the canals. Earlier Irish settlers had been part of George Rogers Clark's army. The later arrivals were a small trickle of the vast exodus who found a new life and a new promise here following the potato famines of the 1840's and 1850's. They have become a vital force in Peoria, where their St. Patrick's Day Parade and "Erin Feis" celebration have become the best-attended ethnic events of the year.

Peoria also has its Swedes, many of whom came here when Cyrus Avery moved his farm equipment factory from Galesburg to Averyville in 1882. There are the Italians, Polish, and Czechs who came to work in area coal mines and the Scotch, Danish, French and Croats. Peoria also has an unusually large settlement of Syrians and Lebanese, most of the latter coming from the small city of Itoo. The fact that nearly half the population of Itoo, a small town in the mountains of Lebanon, eventually came to Peoria is regarded as one of the more unusual developments in the history of American immigration.

First of the Itoo residents to come to Peoria was reportedly Anthony LaHood, who came to America in 1886 and arrived in Peoria a year later. As soon as he had established a business, he wrote to his friends in Lebanon, suggesting that they, too, might like to come here and settle in a community that was receptive to foreigners. Three years later, the Lebanese began to come directly to Peoria. It has been their nature to go into business for themselves and many became active in the grocery, confectionary, and restaurant business, in which they are still notably successful.

Lebanon was at one time a part of Syria and almost indistinguishable from the Lebanese who settled here are the Syrians, whose first member to arrive was Peter Maloof in 1880. The largest number of Syrians came to attend the World Columbian Exhibition in Chicago in 1893. Forty-two came to Peoria as a result of that fair; and by 1939, their numbers here were reportedly 250.

There also are other interesting groups of emigres who settled in Peoria, including 250 who originated on the Isle of Man and are known as "Manxmen"; 150 from Switzerland; and, in 1956, seventy-seven Hungarians, who came after the disastrous uprising against the Russians in that year. They were among the nearly 40,000 who fled Hungary after the Russians crushed the revolt.

While the 1960 census showed the largest national group in Peoria to be German with the United Kingdom second and Ireland and Sweden nearly tied for third, it also numbered sizeable contingents of people from Italy, Yugoslavia, Russia, Lithuania, Poland, the Netherlands, Greece, Austria, Hungary, and Czechoslovakia, France and Mexico.

The census of 1980 designated people racially rather than nationalistically, and reported there were 101,174 white persons living here and 20,177 blacks, along with 189 American Indians, 208 Chinese, 297 Asian Indians, 188 Vietnamese, 81 Japanese, 119 Filipinos, 138 Koreans, 15 Hawaiians, six Guamians, four Eskimos, two Aleuts, and two Samoans. There also were 1105 Mexicans, 109 Puerto Ricans, 57 Cubans, and 455 with "other Spanish origins."

George Fitch wrote years ago that "Peoria is made up of the finest Americans on the continent and all of these finest Americans are of foreign stock except the Indians."

And in 1982, one of the 1956 Hungarian refugees, Val McKnight (originally Mariahegyi) stated even more succinctly the reason that has led so many people from so many foreign countries to this country and to Peoria: "I say God bless America. I say we better preserve it because there's no place to go from here. This is it."

"MUTTER" SLOUGH, WHO ARRIVED IN PEORIA IN 1832.

CHAPTER FIVE

*THE BUILDERS
AND MAKERS:*

From early manufacturing to Peoria's
emergence as a whiskey and earthmoving
capital. Duryea and Greenhut. The early
factories and their evolution and
development. Beer, barrels and tractors. The
status of business and industry today.

THE ABC WASHING MACHINE
ASSEMBLY LINE IN EAST
PEORIA.

68

With its formidable combination of strategic location and abundant resources, the emergence of Peoria as an industrial and business center of middle America was almost inevitable. It was ultimately assured by transportation, the immigration of skilled workers into the area and the natural geographical and agricultural advantages. Yet no one really could have predicted at the dawning of this city on the Illinois River that it would develop into what a SATURDAY EVENING POST writer observed in the 1940's as "the whiskey and earth-moving capital of the universe."

The first business recorded in this Illinois River Valley was the fur trade.

Furs sent out from various posts along the Illinois River in 1816 included those of 10,000 deer, 300 bear, 10,000 raccoons, 35,000 muskrat, 400 otter, 300 pounds of beaver, 500 wildcat and fox and 100 mink. The value was estimated at $23,700.

Once the American settlers began arriving, however, and Peoria began to grow from a rude settlement along the river bank into a town, the necessary services required whenever people gather in one location were introduced. These included carpenters, bakers, storekeepers, masons, preachers, barbers, butchers and undertakers - all required in any civilized society.

Economist Niles Carpenter wrote in 1932 that "the future of any city is conditioned largely by the relation between its location and some of the dominating interest of its time and region. It is also clear that a city whose position makes it attractive for the pursuit of a number of these interests is bound in very truth to have greatness thrust upon it."

The conditions seem to have been met here, for the early growth of Peoria was, if not as spectacular as some gold rush boom town, both steady and remarkable. From the few houses clustered along the riverfront within a decade after the War of 1812, the progress was relentless.

The first steamboat arrived in 1829. Even then the town site and harbor were regarded as the best on the western waters. Settlers, mostly English and Scottish, were already pouring westward, up through Kentucky, across Indiana, up the Mississippi and Illinois Rivers to this scenic and promising location. Roads and bridges were built very early. As a result, Peoria became a dominant commercial center, the shipping point for corn and hogs, a magnet for the produce that was just beginning to pour from the rich, good earth of Central Illinois.

By 1825 there were roads, such as they were, to the borders of Peoria County. A dozen years later, four bridges spanned Kickapoo Creek. Travelers and drovers poured in and Peoria rapidly became an important collecting and distribution center.

Again it was the river that was the vital transmission link. It brought in the new arrivals. It carried out the abundance they produced. In 1834, seven steamboats came to Peoria. By 1845, there were nearly 700 steamboat arrivals and by 1850, a total of 1286.

Already, Peoria had become almost the proverbial boom town. "Situated on the best navigable stream (of its size) in our vast union, with a back country of unequalled fertility, what can prevent its becoming a great commercial metropolis?" asked Simeon DeWitt Drown in April, 1844.

Charles Ballance noted at the same time that "the position of Peoria in a commercial point of view is unsurpassed by that of any town in the state, except perhaps that of Chicago."

Drown's first City Directory, published in 1844, lists an intriguing mix of occupations and practitioners. Among them were William T. Allen, "preacher of righteousness;" John Adams, carpenter, house joiner and general builder; Bartlett & Holland, dealers in dry goods; George C. Bestor, real estate; G. A. Beseman, bread and biscuit maker; William Buckner, fashionable barber and hair dresser; Allan Collings, wagon and dray maker. Also listed were printers, stonemakers, tailors, druggists, justices of the peace, gunsmiths, attorneys, jewelers, hotelkeepers, saddlers and coopers, blacksmiths and laundrymen, millers, painters and undertakers.

The directory lists Isaac Underhill as a dealer in real estate; Walker and Lightner as hardware merchants; Ballance and Cooper as attorneys; Drown himself as a surveyor and mapper; A. O. Garrett as proprietor of the Planter's House Hotel at the corner of Adams and Hamilton; and Alex Labadier, "colored," as a barber and hair dresser on Main Street between Washington and Adams.

These were all predictable and necessary occupations, the kind one might find in any town or city, new or old. Some of the graves of these early businessmen are located in Springdale Cemetery. Some, such as Underhill, Cooper, and Bestor, have streets named after them and retain their places in Peoria's history.

*Couch and Heyle Hardware
    Company
Edward Hine Company
Szold's
Peoria & Pekin Union Railway
Security Savings and
    Loan Association
Illinois Bell Telephone
    Company
Talman Home Federal Savings
    & Loan Association
    — Peoria office
Kavanagh, Scully, Sudow,
    White and Frederick
Wilton Mortuary, Inc.
The Leisy Company
St. Francis Hospital
Proctor Community Hospital
Springdale Cemetery
    Association
Lutheran Cemetery of Peoria
Peoria Hebrew Cemetery
Catholic Cemetery Association
Peoria Mineral Springs
Peoria Board of Trade
Peoria Area Chamber
    of Commerce
Peoria Public Library
City of Peoria
Peoria County
Peoria Public Schools,
    Dist. 150
Academy of Our Lady*

70

But what happened presently was perhaps less predictable. As early as 1832, more roads centered at Peoria than at any city in the entire Illinois valley. And the city over the next generation was to expand into the largest corn-consuming market in the world.

Corn, even then, had an amazing variety of uses. Peoria's products consisted of glucose, syrup, corn sugar, yeast, liquor, alcohol, chemicals, feed, starch and grits. Almost prophetically, whiskey became one of the leading industries, turning the city for over a century into the whiskey-making capital of the world.

The first distillery was built in 1843 and for 140 years, Peoria was perhaps the greatest whiskey town in all of history.

The money that poured into, and out of, the city as a result of whiskey and the taxes levied on it can hardly be imagined. Most of the houses along High Street, once known as High Wine Street, came from whiskey. It is said that Joseph Greenhut, who moved to Peoria not long after the Civil War, arrived with goods valued at fifty dollars. When he left twenty years later to live in New York, he was worth ten million dollars.

J.B. GREENHUT'S HOME, SHERIDAN AND HIGH STREETS. (COURTESY LEE ROTEN).

Greenhut's elaborate, turreted mansion stood at the corner of Moss and High Streets where the stable and house still remain today although the latter has been converted into apartments.

Greenhut served in the Union Army as a private, sergeant and captain. His name is permanently attached to the Grand Army of the Republic Hall on Hamilton Boulevard. In 1881, with Nelson Morris and John H. Francis, he built the Great Western Distillery. Even then, it was known as the largest distillery in the world, a title that was later claimed by Hiram Walker and Sons.

So attractive was this business of turning the area's abundant corn into alcohol and so unlimited were the resources that by 1887, Peoria had a dozen thriving distilleries. Along with the Great Western were the Woolner Brothers Distillery, Monarch, Manhattan, Northern, Peoria, Clarke Brothers, Bush and Brown, Standard, Kruse Brothers, the Great Eastern and Barker.

72

Distilling became the leading industry of Peoria by 1896, largely because of the city's ready supply of superior quality grain, water of the right temperature, coal at low cost, land at moderate prices, and a large river "to carry away the offal." There were six grain elevators in Peoria by then with a capacity of 2.5 million bushels. The population had swelled to 53,000. There were fourteen daily and weekly newspapers -five of them in German - twenty hotels and four sulphur swimming pools.

That same year a writer described Peoria in the most glowing terms. "The busy city with its hum of industry in the foreground, the waters of the lake sparkling in the sunshine, and on the other shore, the bluffs covered with verdure or glowing in the bright tints of autumn form a picture of rare beauty."

One suspects he might have been influenced by Peoria's most notable, and notorious, product. For on some days, the smell of Peoria must have been indescribable. Already this single industry consumed 4.17 million bushels of grain a year in the production of 18.6 million gallons, none of it accomplished

THE WOOLNER NO. 8
DISTILLERY AFTER ITS 1907
FIRE. (RAY BRONS PHOTO,
COURTESY OF CORWIN BERRY).

without powerful odors. Low pressure weather fronts surely suffocated the valley in particular with a noxious and yellowish fog comprised of coal smoke, whiskey fumes, the wet smell of mash, and the mingled scents from slaughter-houses, breweries, and factories.

While distilling was Peoria's leading single industry, it nurtured a host of related activities. Cooperage houses arose where experts fashioned leak-proof white oak barrels in which to age the whiskey. An army of woodcutters worked in surrounding forests. Saws whined. Sawmills hummed. And even little-known tradesmen known as weepers worked with Egyptian papyrus, tapping it into barrels that were leaking ever so slightly.

One of the distilleries' major byproducts, wet corn mash, or slop, made a superior cattle feed. Enormous herds were penned near the distilleries, many near the foot of Western Avenue; and at the peak of the whiskey era in Peoria, the plants furnished sufficient feed for 28,000 animals.

Peoria as a result became an important center for slaughterhouses, meat packing, and dairies. The opportunities kept spreading out, like ripples on a lake. Meat packing required ice. Great ice houses arose, one operated by the former steamboat captain, Henry Detweiller. The ice houses required cutters in the winter who sawed massive slabs from the river. Also needed were sawdust to preserve the ice in the summer, delivery wagons, horses, repairmen, veterinarians, blacksmiths, and farriers. Nobody can conceivably calculate how many people's livelihoods derived in one way or the other from whiskey. The number of farmers, shippers, drovers, stockyard workers, coopers, bottlemakers, packagers, and common laborers must have been staggering.

The industry had two major results. It created an enormous amount of money for the distillery owners and provided immense tax revenue for the United States government.

PEORIA ILLUSTRATED noted in 1893 that this Fifth District of Illinois, of which Peoria is the center, "exceeds by fifty per cent any revenue district in the United States in the amount of revenue tax it pays to the government. This is derived almost entirely from the distillation of spirits, manufactured by the fourteen distilleries with a capacity of over 40,000 bushels of grain, which is equivalent to about 185,000 gallons of spirits every twenty-four hours."

74

DEAD FEEDER CATTLE AFTER A 1904 FIRE AT THE CORNING DISTILLERY. (COURTESY LEE ROTEN).

"Peoria," the unknown author continued somewhat sanctimoniously, "sometimes called by the outside world the 'Distillery City,' uses very little whiskey, but makes the greater proportion of all made in this country and regulates the price. During the year 1891, the Monarch distillery, the largest one in the world, was destroyed by fire, but this made no difference with the output, as idle houses, which along with the Monarch are all owned and operated by the Western Distilling and Cattle Feeding Company, were at once put in operation.

"These mammoth concerns employ an army of men and thousands of cattle are fed here. The Western Distilling and Cattle Feeding Company, which owns all the principal distilleries in the country, has its principal offices here. The officers are J. Greenhut, president; John Beggs, vice president; W. M. Hobart of Cincinnati, treasurer; P. J. Hennessy of Chicago, secretary; and N. E. D. Huggins of Peoria, assistant secretary."

The amount of revenue paid the government the previous year (1892) was over twenty-three million dollars. By comparison, the next largest revenue districts in the entire country were Cincinnati and Chicago, which contributed about ten million dollars each.

So crucial was the distilling industry to Peoria's early prosperity that even some of the money used to found and endow Bradley University had its roots in the distillation of spirits. Both the families of Lydia Moss and Tobias Bradley gained considerable wealth from whiskey. Later in her life, Lydia Moss Bradley's opposition to alcohol was so vehement that not until the late 1970's did alcoholic beverages of any kind officially appear on the campus of the university named after Mrs. Bradley's family. There was for several years, in fact, a virtual ban on establishments which sold even beer in an area extending roughly from Sheridan Road to Western Avenue.

There were other opponents of whiskey as well. In an article entitled, "1818-1918: A Hundred Years of Sunday School History in Illinois: A Mosaic," arranged by Andrew H. Mills of Decatur, it was noted that the Sunday School Association's centennial meeting in Peoria was the subject of some consternation.

"This city," it was noted in the TRANSACTIONS OF THE ILLINOIS STATE HISTORICAL SOCIETY FOR 1918, "like every other city of Illinois has had a dual civilization, its Dr. Jekyll and its Mr. Hyde civilizations....This city was the home of William Reynolds - that mighty man of God...."

THE 500 BLOCK OF SOUTH
ADAMS STREET IN THE 1930'S.

It was also termed "the rich mansion of John Barley Corn,
the greatest enemy of humanity...." whose days are
numbered. "This generation will not pass until old John
Barley Corn will be buried face downward so that the more he
digs the deeper he is buried."

It was to be a prophetic pronouncement, for with the
enactment of prohibition, the great age of Peoria's
predominance in the making of whiskey virtually ground to a
halt. But not quite.

As this story was being played out, Peoria little by little
became a transportation hub of major importance. Railroads
replaced packet boats as the major hauler of grain. The area
developed into the Peoria Gateway, a transit and distribution
point that had the advantage of bypassing the congestion of
Chicago and St. Louis.

78

By 1926, when the population was 94,000, there were 122 passenger trains in and out of the city daily and 158 freights. Since manufacturing tends to establish itself near its chief market, the rise of farm machinery and implement manufacturing was a natural development.

Around the turn of the century, Martin Kingman, one of the most successful plow salesmen in the world, was considering locating a new factory along the Rock Island Railroad in Peoria Heights. Kingman, who had been on Sherman's march to the sea, had bought, in 1882 at a price of $60,000, at least a fourth of the land that later became the Heights. He developed the Prospect Heights Summer Hotel with its eighty rooms at what is now Prospect Road and Grand View Drive. He also founded Peoria's Central National Bank.

But Kingman decided not to build in the Heights. He located his plant instead along the river in Averyville. It later became the Avery Farm Machinery Plant, and it was here that R. G. LeTourneau moved his company headquarters in 1935.

LeTourneau had formed his company in 1921 in Stockton, California, to produce graders and earthmoving machinery. He had started as a garage mechanic and was looking for a

KINGMAN PLOW WORKS. (THE GREAT MIDDLE WEST).

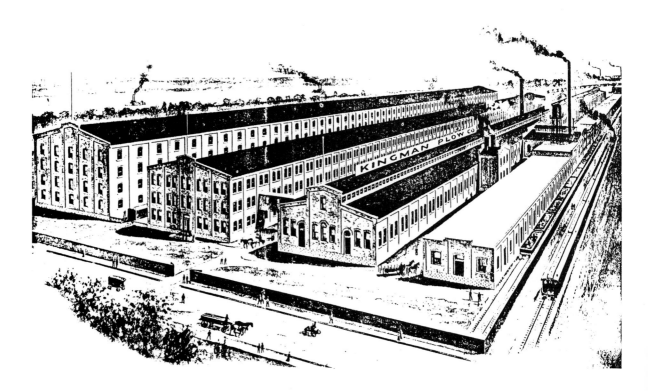

device that would smooth city streets. He found it, and when he moved to Peoria, he quickly established himself as an eccentric industrial genius whose products not only included monstrous "Tournapulls," but welded steel houses, some of which still exist in the area. His slogan was "God runs my business."

More farm-related business grew up in Peoria. Keystone had its beginning in 1889 in Tremont, when Peter Sommer came up with the idea of weaving wire into fencing. The operation that eventually grew up in Bartonville was to become the largest independent producer of wire in the world, employing 2300 workers, with an annual output of 400,000 tons of steel wire.

AN AVERY TRACTOR
CULTIVATING CORN.

80

CHARLES DURYEA IN HIS
FIRST CAR, WITH TWO
NEIGHBOR BOYS FROM
BARKER AVE., ABOUT 1898.
(PEORIA PUBLIC LIBRARY, LEE
ROTEN PRINT).

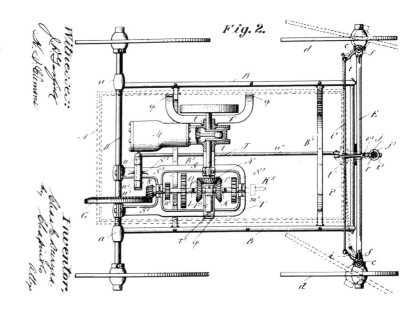

FROM A PATENT ISSUED TO
DURYEA IN 1893.

Back in the Heights, a few of Charles Duryea's horseless carriages, with which he had tinkered at his house on Barker Avenue, had been assembled by Monroe Sieberling at his bicycle plant. Sieberling's factory employed 600 men and was turning out 10,000 bicycles and 25,000 pairs of tires a year. But there was apparently a disagreement between the famous auto pioneer and Sieberling, and Duryea moved his operation to Reading, Pennsylvania. Sieberling went out of business in 1900. The history of bicycle manufacturing is commemorated by the distinctive clock on the side of the Kelly Avenue School in the Heights.

The automobile returned to the Heights, however, in 1911 when J. B. Bartholomew, then president of the Avery Company, acquired Sieberling's old factory and began manufacturing a car called the "Glide." The firm lasted until 1917. Teddy Roosevelt rode in a "Glide" when he came to Peoria and reportedly called the drive along what was then Prospect Heights (and is now Grand View Drive) "The World's Most Beautiful Drive," a motto kept alive by the call letters of radio and television station WMBD. There is, incidentally, a "Glide" in the collection of Harrah's Auto Museum in Reno, Nevada.

J.B. BARTHOLOMEW OF THE GLIDE MFG. CO. (F-STOP SOCIETY).

THE GLIDE SPECIAL 45 ROADSTER, MADE IN PEORIA HEIGHTS AND PRICED AT $2,400. (LEE ROTEN PRINT).

GLIDE SPECIAL 45 ROADSTER - $2400.
45 H.P. - 122 inch wheel base - 36 x 4 wheels and tires.
THE BARTHOLOMEW CO. - PEORIA, ILL.

82

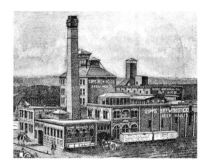

THE GIPPS BREWERY ABOUT 1885. (PEORIA PUBLIC LIBRARY, LEE ROTEN PRINT).

CEDAR STREET BRIDGE FROM THE WATER TANK OF THE NATIONAL WAREHOUSE.

The "Glide" went out of business in 1917, and it was not until 1924 that the Premier Malt Company bought the old Sieberling-Bartholomew buildings and began making malt syrup.

The firm also bought the old Leisy brewery and malt house which was located on the riverfront and had folded with the beginning of prohibition. This building became the grits mill. In 1933, Premier merged with the Pabst Brewery of Milwaukee. It became the Heights' leading employer, paying a fourth of the village's taxes and employing around a thousand people. When the plant closed in February, 1982, the Heights lost its most important source of income and Peoria lost its last brewery.

Before that had come the demise of Gipps, which began brewing beer here in 1881. It closed during prohibition and went back into production with the repeal in 1933, making Gipps Amberlin Beer. After World War II, Gipps was one of the first American breweries to offer a famous foreign recipe, Van Dyck Beer from Holland, starting a trend that continues today. The firm closed its doors in the late 1950's a victim of the trend toward the massive national breweries that now dominate the market.

THE ROUSE-HAZARD CO. IN PEORIA HEIGHTS, LATER THE GLIDE FACTORY.

Old businesses moved out or died. There were once three bicycle makers - the Rouse-Hazard Company at 328 Southwest Adams, F. F. Ide on Fredonia Avenue, and the giant Sieberling firm in the Heights. Robert Ingersoll's former home became the home of the Lewis Single Binder Cigar. There was the Peoria Globe Mill, home of "Pride of Peoria" flour, known for its colorful bags, which bore pictures of famed operatic prima donna Emma Abbott who had been born here and sang at the dedication of the Grand Opera House.

A 1926 survey indicated there were more than 900 articles made in Peoria, among them agricultural implements, washing machines, drugs, chemicals, furnaces, cigars, stock feed and grain products, wire fencing, cordage, cooperage and alcohol. The city also was the home of the largest traffic signal light factory in America, the Essco Manufacturing Company; and this also was among the three leading cities of the world in the production of washing machines.

In 1926, wages for men ranged from forty cents to $1.10 an hour and for women, from twenty-five cents to forty cents an hour.

By 1971, there had been no major change in Peoria's basic industrial makeup. The Chamber of Commerce was still able to proclaim that Peoria was not only home office for the world's largest earthmoving equipment manufacturer (Caterpillar), but the site of the world's largest wire mill (Keystone), the largest bourbon distillery (Hiram Walker) and the world's largest gift mail order company (Foster Gallagher).

LEWIS SINGLE BINDER CIGAR CO., FORMERLY COL. ROBERT INGERSOLL'S HOME, ABOUT 1907.

84

A million bottles of alcohol still poured out daily but tastes were changing. The "light" craze had already begun to set in and sales of the rich, heavy bourbon began to slip. Instead of ordering boilermakers (a beer with a shot of bourbon), drinkers were beginning to sip a little white wine. It signified a drastic change in style and taste that was to doom the distillery. In a frantic last-ditch effort, a new light whiskey was introduced which was paler in color and softer on the palate, but the shift had been made. The Hiram Walker plant that in 1959 was producing 127,000 gallons of bourbon whiskey per day and employing 1150 workers announced its closing by the end of 1981. It was moving into a new $37 million facility in Fort Smith, Arkansas, an area where labor was cheaper and economic incentives more attractive. Peoria's great age as the whiskey capital of the world came to an abrupt and surprising end.

With the closing of the Pabst plant in the early winter of 1982, this once riotous, beer-drinking, whiskey-making river town, with its mingled smells of mash, yeast, malt, and grain

HIRAM WALKER DISTILLERY UNDER CONSTRUCTION. (PEORIA PUBLIC LIBRARY).

alcohol, was literally left high and dry. John Barley Corn had moved to more favorable climes.

Peoria might easily have withered up economically. For the city which had weathered depression and recession with surprising strength with its whiskey, beer, and tractors, suddenly found itself moving with an unaccustomed limp. Not only did Walker's and Pabst leave with over 2000 jobs, but Hyster had closed its plant, Continental Can abandoned the city, and the packing houses went out of business one by one. Already the venerable Peoria Cordage Company had ended its long life, and as massive distribution centers were established, local dairies, bakeries, and grocery stores followed suit.

The world had changed. Huge franchise fast-food chains spread across the country. Supermarkets and shopping centers with nationally-run chain operations replaced the local shoe store and the corner bakery. Three or four gigantic brewing companies dominated the industry. And Peoria, along with the rest of the country, changed drastically.

86

AN EARLY HOLT TRACTOR
DEMONSTRATING ITS
CLIMBING ABILITY.

THIS WORLD WAR I TANK
WAS PRESENTED TO THE CITY
IN 1925 AND LOCATED AT
FRANKLIN AND MONROE. THIS
PHOTO, WHICH PRECEDED
AN ARMISTICE DAY PARADE,
SHOWS MAYOR E.N.
WOODRUFF (4TH FROM LEFT)
AND MURRAY M. BAKER (3RD
FROM LEFT). (COURTESY
CATERPILLAR TRACTOR CO.).

The only remaining giant was Caterpillar, which in the mid 1960's elected to locate its world headquarters building in downtown Peoria and which, despite increasing world competition, has remained the leader in its field.

Some fear, in fact, that Caterpillar has so dominated Peoria's industrial and economic picture that its loss would be calamitous. Peoria's industrial history, however, would have been vastly different without the presence of Caterpillar, which located here almost by chance.

Caterpillar's genealogy goes back to Stockton, California, where the Holt Brothers Stockton Wheel Co. was founded in 1883. Three years later, Holt built its first combine harvester. The crawler dates from 1904 when a Holt steam tractor was fitted with a track-type crawler. It was appropriately called "Caterpillar." In 1906, Holt added the gasoline engine, far more efficient and powerful than the old steam engine, and the gas-powered crawlers went into full production. They were an immediate success.

Holt began looking for a Midwestern site in order to tap into the huge eastern market and the Company very nearly chose Minneapolis. But Murray Baker, a Peoria tractor distributor, contacted Holt and invited the firm to occupy the empty Colean Manufacturing plant in East Peoria. The purchase took place in 1909 and production began the same year. By the end of the following year, the Holt Caterpillar Company had a work force of sixty-five.

The outbreak of World War I in 1914 put the Holt firm into the export business as the Allies used track-type tractors and eventually tanks on the Western Front. Britain and France were to become the company's major customers.

THE HOLT-CATERPILLAR CO.
IN EAST PEORIA.

88

C.L. Best, a Holt competitor who had concentrated on civilian business during the war, approached Holt in 1925 with a merger in mind. It came suddenly. Tractors were to be built in East Peoria and San Leandro, and combines in Stockton, California, a city which over the years seems to have supplied Peoria with considerable industrial muscle. The firm became known as Caterpillar.

By 1931, Caterpillar was selling its first diesel-powered track-type tractors, but the depression hit hard. The firm's sales reached $52 million in 1929 and dropped to $13 million three years later. The company suffered a $1.6 million loss which was its first, and was to be its last, until 1982.

The demand for its product turned upwards in the late 1930's. Sales topped $50 million in 1936 and in 1937 profits hit $10.6 million. Another boost came with another war, when Louis B. Neumiller became president. In the early years of America's involvement in World War II, Caterpillar was manufacturing transmissions and drive assemblies for tanks, plus howitzer carriages and bomb parts. By 1943, however, the government requested that the company return to full-time production of its bulldozers, which proved crucial in the island-hopping South Pacific campaign where runways and other installations required the movement of massive amounts of earth.

After the war, the rebuilding of war-torn countries provided a huge overseas market for Caterpillar tractors and the firm began its expansion with construction of a 1.4 million square foot plant in Joliet in 1949. When Neumiller retired from his full-time duties in 1962, Caterpillar had doubled its plant space and tripled its net assets since the war. Sales and profits had vaulted seven fold and employment had doubled to 35,810. By 1981, growth was even more spectacular. Sales were up thirteen times what they had been in 1961 and profits had increased by almost the same amount. Peoria-area employment by Caterpillar peaked at more than 36,000 in 1979. In 1982, under pressure of world-wide recession and increasing competition, largely from Japan's Komatsu Company, Caterpillar suffered a loss of $179.9 million. The company was involved in a fight for its survival which it appeared to be winning.

The influence of Japan's technology on our own industry is not particularly new or revolutionary. In fact, a Japanese scientist, Dr. Jokichi Takamine, was invited to the United States in 1890 and he was to play an important role in Peoria and later Washington, D. C.

Takamine was the discoverer of a new process for the manufacture of alcohol said to be much cheaper and quicker than the barley malt method used by American distillers. It was inevitable that he would end up in Peoria, headquarters of the massive whiskey trust and home of its president, Joseph Greenhut.

Greenhut hired Takamine on February 18, 1891. His job was to apply his new process to large scale runs at Peoria. It had been estimated that the Takamine process would represent a savings to the whiskey trust of two million dollars a year.

Takamine apparently was in Peoria for almost four years. He conducted his experiments with wheat bran and similar materials in the malt house of the Grove Distillery, which had been built by Woolner Brothers. His work was carried on in secrecy. Guards swarmed about his laboratory to prevent spies from discovering his secrets.

His process finally was used in the Manhattan Distillery here, which had been fitted with new equipment. Curiously, the distillery went bankrupt within two months and the receivers changed the distillery back to the old process. Takamine's contract with the whiskey trust was cancelled.

He went on to found Takamine Laboratory, Inc. in Clifton, New Jersey, and in 1901, he announced the discovery of adrenaline. Perhaps his major fame, however, rests in the fact that he purchased 2000 cherry trees, which were presented to the United States in the name of the mayor of Tokyo and were planted around the tidal basin in Washington, D. C.

A VISIT FROM THE IMPERIAL JAPANESE ARMY'S "AUTOMOBILE COMMITTEE" TO HOLT'S EAST PEORIA PLANT, JANUARY 1919.

HOLT CATERPILLAR 18 USED BY
THE PEORIA ARMY
RECRUITING STATION, 1917.
(CATERPILLAR PHOTO).

92

Along with the industrial revolution that was changing the character of Peoria was a commercial one as well. The vital downtown area began to grow old and change. The post-war rush to the suburbs triggered the decline. Shops followed new families into former corn and bean fields; then came the suburban supermarkets and shopping centers with whole groups of businesses banding together; and finally, there arose the downtown-killing shopping malls. The old central city almost faded and died as a retail center.

No longer were there massive crowds downtown day and night. No longer did the changing of the lights at Fulton and Adams bring swarms of people surging between Block & Kuhl's and Bergner's. No longer were there massive downtown traffic jams. This became almost a ghost town, with empty and littered streets and crumbling pavement. It was threatened with a takeover by the kinds of peripheral businesses which thrive in areas at the point of collapse.

SHOPPERS IN THE 100 BLOCK S. ADAMS ST. IN THE LATE 1940'S. (RAY BARCLAY PHOTO, PRINT BY LEE ROTEN).

94

PEORIA DOWNTOWN, ADAMS
AND MAIN IN THE LATE 1940'S.
(RAY BARCLAY PHOTO, PRINT
BY LEE ROTEN).

DOWNTOWN PEORIA IN 1985.
(VISUAL COMMUNICATIONS
PHOTO).

96

But the people remained and others fought back. The 1967 privately-financed renovation of downtown, sparked by the Downtown Development Council, not only helped bring the Caterpillar World Headquarters into a run-down square block but resulted in the new Savings Tower, the Security Savings Building and the new Courthouse. Perhaps the most important single boost downtown Peoria received came when a group of spiritied citizens campaigned so forcibly that the County Board cancelled its plans to surround the Courthouse with a blacktopped parking lot and instead hired the firm of Scruggs and Hammond to landscape the area.

It has proved an uncommon attraction with its fountains, walkways and trees, not only for its visual splendor, but as a focal point for an ambitious summer series of concerts, artistic demonstrations and the kind of entertainment and cultural events which make a city livable.

Downtown has refused to die. The Pere Marquette Hotel, long abandoned, was restored to its former splendor and reopened in 1983. G. Raymond Becker, a Peoria contractor, not only restored and expanded the former, and long empty, Voyager Inn into an impressive Continental Regency Hotel with parking deck and office space, but erected a matching set of twenty-nine-story condominiums, the Twin Towers, which are bringing residents into the heart of the city once again. And the Peoria Civic Center, with its theatre, convention center, and arena has brought a new and different kind of life and vitality into the downtown.

It is not the same as the 40's and 50's when downtown was the center of everything, when the streets were thronged, when people window-shopped along Main Street or lined up for the Saturday shows at the Madison, the Palace, and the Rialto. But cities change, and so has Peoria, perhaps for the better. The great smokestack, whiskey-making, beer-brewing era has ended here. It is even possible Peoria might no longer be categorized as a blue collar town. No longer are there nights when the smells of mash or malt cover the city like a blanket or those yellow, malodorous smogs cloud the valley. No longer do the whistles of trains sound mournfully or do people set their watches by the factory's noon whistle.

The city moves. A step backwards. Two steps forward. Life is a series of changes for the individual and for the city. The old bustling Peoria grinding out its plowshares, farm tractors, beer, whiskey, rope, and washing machines will probably never return. But the new Peoria, with its balance of industry, business, the professions, and the arts might well prove to be a greater city in the long run.

One of the major factors that helped propel Peoria from its status as an early French village and a small, insignificant American frontier town to its status as downstate's largest and most influential marketing center, has been the businesses and industries that have given it such a lively and continuous economic health.

The river provided the original impetus for business, along with the richness of the soil and the abundance of the harvest. The first business was unquestionably the fur trade back when this was largely wilderness. But with the arrival of the settlers, agriculture created its own needs and opportunities. While the first small businesses grew out of the basic needs of the early Peorians - mills and drug stores, doctors' offices and undertaking establishments, carpenters and shops - these in turn attracted more people to live and work in the growing community.

From such small beginnings, Peoria was to grow into the whiskey and earth-moving capital of the world, a busy, industrial city whose products were utilized in all parts of the world.

But as Peoria expanded physically and economically, the labors and enterprises of forward-looking men and women were at its center. Their businesses, industries and institutions not only nourished the city in its growth, but helped give it a special character, a character that has changed in recent years from a hard-working, smokestack community, to one that, while retaining its commercial strength, has become a more civilized and increasingly appealing place to live and work.

No history of this size and scope could hope to include all the stories of the many firms, institutions, industries and businesses that have helped make Peoria a vital metropolitan center of over a third of a million people. Those firms whose stories appear on the following pages have helped make possible a history of Peoria that is ultimately richer for their inclusion and more reasonably priced than would otherwise be possible. These are enterprises to whom special thanks are due for their part in making this book possible.

PARTNERS IN PROGRESS

98

PROCTOR COMMUNITY HOSPITAL

Back in 1882 when Peoria was a city of 40,000, and horses and buggies, mule-drawn street cars or packet boats were the primary form of transportation, and smallpox, cholera and typhoid were constant threats, a group of Peorians gathered to discuss the need for a community hospital. The project became a reality when Doctors O. B. Willis, John Hamilton, and Thomas McIlvanie acquired a 15-room house on Second Street and opened the Cottage Hospital of Peoria.

The wood house, which was the forerunner of the medical complex known today as Proctor Community Hospital, proved almost immediately to be too small. It was then that John C. Proctor led the formation of a not-for-profit organization to support the hospital. He also was a generous benefactor for its first expansion, a new brick wing that adjoined the frame building and was built in 1893. He was the principal donor when the frame house was torn down and replaced by the 127-bed hospital that opened on February 3, 1902, and remained a familiar landmark in Peoria for half a century. When Proctor died in 1907, the hospital was named in his honor.

By the late 1950's, Peoria was growing northward and the Second Street building was no longer able to meet the community's medical needs. The decision was reached to erect a new building on a 36-acre tract on North Knoxville. And in April, 1959, the building was completed.

Since then, Proctor has undergone four major expansions. The complex, with its attractive landscaped campus, free parking, and convenient adjoining professional buildings, offers complete, state-of-the-art emergency care, surgery and ambulatory surgery, cardiology and cardiac rehab, family-centered maternity care, gynecology, pediatrics, oncology, the innovative Chemical Dependency Center and the area's first Diabetes Care Unit among its many programs.

COTTAGE HOSPITAL, 1982
(PROCTOR PHOTO)

PROCTOR HOSPITAL, 1902
(PROCTOR PHOTO)

PROCTOR COMMUNITY
HOSPITAL, TODAY (1985)
(PROCTOR PHOTO)

Today at Proctor, a physician can "see"into a patient's heart without operating by means of sound waves echoing into a video screen, or into a patient's brain or body to diagnose tumors or other problems using CT scanning. The latest in lasers make possible delicate eye and other surgical procedures more safely and with speedier recovery and less discomfort to the patient. A computer analyzes a patient's history and lifestyle and predicts the probability of a heart attack. Nurses monitor the vital signs of intensive or coronary care patients electronically for precise, speedy handling of their treatment needs. And paramedics can begin life-saving treatment of an accident victim in an ambulance while in radio communication with Proctor's emergency physicians.

Proctor Community Hospital is unaffiliated with any sponsoring organization. It continues to belong to the community. Just as hundreds of area citizens rallied to contribute over $2 million to launch the building campaign in the '50's, the community today continues to provide much of the support of the hospital it recognizes belongs to the people.

PROCTOR'S DIGITAL SUBTRACTION ANGIOGRAPHY SPOTS BLOCKAGE OF ARTERIES, A MAJOR CAUSE OF STROKE. (PROCTOR PHOTO)

COMPUTERIZED TOMOGRAPHY (CT) SCANNING DIAGNOSES TUMORS AND OTHER PROBLEMS IMPOSSIBLE TO DETECT A FEW YEARS AGO. (PROCTOR PHOTO)

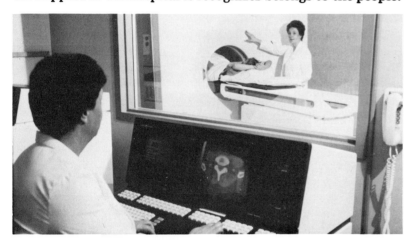

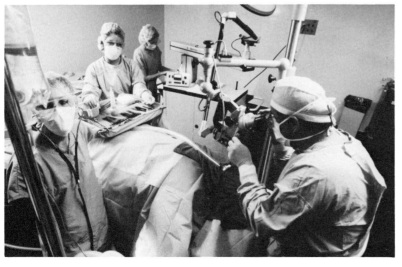

CO_2 LASER IS USED HERE TO REMOVE POLYPS FROM A PATIENT'S VOCAL CORDS. (PROCTOR PHOTO)

100

SAINT FRANCIS MEDICAL CENTER

REV. MOTHER M. FRANCIS KRASSE, FIRST MOTHER GENERAL.

THE FIRST ST. FRANCIS HOSPITAL.

If Otto Von Bismark, the Iron Chancellor of Germany, had not persecuted the religious orders in his native land 110 years ago, it is possible that Saint Francis Medical Center in Peoria might not exist today. But so violent was the pressure brought by his "Kultur Kampf," that a group of 25 sisters and four postulants, led by Mother Mary Xavier, fled to America in 1875 and settled in Iowa City.

Even here, their plight was severe and their poverty relentless. Fortunately, the Rev. Bernard Baak, pastor of St. Joseph's Church in Peoria (now St. Martin de Porres), heard of their hardships and invited them here to set up a much-needed hospital. Five sisters arrived on October 28, 1876, and settled into a two-story frame house in the 700 block of Adams Street.

John Lancaster Spalding, first Bishop of the Diocese of Peoria, presently asked the Sisters to form an independent religious community here, and on July 16, 1877, The Sisters of The Third Order of St. Francis was founded. The Sisters met that day with Bishop Spalding and elected their first Mother General-Mother M. Frances Krasse.

Within weeks, the Sisters raised funds for the building of a new hospital and home, purchased property from Lydia Moss Bradley in what was known as the old Underhill Estate, and laid the cornerstone of their new hospital in the fall of 1877. It was finished the following year and consisted of three stories with a bed capacity of 30.

The hospital continues at the same location today, and has grown to become one of the largest medical centers in the country with admissions of over 25,000 a year and operating expenses of $110 million.

The Sisters' first Mother General died on October 28, 1885. And the last words of Mother M. Frances Krasse are still cherished: "Dear Sisters, keep yourselves in strict accord with the rules and statutes. Live in meekness and obedience. Nurse the sick with the greatest care and love. Then will God's blessing be with you."

Today, the Sisters own and operate six hospitals in Illinois and Michigan, and a continuous care and nursing home in Iowa. There are more than 6,000 employees in their hospitals and the home base. Saint Francis in Peoria has continued to grow until its former European look has all but disappeared behind a proliferation of new and modern buildings.

In 1963, the hospital announced a major expansion plan, which brought the dedication of the "new" St. Francis Hospital in August 1968. The project included the four-floor addition to the Children's Hospital, remodeling of the old A Building, a new eight story D Building and the replacement of the original Center Building with an eight story, 253 bed C Building.

As additional beds and services were needed, the expansion continued. A one-floor addition to the St. Clara Building was opened in June, 1972, to house an intensive care unit and the old convent was opened as the North Building in 1973. A year later, the hospital changed its name to St. Francis Hospital-Medical Center. In 1982, it became Saint Francis Medical Center.

THE PEDIATRIC WARD OF YESTERYEAR AND THE PEDIATRIC INTENSIVE CARE UNIT OF TODAY. (SAINT FRANCIS PHOTOS)

A second parking deck, with a capacity of 650 cars, was added in 1980, and the hospital has launched a cardiopulmonary rehabilitation center, hemodialysis center, Center for Sports Medicine and Health Fitness, and regional poison center. The new E Building, which spans Glen Oak Avenue and will almost double the space of the medical center, will be completed by the summer of 1986 and will include emergency, admitting, surgery, radiology and medical imaging, respiratory therapy, pulmonary services and coronary and intensive care units. It also will become the medical center's main entrance.

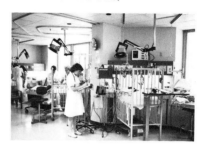

Saint Francis also has become the area's kidney transplant center, and become widely known for its comprehensive and specialized services, including emergency/trauma department, perinatal center, cardiology center, neo-natal services, cancer care and neurosciences.

Saint Francis Medical Center's staff is still inspired by the corporate mission statement of the Sisters who have been here from the beginning..."to fulfill, through a service of love and compassion, a mission of caring and peace consistent with the needs of the Church and the people served. The love of Christ permeates its work as it strives to continue the healing ministry of Christ and His Church to the total person: to be love, mercy, inspiration, tenderness and compassion to those whose lives are entered."

SAINT FRANCIS MEDICAL CENTER, 1985. (SAINT FRANCIS)

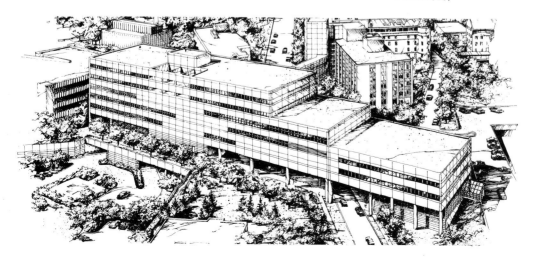

102

WILTON MORTUARY

THE WILTON MORTUARY HAD IT'S BEGINNINGS DURING THE DAYS OF THE HORSE DRAWN CARRIAGE. (C. 1900-1913) THE BUSINESS ORIGINALLY BEGAN HERE AT 1304 S.W. ADAMS BY JAMES BENNETT. (C. 1890) (WILTON COLLECTION)

THE WILTON MORTUARY AT 1212 S.W. ADAMS WAS REMODELED IN 1938. IT HAD AIR CONDITIONING AND WAS THE FIRST MORTUARY IN THE STATE TO PROVIDE ORGAN MUSIC IN EVERY ROOM DURING SERVICES AT NO ADDITIONAL CHARGE. PRIOR TO REMODELING, C. 1930. (WILTON COLLECTION)

Since the preservation of memories, of the past, of history, is one of the important functions of the modern funeral home, Wilton's, as Peoria's oldest and largest funeral home, has a long and impressive tradition. The tradition spans three generations and just over 100 years. From its beginnings on the south side of Peoria before the turn of the century, the firm has continued to expand with services and facilities that are guided by the motto: "Our family serving your family."

Wilton's was founded in 1884 by John B. Wilton, whose descendants still run the firm. Wilton arrived in Peoria that year from Ontario, Canada. He was 22 years old and he went to work for James Bennett, former Peoria County coroner, who had operated a mortuary at 1304 S. Adams St. since the middle 1870's. Wilton married Bennett's daughter and assumed control of the business from his father-in-law. He was joined by his brother, Richard S. Wilton, in 1890. Richard also was an emigrant from Canada. And when Bennett retired in 1894, he turned the entire business over to his son-in-law.

In 1913, the company was incorporated as J. B. Wilton Bro. and Co. And by 1922, the Wilton business had grown so prosperous that the firm moved to a much larger facility at 1212 S. Adams St., where the former D. A. Baker residence was enlarged and renovated to better serve the needs of Peoria.

In 1950, the company name was changed to The Wilton Mortuary and Richard S. Wilton, his son, Ralph, and his son-in-law, Robert Whitmore, were handling the largest share of funerals in the Peoria area.

Wilton's present mortuary at the corner of Knoxville and Republic was opened in 1956. It was carefully designed, even to having no steps, which makes it easy for the elderly and those confined to wheel chairs to move through the entire facility. For nearly five years, the Wilton family operated two mortuaries, the one at 1212 S. Adams and the new one at 2101 N. Knoxville. This, as a result of the long family history and reputation, is the oldest, largest and most highly respected funeral business in the area.

RICHARD S. WILTON POSES IN FRONT OF ONE OF THE FAMILY'S NEW HEARSES. (WILTON COLLECTION, C. 1933)

When Richard S. Wilton died in 1963, his son Ralph became President, and served the firm and the community for several years. At present his son, Robert C., is president of the firm and Robert P. Whitmore is chairman of the board.

Today, Wilton's participates in life awareness seminars and conducts special programs to help children and adults understand death and grieving. They also hold programs on teen suicide, stress and emotional crisis.

To help underscore the firm's appreciation of the past, Robert Wilton selected a series of photos and researched their history in 1984 for a special collection that remains on display to celebrate the firm's 100th anniversary as part of Peoria and to underscore that "remembrance of things past".

THE PRESENT DAY WILTON MORTUARY LOCATED AT 2101 NORTH KNOXVILLE. (WILTON COLLECTION, C. 1984)

104

BRADLEY UNIVERSITY

BRADLEY HALL
(BRADLEY PHOTO)

WESTLAKE HALL
(BRADLEY PHOTO)

Bradley Polytechnic Institute was founded by Lydia Moss Bradley in 1897 as a coeducational, independent, privately endowed institution with the purpose of "furnishing its students with the means of living an independent, industrious and useful life by the aid of a practical knowledge of the useful arts and sciences."

By 1920 Bradley had grown into a full-fledged four-year college, and in 1946, it became a university with graduate work and advanced degrees. Today it is one of the nation's 75 major private universities and the only private, comprehensive university in Central Illinois, offering 10 undergraduate degrees in 63 major areas and 12 graduate degrees in 20 areas.

The University's enrollment is approximately 5,300, of whom 56 percent are men and 44 percent are women. Forty states and 35 foreign countries are represented.

Bradley has received wide national recognition. It was cited by the National Commission on Cooperative Education for having one of the two best cooperative education programs at a private university in the nation. Its accounting program is one of 44 select schools in the nation to have received accreditation from the American Assembly of Collegiate Schools of Business. Its Forensics Team has won both national forensics championship tournaments for four consecutive years, 1982 through 1985. The University's College of Business Administration is one of 200 select institutions of 1,200 business schools in the nation to be accredited by the American Assembly of Collegiate Schools of Business at the undergraduate and graduate levels. The University is one of three in the United States to offer an undergraduate manufacturing engineering program and the State of Illinois has selected Bradley to be one of eight Technology Commercialization Centers.

Bradley's cultural contributions and opportunities are unique for a university its size. Its Meyer Jacobs Theatre in the Hartmann Center for the Performing Arts is the scene of six university theatre productions as well as numerous concerts, ballets and appearances by touring groups, and its newly opened Dingeldine Music Center also is used for concerts and lectures. Peoria's Public Broadcasting classical radio, WCBU-FM, and public television station, WTVP, are housed at Bradley. The University's Cullom-Davis Library has a collection of over 725,000 items and its participation in the Online Computer Library Center gives students access to millions of resources in 2,000 libraries across the nation.

In the rapidly changing business world, principles of good corporate citizenship remain unchanged, and are a source of stability. Caterpillar Tractor Co., resident in the Peoria area since 1909, has sought to help make its home community a better place to work and live.

But perhaps the greatest citizenship contribution Caterpillar can make is to succeed in its basic business activities; to make quality products which compete successfully around the world; to earn a profit and pay adequate dividends to shareholders; to employ people and treat them fairly.

Caterpillar is proud to have helped Peoria become known as "Earthmoving Capital of the World." Actions now being taken at Caterpillar — to maintain quality and financial strength, introduce new and improved products, and reduce costs, — should help Peoria retain that title in the future.

But a vigorously competitive Caterpillar isn't enough. The Tri-County area can benefit from a broader economic base — more industry, more services. That's why Caterpillar is a strong supporter of local economic development and civic improvement efforts.

Through three-quarters of a century, Caterpillar has been a beneficiary of its hometown's natural resources, productive citizens and responsible governments. We're grateful. And we believe that other employers, those already here and those who should be persuasively attracted, can also profit from the Peoria area's many unique assets.

CATERPILLAR TRACTOR CO.

MODERN, STATE-OF-THE ART MANUFACTURING FACILITIES UNDERLINE CATERPILLAR'S COMMITMENT TO—AND CONSIDERABLE INVESTMENT IN—THE PEORIA AREA. HERE, MOLTEN GRAY IRON IS TRANSFERRED INTO A HOLDING FURNACE IN THE COMPANY'S FOUNDRY AT MAPLETON. (CATERPILLAR PHOTO)

LARGE TRACK-TYPE TRACTORS BUILT AT CATERPILLAR'S EAST PEORIA PLANT CAN BE FOUND TACKLING THE TOUGHEST EARTHMOVING JOBS THE WORLD OVER. (CATERPILLAR PHOTO)

FIRST OCCUPIED IN 1967, CATERPILLAR'S ADMINISTRATION BUILDING WAS BUILT IN DOWNTOWN PEORIA IN ORDER TO SHARE IN THE "RENAISSANCE" OF THAT AREA. (CATERPILLAR PHOTO)

106

CENTRAL ILLINOIS LIGHT COMPANY

It was in February of 1853 when the firm that eventually was to evolve into the Central Illinois Light Co., was granted its charter to sell gas lighting for city streets in Peoria. This was the Peoria Gas Light and Coke Co., whose charter was granted the same date as that of Quincy, making it the second or third utility in Illinois after Chicago.

The Company erected a gas manufacturing plant at the foot of Persimmon St., and on November 10, 1855, the gas lights were turned on, illuminating Peoria's principal streets for the first time.

The lamps were kept burning from twilight until dawn. But gas lighting was dim and inefficient, and Peoria's first electric company and second utility was formed by the Jenney Electric Light and Power Co. on September 20, 1883. Jenney obtained a contract from the city for electrical street lighting in November, 1885, which marked the end of gas lights in the city. CILCO was organized in 1913.

The company's 1924 report indicated the bulk of its power came from the East Peoria Plant, with the Liberty Station operating continuously throughout the heating season. More transmission lines were built that year, more gas lines laid and the plant was improved.

In 1932, CILCO contracted to buy natural gas from Panhandle Eastern Pipe Line Company and CILCO discontinued its manufacture of gas. On May 1, 1933, the properties of the Illinois Power Co. were acquired by CILCO, which made the East Peoria generating station, plus the gas, electric and heating properties plus the heating facilities in DeKalb part of the firm.

From 1933 on, CILCO continued to grow. By 1940 the firm had 1,087 employees. R. S. Wallace resigned as chairman of the board in 1947 and the East Peoria Plant was named in his honor.

The company moved its headquarters into the new general office building at 300 Liberty in May, 1959. In April of 1967, operations began at the company's new facility in Pioneer Park.

By 1971, the company's revenues topped the $100 million mark for the first time. It was that same year the Liberty Street Station was dismantled after having served the area for 81 years. The following year, construction started on CILCO's Duck Creek site near Canton.

CILCO really began at Liberty Street Station, located at the site of the old Fort Clark. From here, electricity illuminated Peoria homes for generations, steam-heated many dwellings and businesses and even provided heat to cook food at the old Palace Cafeteria. The company's roots remain in the heart of old Peoria.

CILCO'S R.S. WALLACE POWER PLANT AS IT APPEARED IN 1925. (CILCO PHOTO)

The Commercial National Bank of Peoria has a history that derives, like that of the United States, from "E Pluribus Unum," "one out of many." From the merger of seven different banks in over 100 years, culminating in the 1961 merger with the Central National Bank, the Commercial Bank has emerged as one of the banking leaders of downstate Illinois.

While the roots of the bank date back to the founding of the Mechanics National Bank in 1865, the Commercial National received its present charter in 1885. Its family tree includes such historically famous institutions as the Dime Savings Bank (1886), the German-American National Bank (1883) and the Merchants National Bank (1884). By 1940, the name of the institution had become the Commercial Merchants National Bank and Trust Co., headquartered in the imposing building on South Adams that was built in 1926.

The bank led the way in offering special services to women, whom the 1926 booklet noted, "are rapidly learning the pleasure to be derived from an independent income. As women investors are not always well informed on financial matters, we offer our services to them in an advisory capacity, giving them information which we have gained through years of experience." It was, for its time, a very modern view.

The Commercial National Bank became the cornerstone of Midwest Financial Group, Inc., downstate Illinois' largest bank holding company, under David E. Connor in 1984.

At present, David E. Connor is Chairman and Bank President is Robert T. Stevenson, Jr. The bank celebrated its first 100 years in 1985. It maintains the Main Bank downtown and Bank Park Knoxville and Pioneer offices.

COMMERCIAL NATIONAL BANK OF PEORIA

COMMERCIAL NATIONAL BANK'S SPONSERSHIP OF DEFENSE BONDS AND STAMPS HELPED BUY A BOMBER DURING WWII. (COMMERCIAL PHOTO)

THE INTERIOR AND EXTERIOR OF COMMERCIAL NATIONAL BANK AS IT APPEARED SHORTLY AFTER THE COMPLETION OF CONSTRUCTION IN 1929. (COMMERCIAL PHOTO).

108

WABCO HAULPAK DIVISION OF DRESSER INDUSTRIES, INC.

THE HAULPAK OFF HIGHWAY TRUCK, FIRST INTRODUCED IN 1957, HAS BECOME THE MAINSTAY OF THE COMPANY'S BUSINESS. (WABCO PHOTO)

AN AERIAL VIEW OF TODAY'S WABCO HAULPAK DIVISION OF DRESSER INDUSTRIES. (WABCO PHOTO)

One of the industries that helped give Peoria the title of "Earthmoving Capital of the World" is the WABCO HAULPAK DIVISION of Dresser Industries, Inc., which had its beginning when R. G. LeTourneau moved his company here in 1935.

LeTourneau was one of the innovative pioneers in the earth-moving industry. Back in California in 1922, LeTourneau was a land-leveling contractor who devised a new scraper to move dirt faster and cheaper. So successful was his development that other contractors wanted him to build scrapers for them. By 1929, he was manufacturing more than he was contracting.

He moved his company here from Stockton, California in 1935, to an area between Peoria's old circus grounds and the Avery Farm Machinery Company. So humble were the firm's beginnings, that Mrs. LeTourneau helped her husband unload some of the steel that was to be used in the first manufacturing plant.

LeTourneau purchased the Avery Company in 1941 and during World War II, hundreds of Tournapulls, scrapers, dozers, rooters and sheep's foot rollers poured out of the Peoria plant for military roads and airports in Europe and the Pacific. Then in 1953, LeTourneau sold his Peoria plant to Westinghouse Air Brake Co. which was then purchased by American Standard in 1967. Dresser Industries purchased the construction and mining equipment group from American Standard in 1984.

The Peoria Plant remains the site of many construction and mining industry firsts:

The first two-wheeled prime mover for scrapers was introduced here in 1937.

In 1946, the first electrically controlled, self-propelled rubber tired scrapers were manufactured here.

The Haulpak off-highway truck was introduced in 1975.

The first 120-ton electric drive off-highway truck was built here in 1965 and the first 170-ton off-highway electric truck in 1975. The firm also manufactures the largest production model off-highway truck in the world, the 3200B with a payload of 250 tons.

Today, WABCO HAULPAK DIVISION of Dresser Construction and Mining Equipment is a leading producer of off-highway trucks used in quarries, mines, dams and construction sites around the world and owes much of its continuing progress to the vision of the innovative genius that was R. G. LeTourneau.

EDWARD J. SMITH PRINTERS, INC.

One of Peoria's earliest and longest lasting printing establishments was founded by a journeyman printer named Edward J. Smith in 1899 when he opened his shop at 319 S.W. Washington St.

The commercial printing firm continues today as Edward J. Smith Printers, Inc., and has expanded into foil stamping and embossing and presently does trade work in 16 states.

Smith built a new plant in the early 1920's at 208 S.W. Washington, and remained sole proprietor from 1899 until 1947. That year, he sold the business to Arnold G. Fernsted, who joined the firm as a sales representative in 1917. Fernsted was responsible for most of the firm's larger accounts and its dramatic increase in business over the years. Fernsted remained owner until he retired in 1974.

Mike Fernsted, who joined Smiths as a sales representative in 1947, was responsible for the company's entry into the lithographic field and later the foil stamping and embossing business. Fernsted became owner in 1974 and incorporated the firm in 1978.

Meanwhile, it moved from its old location into the present 12,000 square foot location at 207 Voris in 1963. Michael E. Baer, who joined the company in 1953, became Vice President and Secretary in 1978, responsible for production, purchasing and management. There are presently 12 employees, over 100 commercial customers and more than 60 "trade customers" in 16 states.

THREE MEN HAVE OWNED EDWARD J. SMITH PRINTERS OVER THE YEARS. THEY ARE, FROM LEFT OT RIGHT, EDWARD J. SMITH, FOUNDER (1899-1947), ARNOLD G. FERNSTED (1947-1974), AND MIKE FERNSTED (1974-PRESENT)

110

HAGERTY BROTHERS COMPANY

THE HAGERTY BROTHERS PLANT AS IT APPEARED SHORTLY AFTER THE TURN OF THE CENTURY. (HAGERTY BROTHERS PHOTO)

THE OFFICES AND WARE-HOUSE OF HAGERTY BROTHERS COMPANY, NOW LOCATED IN EAST PEORIA. (HAGERTY BROTHERS PHOTO)

Hagerty Brothers Company dates its presence in Peoria to 1855, six years before the outbreak of the Civil War when the 32 year old Saul Hagerty moved to Peoria to work as a millwright for I. G. Reynolds. By 1860, the year of the firm's founding, the Peoria City Directory listed Saul Hagerty, Millwright, located at 187 N. Adams St. In the 1895 PORTRAIT AND BIOGRAPHICAL ALBUM, he was described as a millwright "thoroughly understanding his trade and excelled by none in the reliable manner in which all his business transactions are conducted and contracts are fulfilled."

It was noted in the Album that every distillery in the city, except one, had been erected by Hagerty.

In 1871 the firm was Lind, Hagerty and Co. The name changed to Hagerty, Hunter & Co. in 1879, and by 1900, the company had changed its name to Hagerty, Graber & Co., which advertised it would "furnish plans and estimates for roller mills, elevators, and distilleries of any capacity."

After Saul Hagerty died on January 11th, 1903, the firm became known as Hagerty Brothers Co. and was operated by his three sons, Almon S., Robert S. and H. Guy. By 1905, it had branched out and was dealing with shafting, belting, pulleys, engine packing and had become sole agent for the Columbus gasoline engine.

When the Eighteenth Amendment (prohibition) closed down the nations breweries and distilleries on Janury 16th, 1920, Hagerty Brothers Company gradually moved into the wholesale steel and mill supply business, supplementing their existing inventory with that purchased from Cummings and Emmerson. During this period, they manufactured a toasted oak chip that was probably used to turn grain alcohol into bourbon. This evidently was very profitable until the repeal of prohibition.

Hagerty Brothers Company survived depression, strikes in the industry, prohibition and economic downturns to be today Illinois' largest downstate Steel Service Center and Industrial Supply House.

In the late 50's and early 60's, Hagerty's moved into its steel warehouse and offices in East Peoria, which have been expanded several times since on the company's property which covers 25½ acres on both sides of Interstate 74.

The present management line of Hagerty Brothers derives from the 1915 marriage of Myrtle Hagerty to John Harvey Flora. Flora's son John Hagerty "Ted" Flora is Chairman and President, and the company, founded in 1860 by the 32 year old Saul Hagerty, celebrates its 125th year.

In Peoria's earliest days, water came directly from the river; but already by 1843, many citizens were buying water from the mineral springs at 801 Seventh St. There was, however, no real attempt to install a municipal water system until after the Civil War. The original Peoria Water Works was located at the foot of Grant Street, opening in 1869 and pumping untreated water from the river directly into the newly laid mains. The quality of the water was understandably questionable, and people who had made sizable investments in their own wells were reluctant to subscribe to the service.

Before long the company failed, and the City of Peoria sold the plant to a group of eastern investors. They agreed to build the present pumping station and main well at the foot of Lorentz Street in 1890, along with a distribution system. The cost, estimated at $1.25 million, escalated to $1.45 million, forcing the company into receivership. It was reorganized in 1898 as Peoria Water Works, the firm from which today's water company is directly descended.

The pumping engines installed in the pump houses were showpieces. They were steam-generated beauties trimmed in oak and walnut and made of polished brass and capable of pumping 7.2 million gallons a day to the Grand Blvd. reservoir on the bluff. These have long since been replaced by electric motors with a pumping capacity of 20 million gallons a day.

But the original pump house and main well buildings, dating from 1890, are still in use today at the Illinois River Treatment Plant, which handles the treatment, purification, storage and pumping of Illinois River water. Part of Peoria's water supply also comes from wells at Dodge St., Griswold St., and the San Koty Well Field.

Peoria's ample supply of good quality drinking water helped give rise to such industries as Pabst Brewery and the Hiram Walker Distillery.

On January 1, 1985, Peoria Water Company merged with the Alton Water Company and Illinois-American Water Company to become the Illinois-American Water Company, Peoria District.

Today, the water company employs 120 people and serves 45,000 customers in Peoria, West Peoria, Bellevue, Bartonville and nearby surrounding townships in Peoria County. It has annual gross sales of over $12 million and maintains a treatment plant at the foot of Lorentz St., a distribution center in Pioneer Park, and business offices at 123 S.W. Washington St. in downtown Peoria.

ILLINOIS-AMERICAN WATER COMPANY, PEORIA DISTRICT

ONE OF THE FOUR RECENTLY RESTORED GARGOYLES CROWNING THE MAIN PUMP HOUSE. (ILLINOIS-AMERICAN WATER CO. PHOTO)

THE MAIN PUMPING STATION, NOW ON THE NATIONAL REGISTER OF HISTORIC PLACES, UNDER CONSTRUCTION IN 1890. (ILLINOIS-AMERICAN WATER CO.)

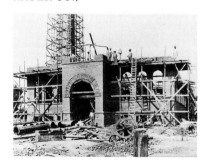

112

ILLINOIS CENTRAL COLLEGE

AN AERIAL VIEW OF PART OF THE ILLINOIS COMMUNITY COLLEGE CAMPUS. (ICC PHOTO)

It was the 1964 Illinois Board of Higher Education study, "A Provisional Master Plan for Higher Education in Illinois", that led to the formation of Illinois Central College. What is remarkable, however, is that in September, 1967, only three years after publication of the study, the college opened its doors with 2,486 students and a full and part-time faculty of 113.

From planning to opening was not as simple as it might seem. The process involved formation of a Tri-County Public Junior College Steering Committee, support of 19 unit or high school boards, formation of a Tri-County Public Junior College District, a referendum, plus selection of a college board, hiring administrators, staff and faculty, building a facility and selecting a curriculum.

From the beginning, it was determined the college would meet the needs of vocational, technical and transfer students. In November 1966, the Board selected and purchased 437.6 acres between East Peoria, Peoria and Washington for the Illinois Central College campus.

Dr. Kenneth Edwards, a member of the Bellevue Junior College faculty since 1947 and dean since 1953, was appointed Illinois Central College's president in December, 1966. The Board and the President made the decision to build temporary facilities instead of delaying the opening. A $99,700 contract for building and leasing interim buildings was awarded to G. Raymond Becker in the spring of 1967. The buildings were ready for fall and several are still in use.

Thirty-eight programs were offered the first year of operation. That fall, the Board recommended $6.06 million be allocated for permanent building construction. In March, 1968, a referendum for a $9.7 million bond issue was approved. And Phase I, classrooms and labs, was ready for occupancy in 1972. Phase II, including the library and administration building and the physical education building, was finished in 1974 at a cost of $10 million. In 1977, the Agricultural and Industrial Technology Building and the 500-seat Performing Arts Center were completed at a cost of about $6 million.

In 1975, Dr. Kenneth Edwards resigned and the new library/administration building was named in his honor. The Board appointed Dr. Leon H. Perley as president.

The college continues to grow, not only in enrollment, faculty and staff, but in the area it serves. It now serves all of Peoria and Woodford Counties and portions of Tazewell, McLean, Mason, Livingston, Bureau, and Marshall Counties. The district encompasses more than 2,000 square miles and it is one of the largest community college districts in Illinois. Enrollment peaked at 15,000 for the 1981 fall semester and is currently approaching 13,000.

AN ICC STUDENT WORKS ON A COMPUTER-AIDED DESIGN PROJECT. (ICC PHOTO)

Back in the 1880's, it was still backbreaking labor to build and maintain split rail fences. Peter Sommer and his two sons, John and Peter W., began to experiment with means of making a practical farm fence from wire in the little blacksmith shop on the farm they worked near Tremont, Ill. By 1889, with son John contributing most of the mechanical genius, the Sommers were turning out an acceptable wire fence with a crude, hand-operated machine. That same year, the machine was installed in a batten-board shed near Tremont and the Keystone Woven Wire Fence Company was in business.

The product was called Keystone Fence because the small stay wires were angled to both sides, giving each aperture a keystone shape. The new fence was a local wonder. It was practical, inexpensive and labor-saving. So successful was this innovation that the company in 1895 moved into a larger building in Tremont. Keystone moved to Peoria's far south side in 1901 and to the site of its present plant in Bartonville in 1907. That same year, the company name became Keystone Steel & Wire Co.

When Peter Sommer developed the world's first woven wire fence, the wire had to be drawn by hand. Keystone now operates one of the largest wire drawing and fabrication plants in the world. The firm produces its own steel from scrap in an electric arc furnace melt shop.

Keystone began using the continuous casting process in the late 60's, and now 100% of its output is made with this energy efficient process. This steel is the raw material for a product line that includes "Red Brand" farm fence and barbed wire, welded wire fabric, hexagonal netting, nails, industrial wire and concrete reinforcing fabric.

The firm has remained a pioneer in bending wire to useful services. It presently employs more than 1,500, has annual gross sales of $150 million and occupies more than two million feet of plant space.

Keystone as well has been a leader in the type of labor management cooperation that has been designed to meet the threat of foreign competition. It has taken a positive approach to labor relations and profit sharing, the latter going into effect when a contract level of profits has been reached.

Keystone Steel & Wire Co. at present is in the midst of an ambitious $10+ million expansion program and is moving into an expanded wire line with new facilities and new equipment. From that little operation on the farm near Tremont, Keystone has become a consistent leader in the wire industry and Peoria's second largest industrial employer.

KEYSTONE STEEL & WIRE CO.

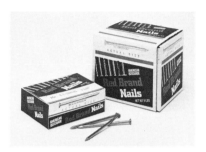

KEYSTONE'S PACKAGED NAILS ARE POPULAR FOR DO-IT-YOURSELF PROJECTS.

RED BRAND HAS BEEN THE LEADING FARM FENCE FOR ALMOST 100 YEARS.

114

KIEFER ELECTRICAL SUPPLY CO.

THE HOME OF KIEFER ELECTRICAL SUPPLY CO. AND ELECTRICAL SPECIALTIES CO. HAS BEEN HALLMARKED AS AN OUTSTANDING EXAMPLE OF HISTORIC PRESERVATION. (JOURNAL STAR PHOTO)

FOUR GENERATIONS OF KIEFERS IN 1942, INCLUDING TODAY'S PRESIDENT, WALTER A. KIEFER. (KIEFER PHOTO)

What is now Kiefer Electrical Supply Co., housed in a distinctive and colorful building on S.W. Washington St., began its business life as an electrical contractor. Its founder, Walter R. Kiefer, a descendant of a pioneer Peoria family from Germany, incorporated his firm on September 26, 1922 in a house at 310 E. Third St.

Since the time of incorporation, three members of the Kiefer family have played primary roles in the growth and development of Kiefer Electrical Supply Co.: Walter R. Kiefer, the Company's founder; Albert H. Kiefer, Vice President and General Manager 1955-1967; Walter A. Kiefer, the Company's current President.

As the firm evolved into wholesale and retail distribution of lighting fixtures and electrical products, it moved to the 300 block of S.W. Washington and then to its third location at 318 S.W. Washington. Its headquarters now located in the former Oakford Fahnestock building at 316 S.W. Washington, were acquired by Walter A. Kiefer in 1969, along with its adjacent parking lot. Ownership of the company started to shift at that time when Walter A. Kiefer, grandnephew of the founder, purchased all of the stock that lay outside the Kiefer family. Later, during the 1970's, he completed the acquisition of controlling interest in the firm.

The renovation of the building, which houses both Kiefer Electrical Supply Co. and Electrical Specialties Co., has been hailed as a prime example of historic preservation. From this building, which is in the heart of the original Peoria, the Kiefer Co. has grown to become one of downstate Illinois' most influential and successful electrical supply firms.

Walter A. Kiefer, a Peorian and graduate of Bradley University, is currently President of the firm. The fifth generation of the Kiefer family, employed by the company as manager of the Engineered Products Division, is Daniel P. Hoppe, great-great nephew of the founder.

In recent years the firm has discontinued its residential lighting, appliance and air-conditioning business and developed a strong position in the commercial and industrial electrical distribution market. Its profile today includes leading edge technology for the development of factory automation equipment in the form of engineering assistance, the industrial control products necessary for factory automation, and the software to tie the total system together.

While its general offices remain in Peoria, Kiefer opened a distribution center in Benton, Illinois in 1975, an office in St. Louis in 1980, and a branch in Lafayette, Indiana in 1981. Kiefer Electrical Supply Co. currently employs 64 people.

The Kiefer building, with the stylized blue and yellow graphic depicting a K on its east wall, is also the home of Electrical Specialties Co.

Electrical Specialties Co. was founded under a separate charter in 1972 by Walter A. Kiefer, who serves as its President. Thomas B. Thomas is Vice President and Plant Manager of the company, which employs 40 people.

Electrical Specialties Co. manufactures electrical wiring harnesses, assemblies and electro-mechanical devices for the industrial market and serves as a job shop, producing special order wiring for the automotive, earthmoving and aviation industries.

Strong emphasis is placed on computerized manufacturing requirements planning. Current projects include those that will allow customer requirements to be received via computer. Parts may then be collated, assembled and delivered for "just-in-time" use by the customer.

As the major industrial manufacturers become more international in their operation, Electrical Specialties Co. is changing and improving in order to maintain growth in an increasingly complex environment.

ELECTRICAL SPECIALTIES CO.

BUILDING AN ELECTRICAL WIRING HARNESS FOR A CATERPILLAR SCRAPER IS AN INTRICATE JOB AT ELECTRICAL SPECIALTIES CO. (CATERPILLAR PHOTO)

116

METHODIST MEDICAL CENTER

THE THREE CO-FOUNDERS OF THE DEACONESS HOME AND HOSPITAL ASSOCIATION, MISS MINNA RIGGS, MISS IDA PHILLIPS AND MISS LUCY HALL. (METHODIST MEDICAL PHOTO)

THE PEDIATRICS WARD IN 1918. (METHODIST MEDICAL PHOTO)

THE METHODIST MEDICAL CENTER OF ILLINOIS TODAY OFFERS ONE OF THE MOST COMPREHENSIVE CORONARY CARE PROGRAMS IN THE MIDWEST. (METHODIST MEDICAL PHOTO)

What has become one of America's most modern, progressive and sizable Medical Centers had a rather humble beginning when it was opened as a 20 bed hospital May 24, 1900. Founded by three Deaconeses of the Methodist Episcopal Church, Miss Minna K. Riggs, Miss Ida Phillips and Miss Lucy Hall, the hospital also started a training school for nurses. Ever since, there has been a constant succession of building programs and medical progress. The Methodist Medical Center of Illinois, so named in 1975, is a large medical complex that reflects the advances made in medicine and health care in Illinois over the past 85 years.

It now includes a 536 bed hospital, one of the largest three-year nursing schools in the state, the St. Jude Midwest Affiliate for treating children afflicted with cancer (the first such affiliation with St. Jude Children's Research Hospital in the nation), the Heidrich Radiation Oncology Center--the only regional radiation therapy facility in Central Illinois, the Methodist Division of the Institute of Physical Medicine and Rehabilitation, the Family Practice Residency Program of the University of Illinois College of Medicine at Peoria, and the Family Physicians' Center.

Since 1975, Methodist Medical Center has launched Peoria's first Ambulatory Surgery Center, one of the nation's busiest, which allows patients to return home the same day for recuperation. It has become one of 59 sites nationwide for the National Cancer Institute's Clinical Community Oncology Program, with the latest care for cancer patients. It has the only Hospice Care program in the Peoria area, offering emotional, psychological, physical, social and spiritual support for terminally ill patients and their families, and it offers special programs for people with sleep disorders, chronic or acute pain or chronic headaches. It has one of the most comprehensive and up-to-date heart programs in the midwest, a comprehensive cancer care program, a laser center and a women's health center.

The Peoria Civic Center is a three-building complex located on 20 acres of land in Peoria's downtown. It is comprised of a 12,000 seat arena, a 33,000 square foot exhibit hall and a 2,200 seat proscenium theater, all unified by a striking glass arcade that enhances the beauty of the complex and provides a climate-controlled corridor for its almost one million visitors annually.

The Center's Carver Arena hosts major sporting and entertainment events that include concerts, Bradley basketball, Riverman IHL hockey, tractor pulls, rodeos, the Ice Capades and the circus. Hundreds of arena events annually generate millions of dollars through ticket sales, facility rental and concession sales. The Exhibit Hall provides floor space for conventions, trade shows, major banquets and meetings. The goal of re-establishing Peoria as a major convention center has been realized in this hall and its 14 meeting rooms. The building has been instrumental in spurring economic growth downtown, such as increased hotel, motel, and restaurant revenues since the Civic Center's completion.

The Civic Center Theater provides a modern and elegant setting for national touring shows and local performing arts organizations. The Peoria Symphony, Peoria Civic Opera, Amateur Musical Club, and Broadway Theater Series all perform on the theater stage. Convention and meeting usage for general sessions has grown as a result of its excellent acoustics.

The impressive Theater lobby provides a gracious location for wedding receptions and social events of all kinds.

The Peoria Civic Center, under the direction of the Civic Center Authority, continues to be an important force in Peoria's economic growth by providing the entertainment and convention facilities that make Peoria a first class city.

PEORIA CIVIC CENTER

118

PEORIA JOURNAL STAR

The taproot of the newspaper that has evolved into the Journal Star of 1985 dates back well over 100 years, to Dec. 1855, when the first issue of the PEORIA DAILY TRANSCRIPT appeared. It was one of three newspapers that ultimately were to converge to form the publication that today is the third largest newspaper in the State, serving a vast area of Central Illinois with its morning, weekend and Sunday editions.

One of the paper's early editors was Eugene F. Baldwin, who was hired as a local editor in 1865. In 1877, Baldwin, along with J. B. Barnes, founded THE PEORIA JOURNAL, which became the second branch of the JOURNAL STAR family tree.

The first edition of the JOURNAL rolled off the presses on Dec. 3, 1877. It was an afternoon edition, and during the first week, the paper's circulation was a mere 1,700. Baldwin left the enterprise for other pursuits and the paper was bought by Henry M. Pindell, former city treasurer of Springfield, Il.

Baldwin's absence from journalism was to be brief. He returned to Peoria to found the PEORIA STAR on Nov. 7, 1897, and the last ancestor of the JOURNAL STAR was in business.

Just over a year later, Pindell bought the TRANSCRIPT and merged it with his paper. It was known as the HERALD-TRANSCRIPT.

Pindell moved into the afternoon field by buying the former JOURNAL in 1900. Two years later, he sold the HERALD-TRANSCRIPT to an out-of-town syndicate, only to buy it back in 1916, when he began publishing the TRANSCRIPT in the morning and the JOURNAL in the afternoon.

#1 NEWS PLAZA...HOME OF PEORIA STAR SINCE 1955. (JOURNAL STAR PHOTO)

After Baldwin's death in November of 1914, the JOURNAL and TRANSCRIPT slowly came to dominate the Peoria newspaper scene while the STAR began a long decline. Pindell's papers became the PEORIA JOURNAL-TRANSCRIPT with morning and afternoon editions. When he died in 1924, the paper was taken over by his son-in-law, Carl P. Slane.

In the early 1940's, the STAR'S financial plight was so serious that a corporation was formed between it and the JOURNAL-TRANSCRIPT. By 1954, the merger of all departments seemed an ideal solution, since the JOURNAL-TRANSCRIPT had a circulation of 70,132 and the STAR 33,152. Following the merger, the new paper came out under the masthead of PEORIA JOURNAL STAR with both morning and afternoon editions.

The new firm began work on its modern plant near the McCluggage Bridge and on Nov. 14, 1955, the first edition came off the presses of the new facility. It was almost 100 years after the founding of the original TRANSCRIPT.

It has approximately 101,000 daily and 117,000 Sunday subscribers.

The he company that is now known as Talman Home Federal Savings, Peoria, started in 1874, when it was chartered on June 12th as the Peoples Loan and Homestead Association. It has therefore been a part of the community for 111 years, although under different names and in different locations. But during its long existence, it has been a major factor in developing thrift and home ownership in Central Illinois.

Peoples Loan was granted a federal charter in 1935 and in 1955 changed its name to First Federal Savings of Peoria. While the firm grew steadily and survived the depression, its major growth came under the leadership of A. D. Theobald, who remained managing officer from October, 1946, until his retirement on July 1, 1971. It became the first savings and loan association in Peoria, growing in the 25 years he was executive officer from about $15 million to $200 million - at least $100 million larger than the next association in the city.

Its specialty was the financing of the development of new residential areas, such as Rolling Acres, Hamilton Park, Lexington Park, Glen Elm, Forest Gardens, Creighton Woods, Vinton Highlands, Illinois Valley Homes and Northaire.

The he association also financed many of the modern type specialized housing for the elderly in the area, large scale apartment construction, land development and multi-family homes. The firm also has been a leader in loans to black families, and in college educational loans. The association is noted for having made the first GI Loan in Peoria and the second one in the state. Shortly after the war, in fact, such GI loans became more than 50 percent of the Association's mortgage portfolio.

In September of 1982, with assets over $450 million, First Federal Savings of Peoria merged with Talman Home Federal of Chicago, from which the firm has taken its new name. Talman had been founded on January 2, 1922 by Ben F. Bohac, the son of Bohemian immigrants, with original assets listed as $692.75.

Today, Talman has over 50 offices located in Chicago and Central Illinois. The office at 111 N.E. Jefferson in Peoria is the main office of the Central Illinois Division, with offices in Northwoods and Sheridan Village, Pekin, Minonk, Lacon, Farmington and Princeville. The Central Illinois Division employs about 165 people. And Talman Home's assets are now listed at over $6.4 billion.

TALMAN HOME FEDERAL SAVINGS AND LOAN

TALMAN HOME WHEN IT WAS PEOPLE'S FEDERAL SAVINGS IN 1952. (TALMAN PHOTO)

THE PRESENT TALMAN HOME FEDERAL SAVINGS, PEORIA AS SEEN FROM COURTHOUSE SQUARE. (TALMAN PHOTO)

120

WESTMINSTER PRESBYTERIAN CHURCH

THE WARM WORSHIP ATMOSPHERE WAS ENHANCED BY A SANCTUARY OF LOFTY BEAMED CEILINGS AND EXTENSIVE STAINED GLASS. ALTHOUGH THE CHURCH BUILDING WAS DESTROYED BY A FIRE IN JANUARY 1985, SERVICES AND PROGRAMS CONTINUE IN ADJACENT BUILDINGS AS THE CONGREGATION PLANS FOR THE FUTURE. (FIRE PHOTO BY JOHN HENDRICKSON)

THE WESTMINSTER INFANT DAY CARE CENTER WAS ESTABLISHED TO PROVIDE QUALIFIED CARE FOR INFANTS WHILE THEIR MOTHERS COMPLETE HIGH SCHOOL. (WIDC PHOTO)

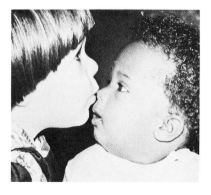

Westminster Presbyterian Church began with one person's concern for the children living in the newly developed area beyond the Sheridan Road city limits. The vision of Miss Elizabeth McKinney in 1884 soon became a widely shared goal among the members of the First Presbyterian Church. Responding to a challenge that had great possibility, a survey committee reported back to the church leadership that the field was open and "ripe for harvest." Soon the Bluff Mission Sunday School had grown large enough to begin a new congregation, and in 1897, twenty-four persons signed a request asking that Westminster be joined to the national denomination.

An area resident, Mrs. Elizabeth Griswold, arranged for her estate to be given to Westminster and that a beautiful church be built not as a memorial to her, but for the purpose of continuing God's work. In excavating for the foundation, the workers uncovered a portion of the walls of a milking barn and churn room, and the builders agreed that these same stones should be used in building the Church's foundation. In June of 1899, the congregation moved from a dilapidated and hard-used frame building into the newly dedicated building on Moss Avenue.

The church and its membership has been highly active in meeting the needs of people in both the local community and the world. It has been a consistent regional leader in mission giving. The approach has been to provide not only assistance to the immediate needs of people, but to work toward eliminating the root causes of poverty, strife, and injustice through support of programs such as the Westminster Infant Care Center, the Grade School Tutoring Program, the Samaritan Counseling Center, and Friendship House.

Public television came to Peoria because of a commitment made by Bradley University in 1961. With the encouragement of President Talman Van Arsdale and the direction of Professor Philip Weinberg, the University helped form the Illinois Valley Educational Television Association. By 1965, a system developed at Bradley served 32 school districts and two parochial school systems with a 4-channel color-capable TV service.

In 1969, the Illinois Valley Public Telecommunications Corporation, parent organization of WTVP Channel 47, became the community license with the cooperation of Illinois Central College, Peoria Public Library, Peoria District 150, Pekin District 108, Lakeview, and Bradley University.

The station went on the air originating from Jobst Hall in June, 1971, with a variety of programs that reached nearly a half million people. By that fall, arrangements were made with the Public Broadcasting Service for interconnection with its network of over 100 stations across the country.

Elwin Basquin, formerly with the Iowa Public TV Network, became Channel 47's first and only station manager in 1972. He helped organize a series of membership drives, canvasses, telethons and auctions and the result was a series of major improvements to the station.

With community support and a matching federal grant, the station bought color cameras, videotape recorders and a mobile unit in 1973, enabling it to provide live coverage of such events as the Heart of Illinois Fair, Marigold Festival Parade in Pekin, presidential visits, Bradley basketball, Peoria Symphony concerts and the grand opening of the Civic Center Theater.

On Sunday, June 21, 1981, exactly 10 years after the station first signed on the air, WTVP dedicated its new $1.5 million transmission facility. Today the station broadcasts over 80 hours a week to more than three quarters of a million people, and serves as a switching center for CONVOCOMS three broadcast stations and microwave system, which connects several colleges and universities, businesses and communities throughout West Central Illinois. On August 5, 1985, a live television call-in program originating in Moline was networked over five downstate public television stations via the control center at Bradley/WTVP.

The station has continued to grow largely because of the commitment and support of the public. At present, a long range plan for the Illinois Valley Public Telecommunications Corp. is being developed to help chart its future course for opportunity and service.

WTVP

WTVP HAS MADE IT POSSIBLE FOR MUCH OF THE PEORIA AREA TO ENJOY A WIDE RANGE OF PROGRAMMING, INCLUDING SESAME STREET, LUCIANO PAVAROTTI PERFORMANCES, AND THE LONG RUNNING, "WALL $TREET WEEK WITH LOUIS RUKEYSER". (PBS PHOTOS)

122

L.R. NELSON CORPORATION

DAVID P. RANSBURG, L.R. NELSON CORPORATION CHAIRMAN HOLDS THE COMPANY'S FIRST PRODUCT, THE PERFECT CLINCHING HOSE MENDER, AND ITS NEWEST, THE RAIN DATE ELECTRONIC WATER TIMER. (L.R. NELSON PHOTO)

THIS BUILDING AT 1722 SW WASHINGTON SERVED AS THE HEADQUARTERS AND MANUFACTURING PLANT OF L.R. NELSON CORPORATION FROM 1918 TO 1972. (L.R. NELSON PHOTO)

If Lewen R. Nelson could return to Peoria, Illinois, he'd be pleased to see that the company he founded 75 years ago has blossomed into one of the country's leading and best known manufacturers of lawn and garden sprinklers and specialty watering devices.

It was Nelson who invented the Perfect Clinching hose mender, and it was that device which enabled him to give birth in 1911 to the L. R. Nelson Manufacturing Company. "That hose mender and several original nozzles are in our catalog today," said David P. Ransburg, Chairman and Chief Executive Officer of the company now known as L. R. Nelson Corporation. Ransburg purchased the firm from the Nelson family in 1972.

Those original products have stood the test of time and have been joined by hundreds of others including 24 patented items.

"We've been able to thrive because Nelson people care," Ransburg said. "You can trace that attitude back to our founder, and it's no less evident in the Nelson people today. It explains our growth into a major manufacturer with a world-wide reputation for engineering innovation, product quality and progressive marketing."

Nelson took root in Peoria in 1911 in a frame facility at 1810 Southwest Washington where it remained until 1918 when it moved into a larger building at 1722 Southwest Washington. That structure served as both its corporate headquarters and manufacturing plant until 1972.

Today's corporate offices and research facilities are located at 7719 North Pioneer Lane, and the company operates a distribution center at 8810 North University to serve the eastern and midwestern states. Materials and components are also stored there until they are needed at the nearby Princeville, Illinois plant.

Nelson also operates regional distribution centers in Gainesville, Florida and Garden Grove, California.

The Human Service Center, one of Illinois' largest comprehensive community mental health centers was incorporated in 1976 with the consolidation of the Peoria Mental Health Clinic, the Stonehedge Foundation, the Peoria Area Council on Alcoholism, and the Comprehensive Mental Health Board of the Peoria area.

The mission of the Center is to help people live their lives well through a variety of services that address the social and emotional needs of all age groups. The Center provides counseling services, substance abuse treatment programs, emergency services, residential programs and services designed to help individuals prevent problems and achieve a happier, more fulfilling life. The Center also has a management division that provides Employee Assistance programs and consultation services to corporations and businesses in central Illinois.

The Center has a history of being a leader in the field of human services. Two of its founding agencies were the first of their kind in Illinois. The Peoria Area Mental Health Clinic (originally Mental Hygiene Clinic) was founded in 1937 and was the first such clinic in the state and the Stonehedge Foundation was the first licensed drug abuse program in Illinois.

HUMAN SERVICE CENTER

HUMAN SERVICE CENTER, FAYETTE OFFICE

Jumer's Castle Lodge, which stands high on the bluff on Peoria's Western Avenue, was conceived with the idea of combining the ultimate in Old World elegance with the most modern guest conveniences. Its German-Bavarian theme is carried out from its exterior architecture to every detail of its interior furnishing and represents a dream come true for James Jumer, whose forebears were a noble family in upper Bavaria with a castle near Regensburg.

Building started on the Peoria Lodge in November, 1969 on the site of the former Kramer's Restaurant. The grand opening was held on Dec. 16, 1970. A 77-room addition was completed in 1979 and another ambitious expansion program that gave Jumers a dramatic new entrance and expanded banquet rooms was undertaken in 1985.

Jumers has consistently received many coveted national awards including the Silver Spoon, Mobile's Star Ratings, and the AAA's Four Diamonds.

JUMER'S CASTLE LODGE

JUMER'S GERMAN BAROQUE SPLENDOR WITH STAINED GLASS WINDOWS, FLOWER BOXES, POSTER BEDS, OIL PAINTINGS, HEAVY WOOD, BEAMED CEILINGS AND ITS WEALTH OF AUTHENTIC ANTIQUES PROVIDE AN ELABORATE GRACE AND CHARM VISITORS FIND DIFFICULT TO RESIST.

124

THE MEYER FURNACE COMPANY

FIVE GENERATIONS OF MEYER FURNACE, FOUNDED IN 1866: A) FRANK MEYER AND WIFE B) GEORGE F. MEYER AND AMALIA MUELLER C) FRANK L. MEYER AND WINIFRED ROGERSON D) GREGORY T. MEYER AND SUZANNE AUGSPURGER E) FRANK L. MEYER III. (MEYER PHOTOS)

PEORIA & PEKIN UNION RAILWAY COMPANY

P & PU ENGINE NO. 9, ONE OF THE ORIGINAL ENGINES IN SERVICE DURING 1883. (P & PU PHOTO)

THE NEW P & PU RAILWAY BRIDGE COMPLETED IN OCTOBER 1984. (HEIDI KLINGELHOFER PHOTO)

While the Peoria and Pekin Union Railway Co. might best be remembered in history for its imposing Union Station and its adjacent train shed (detailed in Transportation Chapter), its major impact on the community and the area has been, and continues to be, its function as the Peoria Gateway. This concept grew out of the confusion created by the massive entanglement that existed 100 years ago when the railroads in Peoria and Pekin ran through and around the towns in a virtual fishnet pattern. From the tangle of trackage, the Peoria and Pekin Union created an orderly flow with an efficiency and logic that remain to this day.

The Railway was founded in 1880 when Peoria was a busy river town with a population of 29,249. It has remained through the great age of railroading and into the present as a vital link in the transportation of raw materials and finished products in this important Central Illinois market.

Big Red and Little Red, Robyn Weaver, VLJ, Ralph Smith, Ira Bitner, Gene Konrad, Mort Cantor are all part of the WIRL heritage.

WIRL went on the air in the late 1940's, under the ownership of the Altorfer Family. In the late 1950's, it was sold to Frudeger Broadcasting and became Peoria's "Big Sound" with top 40 music and contemporary personalities like Stan Majors, who made the Guiness Book of Records with a stay awake stint, and unpredictable Jack Etzel, along with Robyn Weaver and his "Rancid Recipes."

In the early 1960's, WIRL became a part of Mid America Media and continued on the tradition of being the station you were growing up with. WIRL "Good Guy" window stickers graced the rear windows of thousands of Peoria area cars -and Good Guys like Larry Kenney, DJ Dan and Dave Diamond entertained the largest radio audience in Central Illinois.

Now in the 1980's, WIRL has changed as its listeners have changed, reflecting the news and entertainment needs of all those people who grew up with WIRL thru the 50's, 60's and 70's.

In 1972, Mid America purchased WIVC, an FM station owned by the Journal Star. The call letters were changed to WSWT and the blend of relaxing music and the smooth voice of Walter Thurman soon moved FM107 up the ratings ladder.

WSWT has changed with the times. But, it is still the place Peorians tune to for easy listening music.

WIRL and WSWT continue to be a part of Mid America Media, which is based in Kankakee, Illinois, and are part of a group with radio stations and cable TV systems in Kankakee; Indianapolis, Indiana; Davenport, Iowa; Tulsa, Oklahoma; and Hilton Head, South Carolina.

WIRL/WSWT

125

ROBYN WEAVER, WIRL MORNING MAN FOR OVER 25 YEARS. (WIRL PHOTO)

CHAPTER SIX

THE GLORIOUS STEAMBOAT ERA

Accounts of early boats and captains. Steamboat voyages to Peoria. The romance of steamboats. Races and early disasters. Timetables and prices. Details about the Swains, Capt. Henry Detweiller and his role in the Civil War. The packets. The sinking of the Columbia and the arrival of the Julia Belle Swain.

THE STEAMBOAT "MAJESTIC"
ON THE ILLINOIS.

128

It was nearly a quarter of a century after Robert Fulton successfully demonstrated his "Clermont" on the Hudson River in August of 1807 that the first steamboat called at Peoria. But that arrival in the spring of 1830 was to have incredibly far-reaching effects on the future of the city and the area.

Until the steamboat came, with its ability to navigate against the current, river transportation had remained virtually a one-way street. Early French bateaux and later American keelboats were able to make the trip downstream easily, and carried raw material from the interior down to St. Louis and New Orleans.

But the trip upstream was a killing one. Men strained against long poles or oars. Sometimes others pulled the boat with ropes stretched to the shore. On a good day they might make ten miles. On a bad one, three to six. As a result, the transmission of civilization, finished products, and even settlers to areas such as Peoria was seriously restricted.

Once the steamboat arrived, the entire Mississippi Valley was opened. Its rivers became veritable superhighways; and the packet boats which plied these waters in increasing numbers brought emigrants from Europe, grillwork and glass from New Orleans, furniture, architectural ideas, theatre, entertainment. With their coming, the frontier vanished and a way of life dawned that would never quite be recaptured.

As Mark Twain wrote in his LIFE ON THE MISSISSIPPI:

    ❝ Steamboating was born around 1812; at the end of thirty years it had grown to mighty proportions; and in less than thirty years it was dead!....It killed the old-fashioned keelboating by reducing the freight trip to New Orleans to less than a week. The railroads have killed the steamboat traffic by doing in two or three days what the steamboats consumed a week doing; and the towing fleets have killed the through freight traffic by dragging six or seven steamerloads of stuff down the river at a time, at an expense so trivial that steamboat competition was out of the question."

Still it was a phenomenal age while it lasted. Anybody who has taken an excursion aboard the "Julia Belle Swain" has some appreciation for the leisurely grace and elegance of the great days of steamboating, with the green walls of the shoreline rolling past in an endless panorama, the boat gliding silently and majestically with only the slap of the paddlewheel and the trembling caused by the steam engines. On clear summer evenings, the sky and the water turn the shade of saffron and the wake rolls out astern in a satiny ripple.

Twain knew the grandeur of the river; and while he was writing about the Mississippi "pushing its mile-wide tide, shining in the sun," the Illinois, especially at Peoria, was even more spectacular.

On came these first steamboats. By 1831, seven boats arrived here during the season, which lasted roughly from March to December. By 1837, the PEORIA REGISTER announced that seven packets were offering regular service between Peoria and St. Louis with one running from Peoria to Pittsburgh.

ILLINOIS RIVER,
REGULAR PACKET.
1844. ============ 1844.
PANAMA,
A. B. DE WITT, Master.

This well known boat, of a very light draft and superior accommodations, has resumed her regular trips on the Illinois, and runs as a weekly packet as follows:

UPWARD TRIP—DEPARTS FROM

St. Louis every Tuesday,	at 4 P. M.		Sharp's Landing,	Wednesday,	8	P. M.
Alton,	'	8 '	Havana & Spoon r.	'	11	'
Columbiana,	Wednesday,	6 A. M.	Copperas creek,	Thursday,	2	A. M.
Newport,	'	7 '	Pekin,	'	4	'
Montezuma,	'	9 '	Peoria,	'	6	'
Griggsville Ldg,	'	10 1-2 '	Chillicothe,	'	10	'
Naples,	'	11 '	Lacon,	'	12	'
Meredosia,	'	12 M.	Hennepin,	'	3	P. M.
Beardstown,	'	5 P. M.	Arriving at Peru,	'	6	'

DOWNWARD TRIP—DEPARTS FROM

Peru every	Friday,	at 7 A. M.	Beardstown,	Saturday,	4	A. M.
Hennepin,	'	9 '	Meredosia,	'	7	'
Lacon,	'	11 '	Naples,	'	8	'
Chillicothe,	'	12 '	Griggsville Ldg,	'	9	'
Peoria,	'	4 P. M.	Montezuma,	'	10	'
Pekin,	'	6 '	Newport,	'	12	'
Copperas creek,	'	8 '	Columbiana,	'	1	P. M.
Havana,	'	10 '	Alton,	'	6	'
Sharp's Landing,	'	12 '	Arriving at St. Louis,		8	'

AN EARLY STEAMBOAT SCHEDULE. (FROM SIMEON DEWITT DROWN'S 1844 DIRECTORY).

130

THE "COLUMBIA" AT
ECKWOOD PARK. (F-STOP
SOCIETY).

Fully two-thirds of the immigrants were arriving by
steamboat in that year, and a contemporary account noted:

❝❝ Peoria now has twenty-five stores, two
wholesale and five retail groceries, two
drugstores, two hotels and several boarding
houses, two free schools and an incorporated
academy, two Presbyterian houses of
worship and congregations, one Methodist,
one Baptist, one Unitarian and one
Episcopal congregation, six lawyers, a
courthouse and a jail and a population of
from 1500 to 1800, which is rapidly
expanding."

Virtually all the travel from here was southward. Chicago was not reachable by river since the northern point of navigation on the Illinois was Ottawa.

While the great floating palaces, the showboats and the ornate vessels which spawned a whole countryside of steamboat gothic gingerbread all came later, these early boats were primitive, rude, and often dangerous. Most of them lasted no longer than five years, doomed to run aground, to having their hulls ripped open from stumps, snags or collisions, or, worst of all, to suffering an explosion of their boilers with that awful gush of fire and scalding steam.

Neither were the early accommodations anything to rave about. Eliza W. Farnham, an articulate Easterner who traveled up the Illinois in 1846, wrote a description of the packet "Banner" in her LIFE IN PRAIRIE LAND:

    ❝ She was not a very large boat, but what she wanted in size was amply compensated in filth. One flight of stairs between the cabins was carpeted, and sundry small patches still remained on the floor of that in which we ate, being too firmly fastened by mingled grease and clay to be easily removed... The floors were broken, the stairs dilapidated; there was no linen for the berths, the hurricane deck leaked, and its edge was hung with delicate filaments of tar which the warmth of the sun often drew to an inconvenient length and sometimes quite severed, irrespective of the welfare of those passing beneath. The waste of steam was so great that the wheels effected only about four revolutions per minute, and the boat had a strange habit which I could not then fully comprehend, but which has since been satisfactorily explained by a scientific friend, of occasionally running twice or thrice her length with considerable rapidity, and then suddenly lurching so as to throw everything to the larboard. She averaged five of these spasms per day."

132

Another traveler of the period, J. H. Buckingham, son of the founder of the BOSTON COURIER, recounts similar horrors during a trip taken from Peru to Peoria in July, 1847:

" After waiting three hours at Peru in the hope of finding a better conveyance, we embarked on board a small steamboat called the "Dial" to come down the Illinois River. We were loaded with freight and crowded with passengers. The engine was out of doors, on the lower deck, and altogether the prospect of comfort was very small. The captain, however, did his best for the accommodation of everybody and the steward served up a very good dinner. A company of about fifty raw volunteers for the Mexican army were desirous of coming on board, but the captain refused to take them, and thereby deserves our gratitude; for they were excessively noisy and very drunk. We stopped at several small places on the river to take in more freight, particularly at Hennepin and Lacon....We remained at Lacon for nearly three hours, and took on board two hundred barrels of flour and provisions, two hundred bags of wheat and some wool. We started again after dark and arrived at Peoria about two in the morning.

I have heard of flies, and mosquitoes, and bed bugs, and fleas, and sundry other nuisances that are said to infest the western waters. I have heard of the same kind of troublesome vermin being rather numerous in Mexico, but I never could be brought to believe one half of what I experienced on board the "Dial." The boat actually swarmed with them after dark. The heat of the weather and the heat of the boat, and the lights, brought them about us, and I should think that they were, in variety, countless as they were in number.... They came and they stayed; they were brushed off and fell upon the deck but their places immediately supplied by an increased additional number....The floors, the stateroom partitions, the mast of the boat, the ceiling, the freight, the baggage and the passengers were literally covered. We had mosquito nets to our berths, but shutting out the winged insects seemed but serve as a better chance to allow the creeping things to luxuriate. Some people slept! Happy immobility! I tried segar smoke on the upper deck and it had a partial effect; but the enemy was invulnerable, and as soon as possible, I took my baggage in hand and went ashore at Peoria, and laid down on the steps of the hotel at the top of the hill (probably either the Clinton House or the Planters House) to wait for daylight."

Buckingham, upon recovering from the infestation, went on to observe:

❝ Peoria is a beautifully situated town on the right bank of the river and is already the seat of a great business. It commands one of the most grand and interesting views in the world and is built or laid out something in the New England style. It has a large extent of back country to supply, and has increased within a few years almost beyond what it would be considered reasonable for me to state.

THE "FRED SWAIN" AT THE RIVERFRONT. (F-STOP SOCIETY).

134

There must have been happier experiences, even in those primitive days of river travel. The "Avalanche," one of the boats of the Illinois River Express Line, which ran packets between St. Louis and LaSalle, was advertised rather grandly in a gazeteer from the 1830's: "From its superior accommodations, the well-known urbanity and unwearied attentions of its officers to the comfort of her passengers, heretofore the traveling public may rest assured that the "Avalanche" will be the passenger packet of the season."

An account by the Rev. J. P. Thompson of New York in 1851, however, describes these "western steamboats" as very slightly built - "mere shells of pine, shallow, long, narrow, flat-bottomed, open and flaring on all sides. The engines are placed immediately on the lower deck, two large furnaces flaming upon you as you enter the boat, and giving you rather uncomfortable hints of a choice between fire and water in making your exit from the world."

The Rev. Thompson already noted the tides of foreigners, largely Irish and German, pouring into the area by steamboat. "These emigrants have a hard life of it. Poor fare and exposure to the elements on the open deck of the boat, often engender disease among them and break up families before they reach their destined home. There should be an active missionary agency on all the rivers of the west. The deck hands need such an influence for they have no Sabbath and are fearfully addicted to profaneness and intemperance. Their manner of life begs a recklessness of death and of all solemn and sacred things."

"Peoria," he wrote, "is the most beautiful town on the river. Situated on rising ground, a broad plateau extending back from the bluff, it has escaped the almost universal inundation. Indeed, the river here expands into a broad, deep lake that embosoms the rising flood. This lake is a most beautiful feature in the natural scenery of the town, and it is as useful as it is beautiful, supplying the inhabitants with ample stores of fish, and in winter with an abundance of the purest ice. It is often frozen to such a thickness that heavy teams and droves of cattle can pass securely over it. A substantial drawbridge connects the town with the opposite shore. The town is neatly laid out in rectangular blocks, the streets being wide and well-graded. A public square has been reserved near the precise center. The place wears a New England aspect; its schools and churches are prosperous and its society is good. Back of the town extends one of the finest rolling prairies in the state; this region already furnishes to Peoria its supplies and much of its business, which is destined to increase as plankroads and like improvements shall bring the producer nearer to the market."

Rev. Thompson's comments on the morals of the deckhands sometimes might have applied to the captains as well. On a Sunday afternoon in 1839, two steamboats, the "Alpha" and the "Eagle", were observed racing on the river and a newspaper editor wrote: "The question is seriously proposed to a Christian community whether the captains do not deserve a severe rebuke."

I f the competition between boats was at times something less than gentlemanly - the "City of Peoria" at one time was accused of trying to run the "Borealis Rex" into the willows -there was one captain whose name has come to typify the best of that colorful steamboat era, and that was Henry Detweiller.

AN EARLY RACE ON THE RIVER, WITH THE CULTER-PROCTOR STOVE CO. IN THE BACKGROUND. (F-STOP SOCIETY).

136

CAPTAIN HENRY DETWEILLER.

He is perhaps best known for Detweiller Park, which was purchased by his son, Thomas, in 1927 and given to the Peoria Park District as a memorial to his father. At one time there was a bronze memorial at the entrance to the park which read:

> "This memorial erected in memory of Captain Henry Detweiller, a pioneer Peorian and early day pilot and captain, a veteran of the Civil War and a former treasurer of the City of Peoria. Also to honor the memory of the fearless, whole souled loyal co-workers of the good old palmy days of steamboating when the river was rich in romance and glory. It is our duty not only to respect but to cherish and honor the memory of these pioneer steamboat men. They overcame dangers incident in the life of early boating which we do not now have. All of whom have made their final trip and have been wafted to the further shore into a haven of rest on the shores of the Beautiful River that ferries but one way. This park is the gift of his son. Thomas H. Detweiller."

Captain Detweiller, who had been born in France, came to Peoria in 1837 to join his brother, John, who was proprietor of the St. Croix tavern on Water Street. After a series of odd jobs, Henry obtained a position aboard the steamer "Frontier," which ran between Peoria and Peru. He was on board when the boat was sunk after a collision with the "Panama," on September 2, 1842. The captain saved the passengers by running his craft ashore, but the boat was a total loss. In his later life, Captain Detweiller would often relate such incidents as part of speeches he gave before various groups in Peoria.

When the company acquired a new boat, Detweiller was named second in command and in 1847, he took command of his first boat, the "Governor Briggs," which ran between St. Louis and Alton, covering much of the same territory Samuel Clemens was to make famous.

In 1865, Captain Detweiller became part-owner of the "Movastar" and in 1867, he was the sole owner of the "Minnesota."

During the Civil War, Detweiller commanded the "Jenny Lind" and later the "Yankee," ferrying troops and supplies into the middle of battle, where he was often under fire.

He chartered the "Yankee" to the United States for $150 a day. On the night before he sailed from Peoria, he noted in his log: "Shipped up crews and ordered coal and stores on board. In the evening I went to town to buy a new flag for the 'Yankee' and met John Maxwell, Samuel Gulick, Oliver Stone, George Bestor, Jr. and others on Fourth Street, and we had a glorious time together as I was going to leave tomorrow for the enemy south maybe never to meet again. I had bought a beautiful flag and before we parted I told the boys it should never be disgraced or taken by the rebels while I was in command of the 'Yankee'."

After the war, Captain Detweiller commanded the "Beaver" until 1874, and then went into the ice business with N. L. Woodruff. He later operated his own firm as the Detweiller Ice Company.

The Detweillers had seven children and most of them were born and died in the family home on northeast Monroe, a site now occupied by the CATHOLIC POST. When Captain Detweiller died in April of 1903, at the age of 78, it was said he had not a single enemy. He had made his final trip, celebrated by one of his favorite poems by Will S. Hays.

Its first stanza read:
>Mate, get ready down on deck;
>I'm heading for the shore,
>I'll ring the bell
>For I must land this boat forevermore.

And the poem's last lines are:
>For I have made the trip of life
>And found my landing place
>I'll take my soul
>And anchor that fast to the throne of grace.

138

The Detweiller family lasted 110 years in Peoria, not long perhaps as families go, but well-remembered. Detweiller Park. Detweiller Drive. Detweiller Marina. Detweiller Golf Course. Today the family members lie in an intimate circle in the quiet of Springdale Cemetery, gathered around the family monument, a tall obelisk with a rope-twisted anchor on one side and engraved with the family name.

For years, Captain Detweiller's log book from the Civil War was in the possession of the Central National Bank. A model of the "Yankee" which he built himself is located in a glass case just inside the main entrance to the Ivy Club on Galena Road.

While it lasted, the steamboat era was rough, brawling, colorful, dangerous, and somehow grand. It provided, both directly and indirectly, a great many jobs for a great many people. Along with the captain, pilot, engineers, stokers, cooks, clerks deckhands, porters, and roustabouts, it also gave work to boilermakers, tinsmiths, painters, moulders, coppersmiths, glazers and roofers, carpenters, stevedores, harbormasters, clerks, draymen, teamsters, and woodcutters.

The steamboats helped make the river towns into boom towns and brought civilization to the wilderness. One boat, the "Merrimack," which arrived in April of 1839, carried nails, white lead, glass, locks, pulleys, doors, shingles and other items for Bishop Philander Chase's ambitious Jubilee College, then under construction near Kickapoo.

Until the completion of the nine-foot channel of the Illinois Waterway in 1939, steamboats were often at the mercy of low water and sometimes were unable to progress for months at a time. One boat was reportedly marooned near Rome in low water in late fall. Its members waded ashore and went home for the winter to wait for the ice to break up and high water to arrive in the spring.

But when the water ran still and deep, and the wind was fair and the summer storms distant, life on the Illinois was indeed rich and rewarding. There were Fourth of July celebrations, moonlight excursions with brass and string bands, boats bringing opera companies, travelling players, magicians and other entertainers to Rouse's Hall and the Peoria Opera House.

STEAMBOATS IN THE ICE
AT PEORIA. (F-STOP SOCIETY).

Although the rapid spread of railroads following the Civil War ended the great days of the packets, steamboating remained a reasonably busy and thriving trade into our own century. From 1900 through 1909, over a million tons of freight and over 100,000 passengers passed through the Port of Peoria on steamboats. As recently as 1936, Clark B. Firestone wrote of coming to Peoria on a packet after touring the Ohio and Mississippi Rivers:

    “ In the evening we reached Peoria, erstwhile capital of violent liquor, a beautiful and brilliant city, with broad streets, open-air markets, thronged water front, and illuminated pleasure crafts along its glimmering lake. The tall buildings that rose beside the water heightened its resemblance to Battery Park at the foot of Manhattan. Peoria is one of a very few towns in the Old West that turned their faces instead of their backs to the river that mothered them.

140

THE "DAVID SWAIN" UNDER
WAY.

THE "VERN SWAIN" COASTING.
(F-STOP SOCIETY).

THE ORIGINAL JULIA BELLE
SWAIN, ABOUT 1917.
(F-STOP SOCIETY).

By now, the river boats had become mostly a pleasure boat business, even though a few of the packets continued to run. There are still people who remember the Swain boats — the "David Swain," the "Verne Swain" and the original "Julia Belle Swain," and the boats operated by the Eagle Packet Lines, whose faded golden shed was still visible at the foot of Main Street into the 1960's.

But for all practical purposes, the excursion boat business ended in Peoria on the night of July 5, 1918, when the steamer "Columbia" ran aground below Creve Coeur, backed off the bank and sank with the loss of eighty-seven lives.

There were still occasional dances and parties on the river. There was the "City of Peoria" and its barge "Pearl" with weekend galas. But already there were towboats pushing their massive barges along the river in increasing numbers, and in the 1930's and 1940's excursions were limited to occasional passing boats, such as the "Capitol," the "J.S." and the "Idlewild."

AN UNIDENTIFIED PACKET AND THE BARGE "PEARL," WHICH WAS USED AS A FLOATING DANCE PAVILION.

142

THE "COLUMBIA" IN HER
GLORIOUS DAYS. (F-STOP
SOCIETY).

THE "COLUMBIA," SUNK
SOUTH OF PEORIA.

The Sinking of the "Columbia."

By 1918, the era of the packet boats had nearly ended. There was, however, still a thriving steamboat excursion business on the Illinois River at Peoria. On the night of July 5 on that last year of the "Great War," the South Side Social Club of Pekin had scheduled an outing on the steamer "Columbia." According to club records, 563 tickets had been sold for the round-trip excursion from Pekin to Al Fresco Park, which was located south of the present-day Ivy Club. But that night, about midnight, while it was on the way back to Pekin, the steamboat apparently ran into a tree stump along the Peoria shore,

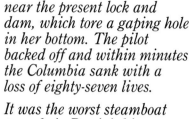

near the present lock and dam, which tore a gaping hole in her bottom. The pilot backed off and within minutes the Columbia sank with a loss of eighty-seven lives.

It was the worst steamboat tragedy in Peoria's history, one that would virtually end the excursion business here.

Whole families were lost in the accident, pinned beneath the wreckage of the once-lavish steamer. One moment they had been dancing, partying. The next moment, following the impact of the steamboat with the stump, there was darkness. The electrical system failed and in the darkness, glass shattered, there were screams, confusion, and people groping wildly in the dark for life preservers.

Most of the victims were from Pekin. Former Peoria City Clerk, William F. Kumpf, said there were twenty-nine persons within a four-block area of his family's home on Second Street in Pekin, who drowned in the disaster. Others were from Peoria, Kingston Mines,

Green Valley, Petersburg, Bloomington, and from as far as Brighton, Iowa, and St. Louis.

So enraged were the survivors and their families that there were threats of violent action against H. F. Mehl, captain of the vessel, and the pilots, Dell Sivley and Tom Williams. Reports told of incensed and belligerent spectators at the scene of the tragedy.

There was talk at the time that the crew of the vessel had been guilty of some misconduct, of using the bar frequently during the evening, and threats were voiced about hanging the captain. It was even suggested that the bars in Pekin be closed following the tragedy to prevent men who had lost family members from becoming inflamed and taking the law into their own hands.

The sinking of the "Columbia," however, virtually brought an end to the excursion business here. Aside from occasional port-of-call stops by such steamers as the "J. S.," the "Capitol," and the "Idlewild," steamboating in Peoria had been dealt a mortal blow. It was not to be revived until the new "Julia Belle Swain" was built in Dubuque, Iowa, and brought to Peoria by Captain Dennis Trone in May, 1971. It was the first steamboat to call here regularly since the "Golden Eagle" had been taken off the St. Louis to Peru, Illinois run in 1935.

144

Until the sinking of the "Columbia," the greatest tragedy on the river at Peoria had been the sinking of the "Frankie Folsom," regarded as the worst calamity in the city's history when it occurred on July 12, 1892. The vessel had brought people from Pekin to Peoria for an evening performance of the elaborate stage spectacle, "Pompeii." The performance ended at 10:15 p.m. and the steamer left immediately, just as a severe storm came up. It was a few blocks from the landing, southbound, when the wind struck the "Frankie Folsom" broadside. It capsized and began sinking rapidly. Twenty-seven people were lost in that accident.

There was a report of an earlier steamboat disaster, on June 3, 1851, when the boilers of the "Dacotah" blew up as it neared Waterworks Park on a test trip. Eighteen died outright and four were fatally injured. The vessel belonged to a party of immigrants from the east on their way to Wisconsin by way of the Illinois River, Illinois-Michigan Canal, and Lake Michigan. They had overhauled the engine at Peoria and were on a test run when the boiler exploded.

Not until Captain Dennis Trone and his brother, Bob, brought the newly built "Julia Belle Swain" here did anything approaching the glory days of steamboating return to Peoria. And here they remain, a faint echo perhaps. But as long as people hear, or even remember, that rhythmic slap of the paddlewheel, the quavery blast of the whistle echoing off the bluffs, that unique sound of the steam engine driving its Pittman arms, that almost silent, majestic passage and the sight of the steamboat coming 'round the bend, the era will never end. Not completely.

A 1920'S RIVER FLOOD WITH STEAMBOATS AT THE FOOT OF MAIN STREET.

THE ORIGINAL "JULIA BELLE SWAIN" ON LAKE PEORIA. (LEE ROTEN PRINT).

146

The "Julia Belle Swain"

On a May morning in 1971, the steam whistle at the top of the pilot house of the "Julia Belle Swain," erupted with an ear-stunning blast. The sound bounced along the bluffs near Grafton, Illinois, rolled across the wide river into Missouri, and faded along the distant bends of the river.

Captain Dennis Trone, her owner and builder, stood on the Texas deck as the lines were let go. The stern wheel bit into the river, her bow swung free, the calliope cleared its pipes with a loud hiss of steam and the tune, "In the Good Old Summertime," echoed through the streets of Grafton.

The steamboat had come back to the Illinois River.

The "Julia Belle Swain" was spanking new, making her maiden voyage from the Dubuque Boat and Boiler Works down the Mississippi to Grafton, then up the Illinois to Peoria. She was to be dedicated May 8 by Julia Belle Swain Shelton, whose name she bore. The real Julia Belle is the daughter of the late Captain Percy Swain, who ran a fleet of boats out of Peoria in the great days of the packets, including the biggest and best of them all, the first "Julia Belle Swain," that ran on the river in the 1920's.

The new boat was the result of a long-time dream of Captain Trone. When he resigned from the Navy in 1963, he and his brother, Robert E. Lee Trone, began operating the "Talisman" on the Sangamon at New Salem, Illinois. It is a small, diesel excursion boat that docks near the sawmill where Lincoln's flatboat reportedly ran aground.

The Trones bought half-interest in the Dubuque Boat and Boiler Works two years later. It is a firm which in its 100-plus years of history has turned out a succession of famous, long-lasting boats. One is the "U.S.S. Ericcson," made in 1894 and regarded as the forerunner of the modern torpedo boat. It saw service in the Spanish-American War and was wrecked in a hurricane in Cuba in the 1930's, still with its original Dubuque engine and boiler intact.

Another was the "Albatross," built in 1907 as a railroad ferry. She was lengthened thirty years later and converted into the excursion steamer "Admiral," which still runs at St. Louis. And the "Sprague," the biggest stern wheel towboat ever made, came from Dubuque. It now lies at Vicksburg on dry land as a river museum.

The idea for a real steamboat came up when a group from the Peoria Chamber of Commerce called at Dubuque. They wanted a sizeable boat to help restore life to Peoria's riverfront. When the Mississippi River ferry boat "City of Baton Rouge" was replaced by a bridge and put up for sale, Trone bought the ferry. He took her to Dubuque, removed her 1916 Gillett-Eaton steam engines for the new "Julia Belle Swain," along with paddle wheel parts and her huge spoked steering wheel. The "Baton Rouge" was towed to Peoria and put into service as a wharf boat.

While the "Julia Belle Swain" was being built, a small, diesel-powered stern wheeler named the "Lady Mim" was sent from Dubuque to Peoria and did a booming excursion business in the late summer of 1970.

When the 400-passenger "Julia Belle Swain" arrived at the foot of Main Street in Peoria on May 8, 1971, heralded by aerial bombs, a parade through the downtown section, and a river flotilla, something exciting had come *back to the river. Julia Belle Swain Shelton of San Francisco was there with her husband, her daughter, and her granddaughter and she cracked a bottle containing Peoria beer and whiskey across the bell on the Texas deck, saying, "I christen thee 'Julia Belle Swain' reincarnated. May her voyages bring pleasure to this generation and others to come." Bands played, bunting snapped in the wind, and the river glinting in the early May sun seemed to have been polished for the occasion. With her whistle sounding its throaty, melodious blast and her calliope piping shrilly, her 55-year old engines whistling softly, and her wheel raising a long swell astern, the "Julia Belle Swain" had come to Peoria.*

It was something special along the Illinois, for the past had come back again and with it an almost vanished sense of the glamour and romance that had once made the river famous, and might again. — Jerry Klein, <u>Peoria Journal Star</u>.

THE PRESENT "JULIA BELLE SWAIN" (PEORIA JOURNAL STAR PHOTO).

CHAPTER SEVEN

TRANSPORTATION: FROM CANOE AND STAGE COACH TO JET

The earliest roads to Peoria, travel by stagecoach and the first trains. Peoria's incredibly busy Union Depot and its fall. The last train. Highways and motorcars, railroads and bridges. The airport and transportation today.

STREET CARS AND TRACTIONS MOVE ALONG A CROWDED ADAMS STREET ABOUT 1920. (CHARLES GIBSON PHOTO, LEE ROTEN PRINT).

150

It requires a massive leap of the imagination for people so accustomed to our intricate network of roads, bridges and highways, to imagine what it must have been like around Peoria 150 years ago.

Virtually all of our transportation today is dominated by the car and the truck and to a lesser extent the airplane. But when Peoria was still a new town and Illinois a new state, the only significant development was that occurring along the rivers and streams. A few miles inland was that vast, almost trackless prairie, bisected by an occasional Indian path or buffalo trail; but otherwise awesome in its isolation and loneliness, and fearsome in its very inaccessibility.

There was land for the taking. Almost anyone settling upon it, however, was bound sooner or later to come up against a river that could not be forded, a mudhole that could not be crossed, or a prairie that no one would venture upon.

Even in the best of seasons, a man on foot or on horseback might cross this rich land, but the use of a wagon or a stagecoach could be a most risky and uncertain business. Farmers, as a result, were confined to a kind of primitive homesteading, supplying their own wants, but having precious little chance of supplying others with their produce. The exception was livestock, which could be driven on the hoof to a convenient river landing and shipped to Peoria or St. Louis.

Even the frequent stagecoaches which served the city were only minimally reliable. These followed what we would hardly regard as roads, but rather Indian trails, often a series of ruts worn into the ground. Grading as we know it was infrequent and drainage left to chance.

AN 1828 STAGECOACH. (PEORIA PUBLIC LIBRARY).

In June of 1825, Miss Ellen Bigelow, a Peoria pioneer woman and sister of lawyer Lewis Bigelow, for whom Bigelow Street is named, wrote of her trip to Illinois from her former home in Massachusetts:

  ❝ We left Chicago in the stage for Ottawa, a route of eighty miles across the prairies, and such traveling never did we behold before. The low prairie about Chicago was entirely flooded with water and the creeks were swollen to rivers. Nothing in the shape of a bridge greeted our eyes. Streams large and small were all to be forded even to the risk of sticking fast in them. On the banks of the Des Plaines, about ten miles from Chicago, we found a multitude of Indians gathered for the great council they have been holding. A more horrible set of grim visages I never beheld...We left Chicago at three o'clock Saturday morning and were until four o'clock Sunday morning reaching Ottawa. In the course of that time we were completely mired six times...In the middle of a slough, or swole, as they call them, you must fancy the coach buried in mud and water above the wheels. The gentlemen all out with their coats off, pantaloons and shirt sleeves rolled up and standing in water about three feet deep, ready to carry the ladies across on their backs, or in any way agreeable to the parties. That being done, they set their shoulders to the wheels of the carriage, the horses kicking and plunging to extricate themselves from the mire, and the driver lashing them right and left and swearing in true stage driver style. You can imagine what a delightful business it must have been to pack ourselves back again, covered as we all were with mud, and nine crowded into two seats as an instance of the inefficiency which characterizes the people of Illinois."

Yet this, for years, was a common, acceptable mode of inland travel.

152

THE OLD FERRY HOUSE ON GALENA ROAD AT THE NARROWS. (LEE ROTEN PRINT).

THE UPPER FREE BRIDGE WITH ITS PLANK FLOOR. (F-STOP SOCIETY).

These early roads, or rather trails, usually depended upon the operation of ferries. Otherwise, during high water, they simply would have dead-ended at the Illinois River. It is believed the first ferry here was operated by the Eads Brothers, Abner and William, as early as 1820. According to James Eads, a son of William, in a recollection recorded when he was more than ninety years old, his father and uncle bought two piroques, or canoes, thirty to forty feet long, lashed them together, and laid rails on them. These they covered with straw. That was the first ferry at Peoria.

There were at one time at least three ferries operating here. One was located by the old French trading house on Wesley Road in East Peoria, another was very close to the site of the Franklin Street Bridge, and a third one was at the narrows at the head of the lower lake in the area known as "Little Detroit."

Lincoln crossed the river on the ferry at the foot of the lake in 1844 during one of his first trips to Peoria. This ferry continued until the first wooden bridge was built in 1849, crossing the river at the foot of Ferry Street, also called Hudson Street, later Bridge Street, and now Franklin Street. The ferry at the narrows apparently was in operation until 1888 when the Upper Free Bridge was built. In late 1825, ferry rates were six and a quarter cents for foot passengers, and twenty-five cents for a man and a horse. Wagons or other four-wheeled carriages with horses and oxen were charged thirty-seven cents and hogs, sheep or goats, four cents.

By this time, the early maps already were showing a road designated "Road to Fort Clark," which was probably the first road leading to the site of Peoria. Other maps show a road about 1822 leading from Peoria to Lewistown, Rushville and Quincy. There is also evidence of a Fort Clark and Wabash trace, leading from here to Terre Haute. There was, as well, the famous Kellogg Trace which ran through Northhampton and Princeton to Galena. Other roads before long carried stagecoaches and horses and wagons from Peoria through Hanover (Metamora) to Ottawa and Chicago and to Springfield and Danville. In 1833, the Illinois Legislature declared the road leading from Peoria to Galena a state road. This became the Galena Road, a part of which goes by the same name to the present day.

But as the very name "trace," or trail, implies, these were literally pathways, either following convenient ridges or valleys, or else those vast beaten-down buffalo trails that ran from the Western plains to the salt licks and bluegrass of Kentucky. Indians followed, as did the fur-traders and early settlers, in one another's footsteps. Some of these paths detoured around big trees or boulders too heavy to move and not until our own day and the construction of the Interstate highway system were some of these otherwise unexplainable kinks and twists removed.

T he first bridge in Peoria County was built across Kickapoo Creek at the ford on the Lewistown Road in 1830. It was 164 feet long and originally rested against two designated trees, each marked with the letter "B."

THE PLANK BRIDGE WHICH SPANNED KICKAPOO CREEK AND WAS RAZED IN 1935. (ERNEST GRASSEL PHOTO, LEE ROTEN PRINT).

154

A STAGE COACH SCHEDULE
FROM DROWN'S 1844
DIRECTORY.

Within a dozen years of Peoria's organization, the major city of the county had become the center of a system of roads leading in all directions - to Springfield, Danville, Ottawa and Chicago, to Galena, Rock Island, Knoxville, Warsaw and Pekin. By the first of April, 1839, stagecoach routes had been established to Ottawa and on to Chicago on both sides of the river, as well as to Galena, Havana, Springfield, Rock Island and Quincy.

An 1844 almanac listed stagecoaches departing from Peoria to Springfield daily, except Sunday, at 4:00 a.m., and arriving at 9:00 p.m. The coach to Ottawa departed from Peoria at 3:00 a.m., arriving at 11:00 p.m. Those customers traveling on the routes east were assured, "The treatment of passengers upon this route has greatly improved for the past three or four years and ladies traveling alone - to say nothing of acquaintances they are pretty sure to fall in with on such great thoroughfares - can consider themselves under the kindest protection during the whole route."

But as Miss Bigelow had discovered, the stagecoach remained a primitive and unreliable form of transportation. No great cities grew up along these stage routes, only small communities surrounding a wayside inn or stagecoach stop.

The farmer remained isolated and remote. It took the coming of the railroad before Illinois was able to reach its economic potential and Peoria once again was at the center of this remarkable development.

It did not, however, come easily. Despite an ambitious plan for a grand internal improvement system that was adopted by the state in February, 1837, the first train that ever turned a wheel in the whole Mississippi Valley did not go into operation until November, 1838. This happened on a tiny stretch of line between Springfield and Meredosia. It was a most significant overture. The effects of the railroad on prosperity and settlement could hardly have been imagined.

In 1850, when the railroads were just beginning to thread their way throughout the state, Illinois had 76,208 farms. Within thirty years, the number had risen to a quarter of a million farms. The assessed valuation of real estate in Illinois was $119,868,336 in 1852. By 1881, it had climbed to $809,995,795. Suddenly, the railroads had opened up the prairies. Towns competed, sometimes bitterly, for the railroad to come through, and more than one community virtually packed up and moved to those gleaming, prosperity-bringing tracks. These brought in settlers, produce, manufactured goods, ready-to-wear clothes and carried out corn, wheat, cattle and lumber. They brought in showmen, preachers,

THE FIRST ROCK ISLAND TRAIN INTO PEORIA, NOVEMBER, 1854. (LEE ROTEN PRINT).

baseball teams; and they made Peoria, with its wonders, into a regional metropolis whose fairs, races, steamboat excursions, opera, and vaudeville houses were only an hour or so away from much of middle Illinois, rather than a day or more.

Peoria's real introduction to the railroad came late in July, 1853, when a group of honored citizens boarded a flat car on the construction train of the Peoria and Oquawka Railroad to ride over four or five miles of completed track. The first locomotive, named "Peoria," had arrived a couple of weeks earlier on a barge propelled by the steamboat "Caleb Cope." Ground had been broken for this railroad in 1851, but money was tight and it was not until January, 1857, that the last rail was laid between Peoria and Galesburg. Meanwhile, the Chicago and Rock Island had brought its track to the Bureau Junction in 1853, and the Peoria and Bureau Valley Railroad was hurried to completion with the first passenger train coming here from Chicago on November 7, 1854. Just over 120 years later, the last passenger train would run over the same route, when the once proud Rock Island "Rocket" made its final, limping run.

156

FROM AN EARLY
ADVERTISEMENT FOR THE
BIG 5.

This was an era when railroads were spreading across the
land like spider webs. Gangs of laborers swarmed along the
right of way, felling trees, grading, ditching, building bridges,
laying ties. Although the first railroad on the Meredosia line
was made up of strips of metal tacked onto wooden rails and
the cars pulled by straining, wood-burning locomotives, the
progress after that was rapid and astonishing. So many lines
were laid into and around Peoria in the era after 1860-1870
that they became a blur of initials and city names.

Eventually fifteen railroads with a total track mileage of over
70,000 miles were located here. So booming did Peoria become
as a rail center that construction was launched in July, 1881,
on a new Union Station at the foot of State Street. This was a
two-story building a hundred feet longer than a football field
and over fifty feet wide. It was officially opened on October
22, 1882. Within a year, a massive train shed covering five
tracks was built. So startling was the increase in passenger
traffic that the depot was extensively remodeled within half a
dozen years of its opening. It was decorated with ornately
carved oak panels, pink marble wainscoting, large murals, and
an impressive sense of elegance. A second train shed, this one
spanning seven tracks, was soon added. The ticket windows
hummed with activity.

Union Depot, Peoria, Ill.

THE UNION DEPOT IN THE
EARLY 1900'S. (LEE ROTEN
COLLECTION).

THE UNION DEPOT'S TRAIN
SHED. (F-STOP SOCIETY).

158

The passengers who surged through this elegant building included the famous and the infamous, everybody from medical quacks and tooth pullers and itinerant peddlers to such people as Madame Schumann-Heink, Mary Garden and Nellie Melba, orchestra leader Paul Whiteman, William Jennings Bryan, Teddy Roosevelt, Herbert Hoover, drummers, showmen, magicians and minstrel singers.

Sie Frankel once stood at the depot ringing a bell to call attention to his clothing store a few blocks away on Adams Street, an establishment which still carries the name, "The Bell." Football specials carried hordes of fans to and from big games at Champaign and South Bend. Thirteen railroads operated their passenger trains out of the Peoria Union Station and at one time there were 128 passenger trains a day. The Peoria and Pekin Union Timetable, effective March 24, 1918, indicated 102 passenger trains operating in and out daily, except on Saturday and Sunday.

Express trains made it to Chicago in four hours. Nearly every city, large or small, could be reached by railroad from here -Buffalo, Dunlap, St. Louis, Indianapolis, Denver, Pekin, New York City, Toulon.

THE TRAIN SHED FOLLOWING THE ACCIDENT THAT DESTROYED IT IN 1927. (F-STOP SOCIETY).

By 1900, a new type of inter-city rail travel started here when the Peoria and Pekin Traction opened its electric line between those two cities. Seven years later, the Illinois Traction System's first car crossed the river into Peoria. The line was acquired in 1928 by the Illinois Terminal System, which ran its electrified "Toonerville Trolleys" to Bloomington, Decatur, Springfield, and St. Louis.

Already, however, passenger service was going into a slow decline. A 1923 timetable at the Union Station showed eighty passenger trains in and out of the city daily, plus the forty Illinois Traction trains.

A MULE-DRAWN CAR ON THE
MONROE-MAIN-SECOND LINE
(LEE ROTEN PRINT).

STREET CAR ON MAIN STREET
ABOUT 1935. (RAY BARCLAY
PHOTO, LEE ROTEN PRINT).

Nothing remains of the once vital streetcar system of Peoria but a few miles of tracks, mostly buried beneath concrete and asphalt streets and only occasionally appearing at the bottom of potholes like some archeologic find.

At one time streetcars were the major form of transportation in the city. They were cheap, reliable, on time, and particularly colorful. No one who ever experienced a summertime ride down Knoxville hill is likely to forget the swaying, careening car, the motorman furiously pounding the foot bell, wicker seats creaking, wind rushing through the open windows—or the trip up Knoxville or Main in the icy wintertime.

160

Even in the 1940's fares on these distinctive trolleys were ten cents, three tokens for a quarter, or a weekly unlimited use pass for one dollar.

They went out of business in the early fall of 1946, when the Illinois Power Company gave up its franchise to the Peoria Transportation Company, which immediately substituted busses for the streetcars. The last streetcar made its run on October 2, 1946.

It was a system which opened on January 15, 1870, when the first horse-drawn car of the Central City Horse Railway made its trip on Adams from South Street to Fayette.

The first electric cars went into service in 1889. For several years various companies operated different parts of the system—the Fort Clark Company, Central Railway, Glen Oak and Prospect Heights Railway, until April of 1903, when all lines in the city were operated by the Central Railway. In the 1930's, the company operating the system was the Illinois Power and Light Service, which later became the Illinois-Iowa Power Company, and finally the Illinois Power Company, with the orange cars marked by the company's badge, an emerald green square with gold lettering.

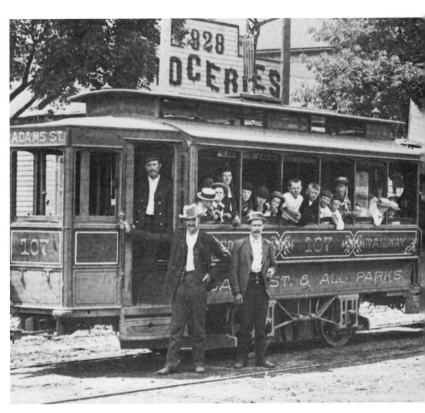

STREET CAR SNOWPLOW ON ADAMS STREET. (F-STOP SOCIETY).

STUDENTS ON THEIR WAY TO THE ST. JOSEPH SCHOOL PICNIC AT CENTRAL PARK IN JUNE, 1890. (PEORIA PUBLIC LIBRARY LEE ROTEN PRINT).

STREET CAR WITH MOVIE ADVERTISEMENT. (LEE ROTEN PHOTO).

STREET CAR AT THE PROSPECT VIADUCT. (LEE ROTEN PRINT).

Something new was happening - roads, cars, and trucks. By 1925, the Good Roads Association so influenced state officials that Illinois ultimately became the state with the best and most complete road network in the nation.

Within a few years, railroad passenger service had dried up to almost a trickle. The last Peoria and Pekin Union passenger train departed from the Union Depot on November 7, 1931. It was not until Pearl Harbor and World War II that the railroad passenger service surfaced for perhaps the final time, with troop trains criss-crossing the country and regularly scheduled trains jammed with sailors and soldiers, their wives, children, and relatives.

The end of the war virtually coincided with the decline of passenger trains in Peoria. The last passenger train to depart from the once teeming Union Depot was a small Peoria and Eastern train on June 25, 1955. Within a few years the depot was converted into a warehouse and was used as work space during the Christmas rush by the Post Office. Then it was boarded up. In August, 1961, it was destroyed by a flash fire. Nothing was left but smoldering ruins and memories. All that remained of the once great passenger service was the Rock Island Railroad, running its single "Rocket" to and from Chicago.

In its best days, this was a crack train, knifing along the banks of the Illinois River in a flash of silver, running from downtown Peoria to the LaSalle Street Station in Chicago in two hours and forty-five minutes. Little by little, the service declined. The tracks were not sufficiently maintained. The speed fell. So did the number of passengers. In its last years, the "Rocket" would creep to Chicago with only a handful of passengers, its speed in some locations limited to a tentative crawl by the condition of the track. In its last days the "Rocket" consisted of two cars jolting violently over a more than four-hour run. The luxury had vanished. The dining car and club cars had vanished. There was only an attendant serving cans of beer from an iced tub. The bar was a plank suspended between the backs of two seats. Its final sad journey came on May 29, 1978. Peoria was no longer a teeming passenger rail hub. It had, in fact, not a single passenger train.

There was a feverish attempt in the following years to institute an Amtrak train on the Peoria-Chicago run and the efforts finally succeeded, on a trial basis. A single train ran

THE WAITING ROOM AT THE
ROCK ISLAND DEPOT.

daily out of a makeshift depot in East Peoria, following the
Toledo, Peoria and Western tracks to Chenoa, then heading
north. This train, the "Prairie Marksman," ran from August
10, 1980, to October 4, 1981; but by now, Peorians had lost
the habit of train travel and the "Marksman" was losing
$200,000 a month. The experiment was declared a failure and
the train stopped running.

But the railroad had served its function. It had opened up
this howling wilderness that had been Illinois, with its
trackless prairies and formerly inaccessible millions of rich
acres. It had brought settlers and civilization into the
smallest towns along its right of way and it had borne the
produce of the land - corn and wheat, pigs, cattle and
chickens - quickly and cheaply to the marketplace. Previously
a trip to market by wagon might have required four to five
days to cover a hundred miles. The railroad made the same
trip in a matter of hours. By stagecoach, it had taken forty-
eight hours for the arduous journey from Peoria to Chicago.
The railroad at its best reduced the trip to less than three
hours.

164

DURYEA'S 1897 AUTO. (F-STOP SOCIETY).

What doomed the railroad more than anything as a passenger carrier was America's growing love affair with the automobile. The "Model T" of Henry Ford was the first great overture in this prolonged romance.

Even then, the roads around Peoria and the streets within the city itself were hardly prepared for the sudden emergence of the automobile and the truck as the major carriers of people and materials. Most of our streets and roads were either dirt or gravel and early car owners faced the same tribulations that beset stagecoaches, particularly in winter or after a long rainy spell and during spring "mud time."

The highways that did exist usually followed old Indian trails or stagecoach routes with right angle curves at section lines and detours around sizeable trees. The few plank roads that were built proved helpful but they were expensive and not noted for their durability. It was not until the end of World War I, when the state-wide road system was launched, that Illinois really prepared for the onslaught of car, bus, and truck traffic that was to develop.

This was a $60 million bond issue, approved in November, 1918, with construction to begin at the end of World War I. One of the first roads completed under the plan was the Peoria-Henry Road, which followed the old Galena Road through Mossville. It became designated as Route 29 and still bears the popular name "Galena Road." Parts of the original road are still in use along the Rome seawall.

OUTSIDE THE FRANKLIN STREET GARAGE.

MAIN AND PERRY, ABOUT 1918.

A dozen years later, some of these first State Bond Issue roads were still incomplete. By then, 9837 miles were paved and open to traffic and another 728 miles were under contract.

A 1931 highway map shows that the road from Morton to Lincoln was still proposed, that Route 116 ended at London Mills, and that Route 24 from Banner to Lewistown had no pavement in place. Some of the roads along the river were the last completed, since travel between cities by packet boat was still fairly common.

Meanwhile, the city of Peoria's streets were gradually being paved with brick. Several methods of paving the city streets had been tried, including gravel and cobblestones, but the brick streets proved to be durable, relatively easy to put down and most economical. Some few brick street stretches still exist. Most, however, have been covered over with concrete or blacktop.

166

While surface transportation was undergoing its drastic revolution from rails to rubber-tired wheels, the airplane was beginning to make its presence felt as a long-distance hauler of mail, people, and freight.

Barnstorming pilots arrived here with their "Jennys" after World War I, a war which had proved the value of the airplane. Flying received its real impetus here in 1925 when Peoria was included on the original Chicago to St. Louis air mail route. Charles Lindbergh was one of the early pilots on the run and before his history-making flight to Paris he had landed his DeHaviland biplane on a field lighted by bonfires near High Point Road. He also landed at the newly developed Varney Airport on Big Hollow Road. Alexander Varney at the time advertised a Peoria-Chicago passenger service at forty dollars for a single person and thirty dollars additional for two or more, with the return flight at ten per cent extra and a dollar an hour for waiting time.

In the early 1930's, the government ruled the Varney airport unsafe and a new location was found at the site of the present Greater Peoria Airport. It originally covered 195 acres and had shale runways. The first airlines to use the field were Chicago and Southern and American Airways. The grand opening was held on December 9, 1932, when President Herbert Hoover sent a message of congratulations to Carl P. Slane, Peoria Airport president.

AT THE PEORIA AUTO SHOW
OF 1910, A SLINN AEROPLANE.

PREPARING A TWA AIRPLANE FOR TAKEOFF AT THE PEORIA AIRPORT. (RAY BARCLAY PHOTO, LEE ROTEN PRINT).

In 1937, the size of commercial aircraft outgrew the field and major airline service was discontinued. Eventually, the runways were lengthened and concrete replaced shale. In 1945, American, TWA, and Chicago and Southern began regularly scheduled flights here. In 1950, the Greater Peoria Airport Authority was formed. Additional hangar space was built and the airport grew to encompass about 900 acres. Ozark began its operations here in 1950 and by 1952, the airport could boast carrying 32,629 passengers a year.

The Peoria Airport since then has evolved into a major transportation hub, second in Illinois only to O'Hare, with passenger service by Britt, Ozark, TWA, Air Wisconsin, and United airlines and freight service by UPS, Purolator Courier Corporation, Emery Worldwide, Federal Express and Air Freight. It now serves about 400,000 passengers a year and has 1363 employees. No longer has the airplane become such a novelty as to attract sightseers who used to come to watch trimotors lifting off at the far end of the runway. It has become today what the railroad was 100 years ago, a major part of the evolutionary process that has carried us from horses, wagons, and stagecoaches, to steam trains and square-fronted cars on narrow, two-lane roads, to Interstate highways, and 600-mile-per-hour jets. And it has all happened in 150 years - a very short time as cities and civilizations go.

168

Peoria's Bridges: A Chronology

1829—The first known bridge in the area spanned Kickapoo Creek about three miles south of the courthouse. It was razed in 1935.

1848—William L. May, ferry operator, obtained a charter to build a bridge at the foot of Bridge Street, near the present Franklin Street Bridge. It was washed away in 1849.

1849—May's bridge was reopened as a toll drawbridge on October 29. It lasted for sixty years. It came to be called the "Cole Bridge."

1888—The wood-floored Upper Free Bridge at the narrows, the former site of "Little Detroit," was opened. It had been designed by George F. Wightman, city architect. On February 27, 1943, the bridge was struck by the towboat, "Sylvia T." It was repaired; but right before its reopening on May 17, 1944, the "Sylvia T." struck the bridge again and put it out of business for good. The United States War Department ordered the removal of debris from the channel, but the city disclaimed ownership and the War Department ultimately removed the debris and the center pier in 1947. The pier on the west side remains in place today.

1904—The Cole Bridge, known in its later years as "Old Toothpick," washed away. It was left until patched up in 1906 and was used until 1912.

1906—The city authorized construction of a steel-reinforced concrete bridge to replace "Old Toothpick." It opened April 11, 1909. Twenty days later, three spans fell into the river at 5:50 a.m. No one was crossing at the time. The bridge builders were bankrupt and the city was unable to recoup its investment of $196,379.33. At this point, "Old Toothpick" was temporarily repaired and put back into service.

1912—The Franklin Street Bridge was opened.

1929—The Cedar Street Bridge was begun. It was known as the "longest bridge in the world" because it had no end. A scarcity of funds delayed its completion. The

state finally provided funds to finish the bridge and it was opened in 1933.

1940—The first two spans of the McCluggage Bridge began. The work was halted in 1942 because of the war. Work resumed in September, 1946, and the bridge was opened in December, 1948. The second span, providing four lanes of traffic, was started in 1975 and completed on October 22, 1982.

1953—Work was started in September on the Murray Baker Bridge. It was dedicated and opened on December 12, 1958.

1970—The first contracts were awarded on the Shade-Lohmann Bridge. Construction was completed in 1973, but the bridge was unused for five years while ramp and interchange work was completed. It was opened on August 30, 1978.

AN EARLY VIEW OF THE UPPER FREE BRIDGE. (PEORIA PUBLIC LIBRARY, LEE ROTEN PRINT).

PEORIA'S FIRST WAGON
BRIDGE, ERECTED IN 1848.
(PEORIA PUBLIC LIBRARY, LEE
ROTEN PRINT).

THE COLE WAGON BRIDGE,
LATER REPLACED BY THE
FRANKLIN STREET BRIDGE.

170

THE FRANKLIN STREET
BRIDGE UNDER
CONSTRUCTION IN 1907.
(F-STOP SOCIETY).

DIGNITARIES GATHER FOR
THE OPENING OF THE
FRANKLIN STREET BRIDGE.
MAYOR E.N. WOODRUFF IS
STANDING IN THE CAR AT
LEFT.

THE FIRST FRANKLIN STREET BRIDGE, AFTER ITS COLLAPSE ON MAY 1, 1909. (LEE ROTEN COLLECTION).

CHAPTER EIGHT

SHOW BIZ AND THE ARTS: OH HOW I WISH'T I WAS IN PEORIA

From the Cotton Blossom to Corn Stock. The great days of vaudeville and the Grand Opera House. Peoria Players. The Peoria Symphony. Lakeview Museum, Bradley and ICC. Opera, ballet, theatre and the Peoria Civic Center. How good it is to be in Peoria today.

PART OF THE CROWD OUTSIDE THE MADISON THEATRE DURING THE WORLD PREMIERE OF THE EARTHWORM TRACTOR FILM, JULY 10, 1936. (CATERPILLAR PHOTO).

JOE E. BROWN AND JUNE
TRAVIS IN A PUBLICITY PHOTO
FROM "EARTHWORM
TRACTORS". (CATERPILLAR
COLLECTION).

THE PEORIA CORN
EXPOSITION, 1900.

There remains to this day a widespread impression that
Peoria is a capital city of the provinces with the worst that
that implies: a dull, uninspiring place that has remained
largely unenlightened by music, the arts, the theatre and even
live entertainment of any but the most menial sort. The
reality is quite the opposite, for even the most casual
examination of the past, and the present, reveals a city with a
rich and varied tradition of excellence and availability of the
performing and visual arts. These flourish in such abundance
that it might be claimed without hesitation that on a per
capita basis, the average Peorian attends more symphony
concerts, plays, art shows, ballets, and operas than the
average Chicagoan or New Yorker.

The Peoria Symphony is one of the ten oldest in the country.
Peoria Players is the oldest community theatre still in
existence. These, along with the Amateur Musical Club's
artists' series, Corn Stock Theatre, The Peoria Civic Opera,
the Peoria Civic Ballet, the Civic Center's Broadway Theatre
Series, the cultural offerings at Bradley University and
Illinois Central College, Lakeview Museum, the Peoria Art
Guild, the Conklin Players Dinner Theatre, the Illinois
Shakespeare Festival at Bloomington and a wealth of other
activities in the area provide an almost endless choice for
anyone seeking something more than mere entertainment or
diversion.

But if there is a certain renaissance in progress, it hardly
compares as yet with the almost phenomenal activity that
once occurred here. Television has diminished live audiences,
to be sure. Yet the numbers remain impressive. These days
the movie theatres in Peoria attract almost a million people
annually. Over 15,000 attend the Peoria Symphony's regular
concerts, another 10,000 hear the orchestra's annual Youth

Concerts at the Bradley Fieldhouse. Peoria Player's audiences number about 15,000 a season and Lakeview Museum outdraws Bradley home basketball games more than three to one.

During the year 1857, when Peoria's population was 17,482, the town's citizens had the opportunity to attend more than 300 productions of staged plays by four professional companies. This was in addition to panoramas, minstrel shows, dramatic readings and other non-legitimate stage offerings.

In that remarkable year of 1857, there were 306 plays - nearly all of them professional - on 144 separate evenings.

The real impetus for this early development came from the river, which was later to carry such showboats as the "Cotton Blossom," "French's New Sensation" and the "Goldenrod" with their melodramas. Not only did the steamboat bring settlers and civilization into Peoria, but it brought theatre and culture as well, most of it from St. Louis. Frontier theatre might not always have been of the highest caliber, much of it consisting of variety shows, magicians, animal acts, gymnasts, minstrels and clairvoyants; but by the early 1850's, Peorians were aware of what was happening in the theatres of St. Louis, New Orleans, New York, and elsewhere through their local newspapers. The exploits of P.T. Barnum, the arrival of Jenny Lind in this country, even the opening of a new theatre in Mobile, were all duly reported here.

"FRENCH'S NEW SENSATION," ONE OF THE HISTORIC SHOWBOATS THAT REGULARLY CALLED AT PEORIA. (PEORIA PUBLIC LIBRARY).

176

By 1845, the Peoria Musical Association was formed. In 1846, the Peoria Brass Band was presenting promenade concerts at the Planter's House Hotel and the following year, a branch of the American Art Union was active here. By 1854, the Germans had organized their active Turner Society, in which they exhibited considerable dramatic, musical, and athletic activities.

While such early halls as Haskell Hall (1850) and Fleck Hall (1852) were pretty much empty rooms in which a variety of entertainments were offered, one of the first real theatres was developed in the spring of 1855 in a building that had recently been erected by Henry Austin on the south corner of Adams and Fulton. It held an upper story which had been used to store agricultural equipment. Boothroyd Emmet arrived that year and leased the room, moved the farm machines aside, installed chairs and benches and presented eighteen different plays in two weeks. The following year, John Huntley arrived in town with an experienced company

THE PLANTER'S HOUSE IN 1840, RENAMED THE PEORIA HOUSE IN 1854. IT STOOD AT THE EAST CORNER OF NORTH ADAMS AT HAMILTON.

from the East that played in Austin's Hall with productions of THE STRANGER, THE LOAN OF A LOVER, and WOMAN'S FAITH. He remained for six weeks with his troupe of twelve professional actors and staged thirty-three performances of twenty-five different plays with his name star Sallie St. Clair.

What helped make 1857 such a year of theatrical abundance was the construction of Rouse's Hall by Dr. Rudolphus Rouse, who was the second physician to open practice here. His hall, which stood at the corner of Main and Jefferson on the site now occupied by the First National Bank, was the first built and furnished expressly for theatrical and musical productions. There were stores and business offices on the first floor. The upper floor, entered by a broad staircase, was fitted with 1200 seats, with a gallery supported by iron rods (which tended to obstruct the vision) and accented with red plush and bright gold trim. It remained the center for Peoria's entertainment for a quarter of a century. In fact, it remained Peoria's major theatre until 1882, when the Grand Opera House was built. Later it became the Main Street Theatre, a popular vaudeville house, and it was razed about 1920 to make way for the Peoria Life Building, which still stands.

ROUSE'S HALL AROUND THE TURN OF THE CENTURY. THE FIRST NATIONAL BANK BUILDING NOW OCCUPIES THE SITE.

178

PEORIA, ILLINOIS, MAY 12TH, 1885.

TUESDAY EVENING,
May 12, 1885.

Engagement of the Popular Tragedian,

Mr. THOS. W.

KEENE,

Supported by a Powerful Dramatic Company, under the Management of Mr. W. R. Hayden, Presenting Colley Cibbies Version of Shakespeares · Historical Tragedy in six Acts,

"RICHARD III,"

OR,

The Battle of Bosworth Field.

CAST OF CHARACTERS.

DUKE OF GLOUSTER, afterwards King Richard III.
....MR. THOMAS W. KEENE
King Henry VI...............................Mr. Carl Ahrendt
Richmond.....................................Mr. P. C. Hagar
Duke of Buckingham.......................Mr. Eugene Moore
Lord Stanley.................................Mr Alexander Corbett
Tressel..Mr. Charles B. Hanford
Norfolk..Mr. Jerry Taylor
Catesby.......................................Mr. Julius Scott
Ratcliffe......................................Mr A. B. Howard
Lieutenant of the Tower.................Mr. Frank Henning

FRANKS & SONS. PRINTERS, PEORIA.

A PROGRAM FROM THE GRAND OPERA HOUSE FOR "RICHARD III" ON MAY 12, 1885. (PEORIA PUBLIC LIBRARY).

Its grand opening was held on May 18, 1857, when John Huntley and his seventeen-member company presented CHARLES I: OR, THE MERRY MONARCH, followed with CHALET as the afterpiece. Among the featured performers were Madame Carlotta Pozzoni from the Academy of Music, New York, and the Philadelphia and Baltimore Theatres; Mrs. Henry Howard from The Broadway Theatre of New York and the Gaiety Theatre of New Orleans; and others from St. Louis, Mobile, and Philadelphia. Tickets ranged from twenty-five to seventy-five cents. During his first month in residence, Huntley and his company performed fifty-eight plays, including three by Shakespeare. Huntley remained for the entire season. So successful was his residency here that he even opened another company in the fall at the old Austin Hall, supposedly directed by Henrietta Irving. Other companies followed, among them one managed by a Mr. Woods from St. Paul, who presented everything from novelty shows to RICHARD III, UNCLE TOM'S CABIN, and THE CORSICAN BROTHERS.

While the resident companies declined with the onset of the Civil War, Rouse's Hall remained a thriving place. Dramatic readings, minstrel shows, concerts, bell-ringers, magicians, and vocal ensembles filled its stage, as well as that of the newly built Parmeley Hall which opened with an Inauguration Ball on September 1, 1858. Here, the major theatrical introduction came from the McVicker troupe of Chicago on September 20, which remained for three weeks with such productions as SWEET HEARTS AND WIVES, UNCLE TOM'S CABIN, and SAM PATCH IN FRANCE.

Orson Parmeley had managed the Frink and Walker Stage Line for a number of years and had opened his own livery business here. His immense stables were built on North Adams and the hall was located on the third floor of the building. It was later known as Howard's Theatre and ultimately burned down.

In 1858, Otto Funke leased the old Austin Hall and launched a full-fledged alteration. It remained for several years as a center of amusement but rarely housed legitimate theatre.

While these early theatres lasted, they were the scenes of far more than stage productions. One early arrival here was the legendary pianist Louis Moreau Gottschalk, who in his time was almost as famous as Liszt. He played in Peoria on December 13, 1864, and wrote in his book, NOTES OF A PIANIST:

" Concert this evening at Peoria. A very ugly
place. The houses are mean and for the most
part one-story. The streets are badly laid
out. The concert hall (unnamed) offers one
peculiarity; the platform, which is like a
theatre, is so high that it gives me the
vertigo to look down upon the audience; we
all fear to approach the edge lest we should
be drawn into the abyss. It slopes so much
that it gives one a sensation analogous to
that of an inexperienced person upon a roof.

Audience numerous and enthusiastic. Hotel
passable. Snow has fallen during the night.
The river is frozen and is covered with
hundreds of skaters, but few pretty women.
Their costumes are indescribable. I forgot to
say that at the hotel the waiters are girls.
Besieged fortress!

PEORIA IMPRESSARIO AND
PHYSICIAN DR. RUDOLPHUS
ROUSE.

Gottschalk later noted that:

" To make a victorious tour of concerts in the
West is for an artist to gain his chevrons.
Bad hotels, snow, mud, railroad accidents,
delays, setting out at three o'clock in the
morning, etc. It requires an iron constitution
and flinty will to succeed at it. I am tempted
to have inscribed at the head of my
programmes: 'G. has made the tour of the
West three times' as the French legions
inscribe 'Arcole, Marengo, Austerlitz' on
their standards.

Conditions, however, were to improve immeasurably with the
building of the Grand Opera House, one of the single most
important events in Peoria's cultural history. It stood on
Hamilton Boulevard from its opening on September 12, 1882,
until it was destroyed by fire on December 14, 1909, a twenty-
one year period when it was hardly unused for a single night
during the fall and winter season.

Rouse's Hall had proved insufficient for many stage
presentations at the time. While it seated 1200, the size of its
stage, bad sight lines, and its limited backstage facilities
caused many touring companies to eliminate Peoria from
their schedules.

180

NEWSPAPER EDITOR EUGENE BALDWIN.

A CARICATURE OF EUGENE BALDWIN IN HIS LIBRARY.

Eugene F. Baldwin, editor of the PEORIA JOURNAL, was the major driving force behind the acquisition of a first-rate opera house for the town. For over a year, he backed the idea almost ceaselessly, convinced it would elevate the cultural level of the community. His campaign seemed almost prophetic, for many of the same obstacles were to surface 100 years later over the proposed theatre for the Peoria Civic Center.

"The feeling in favor of an opera house in this city is decidedly in favor of such an institution," he wrote. "The trouble is that in Peoria it takes an awful amount of talk to get anything on foot. There is here a tremendous amount of wind and very little cider. Everybody is brimful of ardor and no cash to correspond."

There were at least four unsuccessful attempts before the final plans took shape. With each failure, Baldwin became increasingly bitter.

On March 20, 1881, he wrote in the JOURNAL, "We have at last arrived at a dead stop in the matter of an opera house. The whole scheme is at a halt...it is the saddest case of fizzles we have ever seen...Is Peoria so dead that she sits idly by and allows all her chances to drift by without making any effort to help herself? These are questions it behooves us to ask ourselves and to agitate this thing until we get relief, as it were."

Then at last, a group of local investors pledged $7000 to the project. Baldwin purchased the lot on Hamilton, across from the courthouse. Construction finally began on December 8, 1881.

Several Peorians, among them Colonel Robert Ingersoll and opera star Emma Abbott, offered donations ranging from $500 to $1000 so that the new building would be named after them. The Peoria Opera House Company insisted that it not be associated with a particular person or performer and elected to name it "The Grand Opera House."

What they built was to become known as the best one-night stand in the whole Midwest. Its style was Queen Anne. It measured 72 feet wide, 171 feet long, and 60 feet to the roof. Rising above the roof was a forty-foot tower. The interior was lavishly furnished. There were crystal gas chandeliers and wine-colored carpeting. The predominant color of the auditorium was Bessemer blue, a metallic shade named after the inventor of the Bessemer Converter. The ceilings were decorated with frescoes depicting peacock fans,

PEORIA'S GRAND OPERA
HOUSE, FEATURING A
PRESENTATION BY FIELDS
MINSTRELS. BALDWIN'S
JOURNAL OFFICES WERE AT
THE RIGHT.

182

PEORIA'S RENOWNED
SOPRANO, EMMA ABBOT.

pheasants, vases, and flowers in bright colors and golden tints. The hall seated about 1700 in its parquet, dress circle, balcony, gallery, and box seats. Its proscenium arch was thirty-six feet high and thirty feet wide. Above the proscenium was a sculptured figure of the Greek muse of music and lyric poetry. A six-foot stage apron extended in front of the proscenium and in the center of the elaborately decorated fire curtain was a verse from Shakespeare's AS YOU LIKE IT which read:

> Tongues in trees,
> Books in running brooks
> Sermons in stone
> And good in everything.

The theatre possessed a full set of scenery, with forty different backdrops that were stored in a pit. It was judged at the time to be one of the best theatres in the state. Some went so far as to claim it was the best in the world.

At 7:45 p.m. on September 12, 1882, the curtain went up for the first time with a production of the operetta, KING FOR A DAY, starring former Peorian Emma Abbott in the role of Princess Nemes. The elaborate costumes were made by a noted French costumer, and Miss Abbott's first entrance as the princess was in a palanquin borne by four natives.

Despite the grandeur of the occasion, it was not exactly a hit. Even Baldwin, in his review, admitted: "There has been some little dissatisfaction expressed at the opera selected for the opening night and the more astute musical critics have not been slow to find fault with its rendition." Baldwin suggested the main reason for the cool reception was the newness of the work. "Music is much like wine," he wrote, "It's chief excellence is given by its age."

Two successful performances by Miss Abbott, in COLLEEN BAWN and MARTHA on September 12 and 13, received considerably warmer receptions and her share of the receipts for the opening productions was reportedly $5700.

While it was called the "Grand Opera House," few grand operas were performed. Seldom were more than two presented during the same year and these were only the most popular, such as LA TRAVIATA, FAUST, FRA DIAVOLO, IL TROVATORE, LOHENGRIN, and PARSIFAL.

Operettas, however, were presented as often as twice a week. Among these were such forgotten gems as OLIVETTE, THE MERRY WAR, and ADONIS along with such still popular offerings as THE MIKADO and H.M.S. PINAFORE.

Solo artists were also a rarity. Among the few who appeared at the Grand Opera House were Blind Tom Boone, a pianist; Professor James E. Murdock, an elocutionist; and Professor Flint, magician and hypnotist. There also were occasional lectures. Considerably more popular were minstrel shows and extravaganzas. Among the latter were J.A. Little's THE WORLD, which was advertised as having $10,000 worth of scenery with a life-sized raft onstage. Lee Hanlon's VOYAGE EN SUISSE featured an onstage bus wreck, a scene aboard ship in a storm, an exploding pullman car, and a chaotic banquet scene in which a character plummeted through the ceiling onto a table filled with food.

The most frequently seen productions were legitimate plays, ranging from Elizabethan to contemporary comedies, tragedies, and melodramas. Booth's New York Company appeared regularly at the Grand Opera House, as did the companies of David Belasco, and Klaw and Erlinger. The Hoyt Company played here more often than any other group.

Some of the more famous actors and actresses of the era appeared regularly at the Grand Opera House - Joseph Jefferson, John Drew, Edwin Booth, Maurice and Ethel Barrymore, John McCullough, Mrs. Fiske, and Otis Skinner.

AN 1890 GRAND OPERA HOUSE PROGRAM. (PEORIA PUBLIC LIBRARY).

184

**A TOP-HATTED GROUP
ADVERTISING THE
COMMERCIAL TRAVELERS
ASSN. MINSTRELS IN FRONT
OF THE GRAND OPERA HOUSE.**

Minnie Maddern Fiske was one of the most beloved performers to hit Peoria during the years of the Opera House. She first appeared as Becky Sharpe in VANITY FAIR on Christmas night, 1900. After that she appeared annually and the lines of ticket buyers invariably extended around the foyer, out onto Hamilton Street, and on to Jefferson.

Most of the plays given at this splendid location have long sunk into obscurity. But there were classics as well. Edwin Booth appeared in JULIUS CAESAR and THE MERCHANT OF VENICE and the widely hailed Thomase Salvini triumphed in OTHELLO.

So successful was the Grand Opera House that its influence extended to merchants and nearby businesses. The sale of opera cloaks became rather brisk during the era. Stores added opera glasses to their stock. An enterprising proprietor of the Gem Cigar Store, George Clark, sold special cigars, labelled "Grand Opera House Brand."

While the fashionable crowd arrived at the Opera House in their own carriages, others would walk. Neither were there regulations concerning dress. Even before the first grand production, a notice ran in the PEORIA JOURNAL: "There is a feeling abroad that people cannot afford to attend the first night unless they are apparelled like the lilies of the valley. This is a mistake. There are and will be no regulations concerning dress. Everyone can attend in such garb as is to him most comfortable and feel at home."

Still, there must have been a certain sense of occasion that went along with a performance. One old photograph from the collection of Ray Brian shows a group of citizens standing outside the place in their tall silk opera hats looking almost like Parisians.

Seats in the gallery sold from twenty-five to fifty cents. There were only benches there to sit on, but it became a favorite hangout for the young people of school age.

Not always were manners what they might have been. When the Cherry Sisters appeared on April 18, 1909, some people simply left quietly. Others responded with yowls and catcalls and still more took to banging tin pans, blowing horns, and throwing pieces of wadded-up paper onto the stage.

Leonard Worley, who worked at the Opera House and later managed the Madison Theatre, recalled that many members of the audience left at intermission for a nearby bar. "It was my job to punch a buzzer backstage a few minutes before the show resumed. That part was easy enough. The hard part was

LOOKING SOUTH ALONG
ADAMS AT MAIN STREET ON
AUG. 24, 1905. (LEE ROTEN
PRINT).

188 A MINSTREL PROGRAM FROM MAY 7 AND 8, 1902. (PEORIA PUBLIC LIBRARY).

∞ K. F. M. ∞
MINSTRELS

Wednesday and Thursday Evenings, May 7th and 8th, 1902.

. ST. PATRICK'S HALL .

PART I.

SOCIAL SESSION, K. OF F. M.

OVERTURE
arranged especially for the occasion by
PROF. ELLIOTT J. STRAWN.

Chairman of the Evening, MR. CHAS. CLEMENTS.

Guests of the Evening,

BONES.	TAMBOS.
MR. F. COOPER,	MR. G. GRUBER,
MR. F. LIDLE,	MR. A. SINCLAIR.

THE FOLLOWING VOCAL SELECTIONS WILL BE RENDERED DURING THE FIRST PART BY THE FOLLOWING WELL-KNOWN SINGERS . . . .

"When the Blue Sky Turns to Gold"........MR. M. J. PURFIELD
"I'm Goin' to Live Anyhow until I Die"..........MR. G. GRUBER
"In the Shade of the Palm"............MR. JAMES T. GALLAGHER
"My Heart's Desiah"................................MR. FRED COOPER
"Wait"..MR. JAS. MURPHY
"Maisy, My Dusky Daisy"............................MR. FRED LIDLE
"Down Where the Cotton Blossoms Grow"...MR. JOS. DOWNS
"I Just Can't Help from Lovin' That Man"...MR. A. SINCLAIR

OLIO OF NOVELTIES.

ALONZO BRANDOW,
THE FORTUNE-TELLING MAN.

MR. CHAS. RODECKER,
OUR BONE WONDER.

J. — NORVELL AND POWELL — C.
SONG AND DANCE ARTISTS.

H. — SHAFER AND STEINBACH — L.

when I had to rush from the theatre and run and hustle the crowd out of the popular National Bar. And some of them would just refuse to go back to the theatre."

While is lasted, the Grand Opera House had something for everybody. There was a lecture on "Decomposition" by Professor M. L. Seymour on April 26, 1884; a concert by the Mendelssohn Quintette Club of Boston; a Junior Class play from Peoria High School; an appearance by Grau's English Opera Company; Emma Abbott in THE LAST ROSE OF SUMMER in September of 1884; a lecture by Ingersoll; a concert by Spencer's Band; Otis Skinner in PRINCE RUDOLPH in November, 1897; Princess Go-Won-Go in THE FLAMING ARROW in April, 1902; Ethel Barrymore in COUSIN KATE on August 31, 1904; Eva Tanguay in THE SAMBO GIRL, November 23, 1904; Chauncey Olcott in EDMUND BURKE on April 14, 1906; Lillian Russell in THE BUTTERFLY on March 4, 1907; Maude Adams in THE JESTER on May 5, 1908; and on December 14, 1909, Professor and Mrs. Flint with their magic act.

That evening after the performance, somebody apparently dropped a lighted cigarette in the men's rest room. The fire that resulted destroyed the building.

The PEORIA REVIEW printed the following account of the incident:

"The Grand Opera House Building, meeting place of cabbages and kings, was destroyed by fire at 1:30 yesterday morning. The flames likely started from a cigaret stub tossed in the after-show rubble ..... by some gallery god during the performance of Professor Flint. The damage was figured at $200,000."

For half a dozen years thereafter, the shell of the building remained as a downtown blight, a repository of memories. It was finally converted into a parking garage, which remained until 1922 when an appliance store was built on the spot. This was later razed and the site of the Grand Opera House is now occupied by the parking lot next to the county jail.

The sudden and shocking end of the Opera House, however, did not affect for long the cultural and entertainment climate of the city. Times were already changing — new theatres were going up, and Peoria was poised for its great plunge into the age of vaudeville.

MARCHERS IN A PARADE ALONG MAIN STREET.

190

INTERIOR OF THE PALACE
THEATRE WITH ITS LAVISH
CHANDELIER.

A 1933 PROMOTION AT THE
PALACE FEATURING A NEW
CHEVROLET GIVEN AWAY BY
THE LARKIN STORES (F-STOP
SOCIETY).

While all the great vaudeville and show business stars played in the theatres of Peoria, the Palace was the last of the vaudeville houses and its stage was home to some of the most familiar names. It was known as Ascher's Palace when it had its formal grand opening on January 6, 1921, with a 6:30 p.m. performance that included the gorgeous spectacular "Syncopation in Toyland," followed by "Novelty in Music" with Miss Freda Leonard and Her Jazz Band, Frisch, Rector and Tool in "Three Boys from Harmony Land" and the comic novelty, "Hector and His Pals." Other acts included Britt Wood in "The Boob and His Harmonica" and "Dance Creations," which was described as a "sensational terpsichorean fantasie enhanced by

magnificent costuming and scenic effects by members of the Metropolitan Grand Opera Ballet."

Among the big names who played the Palace were Duke Ellington, Lawrence Welk, Spike Jones, Gene Krupa, Paul Whiteman, Sally Rand, Burns and Allen, Ozzie and Harriet, Dick Powell, Joe E. Brown, Eddie Cantor, Sophie Tucker, Blackstone the Magician, and Fibber McGee and Molly (who grew up here as Marian Driscoll and Jim Jordan), Amos and Andy, and the Dead End Kids.

The Theatre's billing ledger shows Marian and Jim Jordan playing on July 31, 1926 for $142.85; Miss Raffin and Monkeys on April 13, 1927 at $142.85; Will Higgie and the Higgie-Jig Girls on August 3, 1927 at a cost of $342.85; Two Dozen Peaches, an all-girl show, which played February 19-22, 1928 at a cost of $1627.55 (net) plus $100 for fare and baggage; Edgar Bergan and Company on September 24, 1928 for $192.85; Peoria's famous harpist Roxy La Rocca on October 7, 1928 at $214; Fink's Mules on November 18, 1928 for $192.85; and the comedy team of Olsen and Johnson December 18, 1928 for $1071.40.

THE EARLY MAJESTIC THEATRE, BEFORE IT WAS INCORPORATED INTO THE JEFFERSON BUILDING. FEATURED WAS "JUST MARRIED"..."THE LAST WORD IN LAUGHS". (LEE ROTEN PRINT).

192

THE MAIN STREET
VAUDEVILLE THEATRE,
FORMERLY ROUSE'S HALL.
(LEE ROTEN PRINT).

194

Weast's Theatre, later called the Lyceum, was built in 1900 on Fulton, where it remained until it was demolished in 1959 to make way for the Illinois Bell Telephone Building. The Majestic, housed in what is now the Jefferson Building, opened on December 21, 1906. The Orpheum on North Madison was opened by Peoria industrialist and brewer Ed Leisy in 1910, and the Hippodrome, which later became the Rialto, opened in 1909.

Part of Rouse's Hall was converted into the Main Street Theatre and lasted until Peoria's most distinctive skyscraper, the Peoria Life Building, was built on the spot in 1920. This building is now occupied by the First National Bank. Later came the Palace and the Madison, which are best remembered as movie houses.

Into these many theatres poured the best of the nation's entertainers and virtually hordes of Peoria and area audiences. The Majestic offered everything from a production of Maeterlinck's, THE BLUEBIRD, to early Orpheus Club concerts, an appearace by Calvin Coolidge, and Golden Gloves boxing matches. In the Orpheum, one could find almost anything to suit his fancy from Rudolph and Lena, Yodlers and Singers ("If you like this act, please applaud"), to Peoria's own Roxy LaRocca, "The World's Greatest Harpist", to novelty canine equilibrist or Douglas Fairbanks and Anna Mae Wong in THE THIEF OF BAGDAD.

There were ventriloquists, midgets, comics, imitators, acrobats, dancers, mind-readers, magicians, and even motion pictures.

Fay Bainter, David Warfield, Alfred Lunt, and Lionel Barrymore all appeared at the Majestic. The Hippodrome was the home of the Gifford Players with a resident orchestra conducted by Tony DeNufrio. The Orpheum had its own orchestra as well, directed by Rud A. Born; and during the golden days of vaudeville, Will Rogers, Al Jolsen, Sophie Tucker, Fannie Brice, Jack Benny, Gallagher and Sheen, George M. Cohan, the Fulford Family and prize-fighter Jim Corbett all played here.

The Orpheum had 1400 seats that were filled every night of the week. A box seat cost thirty-five cents and a dime gained one's entry to the balcony for a matinee. This became a part of the far-flung Orpheum Circuit which eventually opened the Palace in New York. That became the ultimate goal of all vaudeville performers and playing in Peoria was only a short step from the top.

**THE ORPHEUM, WHICH
OPENED IN THE 100 BLOCK OF
NORTH MADISON IN 1910.**

196

THE ORPHEUM, ADVERTISING
A MATINEE PERFORMANCE BY
IRWIN AND HERZOG.

Vaudeville died its slow death with the coming of the movies, and so did the Orpheum. It was abandoned in 1926 and remained as a dusty warehouse until 1952, when it was torn down to make room for a parking deck. The Lyceum became a saloon, WMBD radio and television took over the space occupied by the Majestic, and the Palace and Rialto installed projectors and became movie houses.

By the 1920's, most of the old halls where live theatre and vaudeville had been performed were gone. One could no longer find traces of the Germania Hall on Water Street, Haskell Hall, Austin's Hall, Parmeley's Hall (built above his stable on North Adams), the Adelphi, Dempsey's Folly on South Adams, or the Auditorium on South Adams. Now there were movie theatres downtown, such as the Deluxe, the Lyric, the Empress, the Cort, Elysium, Apollo, Princess, Columbia, the Star and the Sangamo. As a postwar exodus to the suburbs began in the later 40's and 50's of the twentieth century, the downtown theatres began to disappear one by one. The Hippodrome (Rialto) fell to make way for the Civic Center arena, the Palace went to make room for the Twin Towers complex; and today only the Madison remains with its baroque-rococo splendor, still awaiting a tenant worthy of its grandeur, dank and faded though it may be.

THE PRINCESS, ABOUT 1937.
(LEE ROTEN PRINT).

INTERIOR OF THE APOLLO,
313 MAIN STREET.

198

CONSTRUCTION SCENE IN
GLEN OAK PARK. (F-STOP
SOCIETY).

(FAR RIGHT)
THE GLEN OAK LAGOON IN
EARLIER DAYS. (F-STOP
SOCIETY).

YOUNG WOMEN IN A STYLIZED
DANCE SET IN THE GLEN OAK
SUNKEN GARDEN. (F-STOP
SOCIETY).

As opera, theatre, minstrel shows, and vaudeville passed through their evolution into movies and television, newer traditions were being forged that would propel Peoria again into a position in the arts and entertainment arena that would be formidable, if not predominant.

For while Peoria was gaining a certain enviable fame as a show business town, the more durable and less commercial expressions of art, theatre, and music were flourishing as well.

As far back as 1851, the new Germans of Peoria, who were to become so vital to its cultural development, had founded their singing society known as the "Liederkranz." The Peoria Women's Club was launched in 1886 and its Club House on Fayette built in 1893. It served for over fifty years as a location for concerts, exhibitions, and plays; and the building remains standing today.

The Peoria Art League began in 1888, and two years later, when the population was 41,024, the Peoria Conservatory of Music was launched. Bradley University first opened its door in 1897 as Bradley Polytechnic Institute; and in 1898, the Peoria Civic Orchestra was formed under the direction of Harold Plowe.

HAROLD C. PLOWE, FOUNDER OF THE PEORIA SYMPHONY ORCHESTRA.

PLOWE AND THE PEORIA SYMPHONY ONSTAGE AT THE ORPHEUM. (BERT POWERS PHOTO).

Plowe, with his brother Eugene, had founded the Peoria Conservatory of Music at Fifth and Franklin Streets. Eugene was head of the music department at Eureka College and director of the St. Paul's Episcopal Choir. Another brother, Jay, had a distinguished career as a flutist, becoming first flutist of the Royal Berlin Opera and later the Los Angeles Symphony and Hollywood Bowl Orchestra.

But it was Harold who became the father of the Peoria Symphony, which was formed under the auspices of Bradley Polytechnic Institute. He played and taught violin, cello, piano, and organ. He was a restorer of stringed instruments. He also introduced archery to Peoria and was known as an inventor and manufacturer of fireworks and rockets.

Plowe, slight and bespectacled as he was, emerges as a heroic figure for the sheer feat of keeping his orchestra together and playing through seasons so dismal that his salary was $250 and the budget so constricted that in 1917, the orchestra wound up the season with a treasury of $1.70. At one time in the middle 1920's, the orchestra was known as the "Arcadia Little Symphony" and gave a single concert at the Arcadia Avenue Presbyterian Church. By 1929, the orchestra was down to a single concert given at the Majestic Theatre on March 31. So crushing were the burdens of the depression, that the Symphony might have folded but for the offer of sponsorship made by the Amateur Musical Club in the summer of 1931.

Eventually, further support arrived from the Intercivic Council, which sponsored the performance on January 14, 1936, at the Majestic with promotion supplied by WMBD Radio.

As late as 1940, Plowe, then emeritus conductor and a very old man, was still conducting at least a single work each program. But until 1946, the Symphony remained at best a musical organization held together by the unwavering determination of its founder. After his death, the orchestra moved into its modern era under the baton of Rudolph Reiners, former violinist with the Chicago Symphony. Reiner's first concert was held January 4, 1948; by the following year, the orchestra was up to a five-concert season with impressive financial backing from merchants, industrialists, lawyers, and doctors. Money-raising events proliferated and the orchestra became known as the musical voice of the city.

THE MEMORIAL TO LAURA BRADLEY, WHICH FORMERLY STOOD ON MAIN STREET NEAR PARKSIDE DRIVE.

THE SHRINE MOSQUE IN 1937. (LEE ROTEN COLLECTION).

The Symphony played its concerts at Woodruff High School in the late 1940's before moving into the Shrine Mosque and into the big time. It remained there, except for a few seasons at the new Manual High School auditorium, until it moved into the new Civic Center Theater under conductor William Wilsen for the 1982 season.

"Two things can happen," Plowe said while this was still a very young orchestra with an uncertain future. "Either we can die or grow into a first-class symphony." To say that the latter has happened might be chauvinistic. But it has.

202

WORLD WAR I BILLBOARDS
IN THE COURTHOUSE LAWN.

Somehow, Plowe's spirit must have been there when the symphony he founded, now the tenth oldest in the nation, received a roaring, standup ovation after playing before the distinguished delegates of the American Symphony Orchestra League's national convention in Chicago's Palmer House in the summer of 1983.

The saving of the orchestra in the 1930's by the Amateur Musical Club is only one of the many benefits this group has brought to the city. The name of the Club is so misleading that a Peoria correspondent for VARIETY was once instructed not to cover their offerings. The Amateur Musical Club began here in 1907 with the simple goal of advancing and promoting musical art in Peoria. Part of this is achieved through music appreciation classes; member's concerts; altruistic programs in children's homes, nursing homes and hospitals; and the support of all civic musical groups and affairs. The Club's major impact, however, has been its sponsorship of some of the best artists, performers, and orchestras in the world.

The list is far too long to detail, but under the sponsorship of Amateur Musical, pianist Vladimir de Pachmann played here in 1912, Ferrucio Busoni in 1915, Alexander Brailowsky in 1926, Robert Casadesus in 1940 and 1960, Dame Myra Hess in 1949, plus William Kapell, Byron Janis, Artur Rubinstein, Rudolph Serkin, and Vladimir Horowitz.

Virtually all the great violinists have played here as well - Sol Cohen, who lived and worked in Peoria before World War I; Zino Francescatti; Jascha Heifitz; Yehudi Menuhin; Nathan Milstein; Itzahk Perlman; Isaac Stern; and Joseph Szigeti. Countless others, such as Marcel Marceau, Andres Segovia, the Royal Winnipeg Ballet, the Gewendhaus, the Chicago and Leningrad Symphonies, Helen Traubel, Rosa Ponselle, Gregor Piatigorsky, the Dresden Staatskapelle, and the Philadelphia Symphony have appeared before Peoria audiences.

While opera houses have burned and theatres have been destroyed, Peoria has kept its tradition and its heritage alive up to the present time - hopefully a renascent one - largely through organizations that have survived and become historical, if not venerable, by their very longevity. The Symphony and Amateur Musical are two. Peoria Players is another.

It was June 27, 1919, when a small notice appeared in the PEORIA TRANSCRIPT that plans for a little theatre had been launched at a meeting of thirty-five Peorians at the home of William Hawley Smith. Their players group would consist of amateur actors, writers, painters, and electricians. Talks went

PEORIA PLAYERS ORIGINAL
THEATRE ON JACKSON STREET.

on through the summer and on October 6, Peoria Players presented its first program at the Peoria Women's Club. There was an introductory talk by William Wittick, president of the group; a speech by Laura Sherry on "The Little Theatre Movement;" and a presentation by Group One, directed by Mrs. O. P. Applegate, of Oliphant Down's THE MAKER OF DREAMS with Nina Alice Dodge, James Wilton, and Joseph Cowell as the players.

Some of the best-remembered names from these early Peoria Players years include Mrs. Frank Gillingham Morrill, Leonard Fritz and Louise Bliss (who later married each other), Julia Proctor White, Dorothy Powers Blomeyer, and the Bourland family, whose members have been active in the theatre for four generations.

By 1929, Peoria Players had outgrown the limited staging capacity of the Women's Club and was at the point of moving into its own theatre in the former fire house on Jackson Street, when the stock market crashed and the country was plunged into the Great Depression. While plans for the new building went ahead somewhat more subdued, the theatre continued at the Women's Club, with an occasional offering

204

THE FIRST AUDIENCE
ARRIVES FOR CORN STOCK'S
OPENING PRODUCTION OF
"GIGI" ON JULY 27, 1954.
(COURTESY CORN STOCK
THEATRE).

at the Majestic. It was not until Easter Monday of 1933 that Players moved into its Little Theatre on Jackson with its production of BERKLEY SQUARE, directed by Mrs. Morrill.

Most of these early plays were directed by women, among them Mrs. Morrill, Mrs. Francis Wittick, Mrs. Halcyon Allton Bryant, Gretchen Hulsebus (later Iben), Helen Wallace Young and Ethel Avery being among the most active.

By May, 1947, Peoria Players had paid its debt to the city and owned the building on Jackson. It had $7000 deposited in the bank for a building fund. The 36th season, that of 1954-1955, was to be the last on Jackson Street. The state had announced plans for the new Interstate 74, construction of which would so reduce the building as to make it impractical for further use as a theatre. Directors that year were Wayne West, Alan Foerter, Gretchen Iben, Milton Budd, Ken Camp, and Louise Fritz; and the last show on Jackson Street was DIAL "M" FOR MURDER, directed by Don Ford and opening on December 3, 1955.

For a time, the Peoria Players returned to the Women's Club while its new building, designed by Leslie Kenyon, was constructed in Lakeview Park. The grand opening was held on November 30, 1957, with TEAHOUSE OF THE AUGUST MOON. The play's author, John Patrick, was on hand to dedicate the new facility.

Since its beginnings sixty-six years ago, the theatre has survived storms and crises to become one of the longest-running theatre groups in the country and in these middle 1980's, its health and future would seem to be assured.

In the meantime, Peoria's outdoor summer theatre, Corn Stock, was launched on March 7, 1954, with the first meeting of the new group in Cilco Hall, headed by Gretchen Iben, Richard Chandler, Bill Muma, Bill and Alice Oakley, Betty Lou Hornbaker, Robert Schmidt, Mort and Edna Bowman, and Madison Meyers.

Its season opened on July 27 that year, with the area's first theatre-in-the-round production, GIGI, held in Detweiller Park. Sidney Baldwin, daughter of Eugene Baldwin who founded the Grand Opera House, played the part of the grandmother, with Miriam Beyer Cartwright as "Gigi," Virginia Lott as her mother, Charles Mulvahill as the uncle, and Jack Lawless as the butler. There were nightly interuptions as the Rock Island Rocket roared by and the performers "froze." Corn Stock also did THE SILVER CORD that summer in Detweiller. The following year, Corn Stock moved into the Bradley Park Tent with Richard Chandler as the first theatre manager. Chandler later moved to New York to become associated with producer Cheryl Crawford. His play about a Peorian in Greenwich Village, THE FREAKING OUT OF STEPHANIE BLAKE, was set to open on Broadway during the 1967 season when its star, Jean Arthur, "freaked out" at the last moment and the play never opened.

Later Corn Stock managers included Eugene Holmes from 1960 to 1966, Williams Shrier from 1967 to 1969, Robert Miller in 1970, and Thomas Joyce from 1971 through 1978.

While this amateur local theatre was attracting increasing crowds, professional touring theatre made its return to Peoria with the launching of the Broadway Theatre League at the Shrine Mosque in 1959 with a rather heavy season that included LOOK HOMEWARD, ANGEL.

The 1960's and 70's were good years for the performing arts in Peoria. Although the Peoria Symphony, Orpheus Club, Amateur Musical, Peoria Players, and Corn Stock had supplied the majority of concerts and plays, new organizations were founded and new halls built, and with each opening came a wealth of new offerings. These were the years when the Peoria Civic Ballet was founded, with Jack Slater as its first artistic director. The Peoria Civic Opera began in the Bergan High School Auditorium in 1972 with small, staged operas presented by its artistic director and founder, Cybelle Abt. She revived a tradition that had been dormant in Peoria since the days of the Grand Opera House and the "Gay Nineties," when the Andrews Opera Company presented its outdoor fare in Sylvan Park, near what is now St. Augustine Manor.

Aside from touring opera and a short-lived opera group at Bradley around 1950 that was directed by Lawrence McKenna, the only opera seen here was that given by mainly second-rate touring companies.

Illinois Central College's ambitious new Performaning Arts Center was opened on January 14, 1978 with the Mid-America Dance Theatre (formerly and later the Peoria Civic Ballet) presenting "Le Patineurs" and part of "Coppelia" under the direction of Mark Ligon.

Bradley University, too, began to move away from its historic emphasis on basketball, business, and engineering, first by locating its music school in Constance Hall; and in 1979, by converting the old gymnasium, one of the college's original buildings, into the new Hartmann Center for the Performing Arts. It opened on September 7, 1979, when Richard Marriott directed MAN OF LA MANCHA starring Tom Joyce as "Cervantes."

THE PEORIA CIVIC BALLET IN ITS 1984 PRODUCTION OF "THE NUTCRACKER" AT ILLINOIS CENTRAL COLLEGE. (COURTESY R. & K. PHOTOGRAPHY).

206

PEORIA SYMPHONY POPS
CONCERT, 1985. (JOURNAL
STAR).

**Bradley also converted the former Church of Christ Scientist
on Barker Avenue into its new Dingledine Music Center,
which had its dedicatory concert on September 25, 1983, with
Bradley graduate Jerry Hadley of the New York City Opera
as featured performer.**

If the opening of the Grand Opera House had been one of
the high points of Peoria's cultural history in the nineteenth
century, the dedication of the new Civic Center Theater on
September 11, 1982, probably represents the peak of the
twentieth century. It occured, curiously, one day less than
100 years after the Grand Opera House opening ceremonies.
The Peoria Symphony Orchestra, under the baton of William
Wilsen, played Peoria composer Dean Howard's
"Celebration," which had been commissioned for the event.

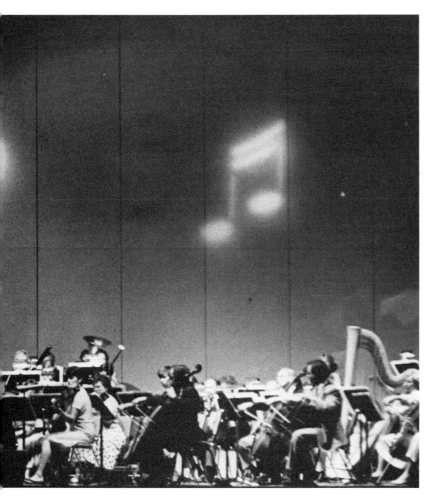

The orchestra followed this with the final movement of the Beethoven Ninth Symphony with Peoria Civic Opera soloists Nancy Amini, Susan Floreen, Michael Sylvester, and William Rhodes plus a chorus made up of members of the Bradley-Community Chorus, and Orpheus Club, and the Philharmonic Chorale.

The Peoria Civic Ballet followed with excerpts from SWAN LAKE and SLEEPING BEAUTY with soloists Cynthia Harvey and Ross Stretton; and the Peoria Civic Opera presented Act II of LA TRAVIATA, with Jo Ann Lacquet Sims joining the soloists who had earlier sung in the Beethovan selection.

Along with such premiere season attractions as The Royal Winnipeg Ballet, the Chicago Symphony, Itzahk Perelman and A CHRISTMAS CAROL, was the nude play, O CALCUTTA, which stirred considerable public controversy. The Theater has since settled down to become the home of the Peoria Symphony, Amateur Musical Club artist concert series, the Civic Opera, Broadway Theatre series and other high calibre offerings.

208

THIS OBSERVATION TOWER WAS BUILT BY THE PEORIA PARK DISTRICT ON GRAND VIEW DRIVE IN 1906. IT WAS DISMANTLED IN 1942 AND ITS METAL USED DURING THE WORLD WAR II SCRAP DRIVE.

If the building of the Civic Center, with its impressive theatre, was a culmination point in the history of the performing arts in Peoria, also very crucial to the city's cultural climate was the completion of Lakeview Museum, then known as Lakeview Center, in 1965. It was to focus an enormous amount of artistic activity beneath a single roof. Arts groups had flourished in Peoria since 1888, when the Peoria Art League was founded. That group evolved into the Peoria Society of Allied Artists in 1913, a loose confederation made up of the League, the Manual Arts Department of Bradley, and the Art and Literature Department of the Peoria Women's Club. This group was succeeded by the Art Institute of Peoria in 1923, which, for a time, occupied a house at Hamilton and Randolph. It was reorganized in 1949 with headquarters and an art school and gallery at 317 Main Street, and in 1952 moved into the Glen Oak Park Pavilion, which was its last stop before Lakeview.

The visual arts, however, do not depend as much on structure or organization as do the performing arts, and much of the city's artistic heritage derives from men and women who worked alone and exhibited where they could. There were active potters, portrait painters, silversmiths, and others who passed through while this was still a pioneer village. Among those who remained was Daniel Greenbach, who moved here in 1861 and began producing mottled-ware pitchers and mugs and, later, stoneware. By 1880, the Peoria Pottery Company was the largest manufacturer of glazed stoneware in the country.

Another influential artist who lived here for a time was James F. Wilkins, who returned from the California Gold Rush to produce a huge painting called "The Moving Mirror of the Overland Trail," a panorama in three reels that was shown

A BROADWAY SERIES PRESENTATION OF "SOPHISTICATED LADIES" AT THE CIVIC CENTER THEATER. (COURTESY PEORIA CIVIC CENTER).

here for two weeks before eager crowds. Wilkins remained
here in the early 1850's to paint large portraits of the Charles
Ballance and John Reynolds families.

In 1882, a young silversmith and engraver, who was to have
a lasting effect on his adopted city, moved here from England.
He was Hedley Waycott and his first job was in an art store
where the Palace Theatre used to stand. Waycott began
painting with oils and for over fifty-seven years was the city's
best-known painter. While his works won critical acclaim in
New York and Chicago and he sold over 800 works, the
framing business provided his livelihood. Many of his
paintings have a pointillistic style, suggestive of late
Impressionism. Some of these are now hanging at the Buehler
Home, in Peoria high schools, and in private collections.
Waycott's last home was a modest frame building at 218
Wisconsin Avenue, which was identified by a small, palette-
shaped sign in the front yard, "Hedley Waycott. Painter." He
died in 1937. A restrospective of his work was held at the
Peoria Art Center in Glen Oak Pavilion in 1964.

Other significant and enduring work was contributed to the
city by Frank Charles Peyraud and Hardesty G. Maratta,
who painted several murals in Peoria, including a series of
wall-sized murals for the former Peoria Public Library. They
also reportedly painted an eight by nine panorama of the
Civil War Battle of Missionary Ridge, done in payment for a
bar bill. It hung in a downtown saloon until prohibition, but
has apparently disappeared.

Perhaps Peoria's most famous sculptor is Frederick Triebel (1865-1944) whose major work here is the War Memorial in Courthouse Square. Triebel grew up in Peoria and moved to Rome, Italy, where he received the Galileo Award in 1891. His largest Peoria work was cast in Italy, shipped to Peoria, and assembled by the artist. It was dedicated in 1899 by President McKinley. The monument had its critics: a Peorian, John McGinnis, termed it "a travesty on art and a jest to war and should not be tolerated in our fair city." Triebel's other major Peoria works include the statue of Robert Ingersoll which stands at the lower entrance to Glen Oak Park, the bust of Lydia Moss Bradley owned by the University, and the sculpture entitled "Love Knows No Cast," now in City Hall.

Triebel's Courthouse work was the forerunner of succeeding major public art projects in the city, some of which were to provoke considerable controversy. Such public art did not precisely proliferate here, its chief expression being found locally in just a few works. These are the "Peace" and "Harvest" statues by Mary Anderson Clark, a WPA artist from the 1930's, which stand in the Courthouse Square; Peorian Nita Sunderland's works the "Birds of Prey," which stand near Bradley University's Book Store, and her dragon, "Cedric," which formerly stood before City Hall; and in the Trova "Gox" at the Peoria School of Medicine.

But the voice of people erupted with extraordinary ferocity when nationally-famous artist, Richard Serra, unveiled his proposed "Shaft," which was commissioned to stand before the new Civic Center. The project had been launched by the Junior League of Peoria during the Bicentennial Year. The League raised $50,000, which was matched by a grant from the National Endowment for the Arts; and a panel of experts chose Serra as the artist to execute the work.

So vehement was the public response to his proposed slabs of intersecting Cor-Ten steel that Serra ultimately was scratched as the artist and the search for a new scuplture was launched. Peoria became the object of considerable ridicule because of the uproar, but there was something almost prophetic and justifiable in the refusal to accept the "Shaft," for similar Serra works which were erected in New York and St. Louis have triggered massive petitions for their removal as "civic eyesores."

211

What finally was erected as Peoria's Civic Center sculpture was a major work by Ronald Bladen entitled "Sonar Tide," a black, curving, expressive work which has met with a considerable amount of public reception, very little hostility, and, to date, no vandalism.

Perhaps too often overlooked as part of Peoria's cultural mix is the presence of public television, Channel 47, and WCBU, FM-90, which almost continuously broadcasts classical music and superior programming.

The history is incomplete. But what has emerged from this long and sporadic ascent from a frontier town and river city with its intinerant limners and portrait artists, ventriloquists, touring players, vaudeville, and one-night stands is a highly civilized city whose artistic and cultural heritage have helped make life in Peoria extremely rich and rewarding. To those who know the city and its attractions, the old vaudeville song, "Oh, How I Wish't I Was in Peoria," is not an insult as much as an expression of envy.

THE IVY CLUB DURING HIGH WATER. (F-STOP SOCIETY).

CHAPTER NINE

PEORIA'S PEOPLE, FROM SAINTS TO SINNERS

From politicians to painters. Lincoln, Ingersoll and Spalding. The E.N. Woodruff era. Hedley Waycott, Betty Friedan, Fibber McGee and Molly and the Shelton Gang. The people who influenced Peoria and were, in turn, influenced by the city.

THE AMERICAN LEGION FLAG BEARERS PARADE IN THE 100 BLOCK OF S. ADAMS BEFORE WORLD WAR II. (RAY BARCLAY PHOTO).

214

Any city is a sum total of its people. It takes its character from their presence, their work, their interests. And somehow, uniquely, it fixes its own stamp upon them as well. While no one can really calculate which citizens most influenced the city or were influenced by it, a rich and colorful cast of the famous and infamous emerges in the three-hundred-plus years since the French arrived and built their ill-fated fort.

Peoria has been a French frontier village, a booming river town, a whiskey capital, a show business and vaudeville center, a wide-open city famous for its red-light district and tolerant ways, a throbbing manufacturing center, and the hub of a major commercial and agricultural area with a proud heritage and new hope for the future.

Jean Baptiste Maillet might properly be termed the founder of Peoria, but the honor of being its first citizen belongs to Josiah Fulton, who settled here in 1819 and remained for the rest of his life. He was the only one of the original group to become a permanent resident. His life spanned much of Peoria's history. When he arrived, there was nothing but the remains of Fort Clark, a handful of Indians, and a few Frenchmen. When he died in 1894, at the age of ninety-four, the city was a distilling and railroad center with factories, streetcars, a bustling downtown, and its Grand Opera House. It may be difficult to imagine what this site looked like when Fulton arrived here, but the Peoria of the 1890's has a certain familiarity. Much of what is here now was here then. Fulton's fame does not rest so much on his longevity or the properties he owned, but on the fact that he came first and stayed the longest. He must have known virtually every major figure who lived or made his mark in Peoria during all but a few years of the nineteenth century.

Easily the most famous of these was Robert Green Ingersoll, who is best known today for his radical agnosticism but who in his time was so sought after as a speaker that he earned as much as $3500 for a single talk. After hearing him speak, Mark Twain once said, "It was just the supreme combination of English words that was ever put together since the world began....Lord, what an organ is human speech when played by a master."

They called him "Royal Bob" and "Peoria's Pagan," although he was not a Peorian by birth but by choice. He was born in Dresden, New York, on August 11, 1833, and followed his family westward. He was admitted to the Illinois Bar in 1854, and three years later moved to Peoria, where he remained for twenty years. He served in the Civil War as a colonel of the Illinois volunteer cavalry until he was captured during the battle of Shiloh in 1862.

"What do you want to shoot me for?" he supposedly said when he was surrounded by rebel troops; "I've been wanting to acknowledge your old confederacy for the last two seconds." Whether because of his speech or his bearing or the mercy of General Nathan Bedford Forrest, Ingersoll was paroled and he returned to Peoria.

His house originally stood at the corner of Hamilton and Jefferson and later was moved to the middle of the block to make way for the construction of the National Hotel. The hotel burned in 1911, and the New National Hotel was built around the Ingersoll house.

COL. ROBERT INGERSOLL.

216

TRAFFIC POLICEMEN ON S. ADAMS STREET IN 1937. (RAY BARCLAY PHOTO).

When Susan B. Anthony came to Peoria in 1854, Ingersoll was on hand to speak in her behalf, saying, "We favor the extension to women of all rights now enjoyed by men as quickly as possible."

While he gained most of his notoriety as a baiter of religion, particularly that of the "hellfire and brimstone" variety, he was a lawyer, orator, author, poet, philosopher, and humanitarian. His creed was, "The place to be happy is here, the time to be happy is now, the way to be happy is to make others so."

While he seemed to be almost satanic in his attacks on religion - "with soap, baptism is a good thing" - he was devoted to his family and his home, would never turn a beggar away from his door, and was known for his charity and compassion.

"If there is a God," he once said, "He will be merciful to the merciful." In an oration at a child's grave, he said, "We do not know which is the greater blessing, life or death. We cannot say that death is not good. We do not know whether the grave is the end of this life or the door to another, or whether the night here is not somewhere else a dawn....every cradle asks 'whence?' and every coffin 'whither?'. Death at its worst is only a perfect rest. We, too, have our religion and it is this -help for the living, hope for the dead."

In one of his highly-paid speeches, this one given at the Palmer House in Chicago, he responded to a toast with the words, "....to all the dead, to Sherman, to Sheridan and to Grant, the foremost soldiers of the world; and last, to Lincoln, whose loving life like a bow of peace, spans and arches all the clouds of war."

Ingersoll is the only Peorian who can be found in an encyclopedia. His famous "plumed knight" speech in favor of James Blaine supposedly caused that political figure to cast his shadow over the White House for sixteen years.

When he died in New York on July 21, 1899, his housekeeper called him "the loveliest man in the world."

MOTORCYCLE POLICEMEN LINED UP FOR INSPECTION BEFORE THE ARMORY ON NORTH ADAMS ST., 1937. (RAY BARCLAY PHOTO).

The only memorial to Ingersoll remaining in Peoria is Fritz Triebel's lonely statue that stands at the lower entrance to Glen Oak Park. It is inscribed, simply, "Ingersoll."

The Lincoln that Ingersoll so admired can hardly be called a Peorian, but we was here often enough and his presence was important enough to deserve inclusion as one of the major figures in the city's history.

One of Lincoln's greatest debates with Stephen Douglas, the one some claim launched him on the road to the presidency, took place within a stone's throw of Ingersoll's future home. It was October 16, 1854, and according to B. C. Bryner, who saw the debate as a boy, there was, at the time, "not a completed railroad in Peoria, no telegraph, no sewing machine, no telephone, tallow candles for illumination, butter, eggs and milk lowered into the cistern to keep fresh. Amid such scenes Lincoln and Douglas first met in debate in Peoria, October 16, 1854."

It was not Lincoln's first visit here. He came through in 1832 when he was twenty-three and on his way back to Springfield from the Black Hawk War. His first real recorded visit here took place on February 10, 1840, when he attended an all-day political rally of Whig party leaders. In 1844, Lincoln was in and out of Peoria several times addressing a "Henry Clay for President" meeting, deriding a Springfield Democrat, John Calhoun, who was running for presidential elector; and taking part in a divorce case in court. He also was here on October 9, 1848, campaigning for General Zachary Taylor for president. He frequently took a room overnight at the Peoria House, a popular hotel at Hamilton and Adams. His most historic visit occured in October of 1854, when he made his renowned "Peoria speech."

Lincoln here directed his attack at the Kansas-Nebraska bill, which not only created these two territories, but allowed the inhabitants to decide whether they should be slave or free.

"The genius of discord himself could scarcely have invented a way of again setting us by the ears but by turning back and destroying the peace measures of the past," said Lincoln. "Repeal the Missouri Compromise, repeal all compromises, repeal the Declaration of Independence. Repeal all past history, you still cannot repeal human nature. It will still be the abundance of man's heart that slavery extension is wrong, and out of the abundance of his heart his mouth will continue to speak....Stand with anybody that stands right. Stand with him while he is right and part with him when he goes wrong."

Today a bronze plaque in the Peoria Courthouse Plaza commemorates that day and that speech with Lincoln's words, "The people's will is the ultimate law for all."

218

Among those who had invited Lincoln to the debate was the historian, lawyer, and land-owner Charles Ballance. Ballance's major claim to fame lies in his 1870 history of Peoria and in his long fight to disprove the French claims. He seems, in retrospect, to have been one of those distant and proper figures quiet beyond reproach, but he gains a certain humanity and appeal through some far more earthly qualities. One of these involved a dispute with a neighbor over a fence. This dispute involved a certain amount of violence and led to Ballance being charged with battery. He also recounts certain incidents which tend to make history far more approachable and understandable than is usually the case.

One in particular involved an argument over the possession of a ferry between Abner Eads, one of the 1819 settlers, and attorney John Bogardus. Eads, who was winning the fight, was wearing a mackinaw blanket-type overcoat with heavy iron buttons. Bogardus, getting the worst of it, drew a small revolver and fired point blank at Eads, who fell back appearing to be mortally wounded. It happened, however, that the bullet struck one of the buttons and drove it into the thick coat, a piece of luck which spared both these early settlers the ignominious fate of being remembered best for a fatal brawl.

There obviously was no such thing as a typical Peorian of the nineteenth century. The citizens ranged from lawyers and educators to the great Ingersoll and a churchman, John Lancaster Spalding, who was the first Catholic Bishop of Peoria and a friend of the famous agnostic. Bishop Spalding is best known today for his namesake, Spalding Institute, which he built and equipped out of his own considerable pocket. During his life he was a controversial theologian, writer, and lecturer known almost as well in the ecclesiastical circles of Europe as in the churches of Peoria and the East.

THE S. PEORIA VOLUNTEER
FIRE CO. NO. 1 IN 1909.

There is a temptation to regard most characters from the historical past as men and women of unimpeachable righteousness—stern, humorless, sober, law-abiding, etc. But the pioneer lawyer, Charles Ballance, in his journal, reveals an almost unexpected side to the usually venerable patriarch when he relates a story about a fight over a disputed piece of land on which he had a garden and three houses:

"Underhill (Isaac) some time ago threatened to tear down my garden fence, but from assurance I gave him he became apprehensive there might be some danger in (sic) and hired George Depree, a low-life bully, to do it. Depree undertook it three or four weeks ago when I was planting some things in the garden and I struck him a lick with the hoe which proved sufficient to stop him. On Monday late, Underhill hired an Irishman to do it and armed him with a pistol he himself guarding the man with a gun. As soon as I learned what was going on, I went on the ground with a gun and two pistols. On my arrival, he cocked his gun and his man cocked his pistol. I ordered the man to desist from tearing down the fence. Underhill ordered him to proceed and raised his gun at that instant I fired my gun at Underhill and he fired his at me and his man Thompson drew his pistol; but before he had time to shoot, I had fired a pistol at his head which made him retreat a short distance; but supposing I had no other pistol, he rallied with his pistol presented but seeing I was ready with another, he retreated. I then commenced reloading my gun upon which he approached me again with a cocked pistol but I kept him at bay with mine until I had loaded my gun. He then retreated and left the field, Underhill having retreated before. They then made complaint upon oath to a justice of the peace who after hearing their statements, ordered me to enter into bonds which I did for my appearance at the next circuit court since which time my fence has remained unmolested. During this day I was not only lame with the rheumatism, but also had a large blister of catharides on my ancle insomuch that I had to fight on crutches but what made the case I was otherwise quite unwell."

Ballance recorded that he was eventually acquitted.

HISTORIAN AND LAWYER
CHARLES BALLANCE. (PEORIA
PUBLIC LIBRARY).

220

JOHN LANCASTER SPALDING,
FIRST BISHOP OF PEORIA.

He was born June 2, 1840, in Lebanon, Kentucky, a nephew of Martin John Spalding, Archbishop of Baltimore. His paternal ancestors had fled from religious persecution in England some time before 1650, and his mother's family, the Lancasters, traced their lineage to Edward III.

Spalding studied for the priesthood at Louvain, Belgium, and was ordained December 19, 1863, at Malines. He spent six years studying and traveling in Europe before he was assigned to the Cathedral at Louisville as a rector. He later became chancellor of the Louisville Diocese and following that, was transferred to New York City.

When the Diocese of Peoria was formed, Father Michael Hurley, pastor of St. Patrick's in Peoria, was the original choice for bishop. He declined, and Spalding, the second choice, was consecrated as bishop in New York on May 1, 1877.

His first major project was the construction of St. Francis Hospital for which he laid the cornerstone on September 30, 1877. He also invited the Cincinnati Franciscans into the Peoria area, where they remain to this day. He laid the cornerstone of the present St. Mary's Cathedral on June 28, 1885. While he was an intellectual aristocrat who was not particularly approachable, he was regarded as the founder of the Catholic University of America in Washington, D. C., and an endless champion of Catholic education. Ingersoll was one of his friends, unlikely as it might seen considering their backgrounds and beliefs; Theodore Roosevelt was another. It was upon Bishop Spalding's invitation that Roosevelt came to Peoria for the Columbus Day Banquet in 1910.

Bishop Spalding refused several chances for advancement, turning down opportunities to lead such major archdioceses as Chicago and New York in his preference to remain in Peoria. Because of his writings, he was regarded as the greatest literary artist in the entire history of the American Catholic hierarchy and it was said that he accomplished for the American church what Cardinal Newman had for the church in England. He suffered a series of strokes and resigned in 1908, but continued to live in the bishop's residence on Glen Oak Avenue until he died on August 25, 1916.

THE JUDGE FLANAGAN HOME
ON GLEN OAK, DETERMINED
TO BE PEORIA'S OLDEST
HOUSE, BUILT IN 1837. IT IS
NOW OWNED BY THE PEORIA
HISTORICAL SOCIETY.
(RICHARD ETTER PHOTO).

HOME OF JOSEPH GREENHUT
AT HIGH AND SHERIDAN,
AROUND 1920.

222

THE EUGENE BALDWIN HOUSE
AT 245 NE PERRY, BUILT IN 1877
BY DAVID C. PROCTOR AND
PURCHASED BY BALDWIN IN
1912. BALDWIN'S 3,000 VOLUME
LIBRARY WAS SAID TO BE ONE
OF THE LARGEST IN THE
ENTIRE STATE. THE HOME IS
NOW HEADQUARTERS FOR
AN ADVERTISING AGENCY.
(LEE ROTEN COLLECTION).

THE ROCKY GLEN TAVERN
AT 3522 W. LINCOLN IS ONE OF
THE OLDEST BUILDINGS ON
THE SOUTH SIDE. IT WAS AN
INN IN THE 1840'S. (PEORIA
PUBLIC LIBRARY, ERNEST
GRASSEL PHOTO).

FRANCIS W. LITTLE HOME,
BUILT BY FRANK LLOYD
WRIGHT, 1902. NOW THE
RESIDENCE OF MR. AND MRS.
WALTER SWARDENSKI.
(JOURNAL STAR PHOTO BY
LARRY BROOKS).

ERASTUS B. HARDIN HOUSE,
511 HIGH STREET, BUILT 1859.
(LEE ROTEN COLLECTION).

THE SAMUEL WOOLNER HOME
AT 317 N. PERRY WAS BUILT IN
1877 BY PORTIUS WHEELER,
AND LATER PURCHASED BY
WOOLNER, WHO ORGANIZED
THE ATLAS DISTILLERY. IT
HAS BEEN REFURBISHED.

RESIDENCE OF C.P. KING,
205 N. MADISON. (LEE ROTEN
COLLECTION).

THE JOHN GRISWOLD HOME
ON MOSS AVE. (PEORIA PUBLIC
LIBRARY, LEE ROTEN PRINT).

224

BISHOP PHILANDER CHASE.
(PEORIA PUBLIC LIBRARY).

While a host of notables from nineteenth-century Peoria are worthy of attention and seem to be clamoring for it, two in particular have had a long-lasting impact on the city and the area, one for a college that failed and the other for an institute that grew into a university.

Bishop Philander Chase was perhaps a man ahead of his time with his visions and his hopes, while Lydia Moss Bradley was a woman in step with hers. They both suffered tragedies of a different sort, and yet they each fashioned something unique which remains, each vital in its own way.

Bishop Chase was, of course, the inspiration behind, and the founder of, Jubilee College, a pioneer Episcopalian Church school which marked the first attempt to bring higher education into the Illinois wilderness. The bishop, strictly speaking, was not a Peorian, but his story belongs both to the city and the county. The Chases, like the Spaldings, arrived in this country long before the Revolutionary War. Aquila Chase settled in New England in 1640, and five generations later Philander, the fifteenth child of Dudley and Allace Chase, was born in Cornish, New Hampshire, December 14, 1775.

He was ordained to the priesthood in St. Paul's Church, New York City, on November 10, 1799, where he served until being dispatched to New Orleans in 1805, where he was assigned to Christ Church. He later served a most happy time in Hartford, Connecticut, and was named the first Bishop of Illinois in 1835. While he was also the Bishop of Ohio at Worthington and founder of Kenyon College, his most noteworthy and certainly most heroic accomplishment was the building of Jubilee College in what was then a total wilderness near Kickapoo. He built his first "Robin's nest" near here in 1836, so called because it was built of mud and sticks and was full of young ones. The chapel was erected at nearby Jubilee in 1840-1841, and by 1843, the building called "The Cottage" was constructed. On the eighth of July, 1847, five students of the college received their bachelor's degree.

CHASE HALL, THE ORIGINAL
BUILDING AT JUBILEE
COLLEGE.

All this had been made possible by the Bishop's ceaseless efforts to raise funds and support in the South, in the East, and from old friends in England. When he died on September 20, 1852, he remained certain that this great gift to his diocese, his church, and his Illinois wilderness was to be a lasting memorial.

Although it became an embarrassment and a ruin during the earlier part of this century, it has been spared the fate of oblivion by its recognition as the first national historic shrine in the area, and by its development as a state park. Reconstruction of the buildings is continuing under the constant urging of the Citizens Committee to Preserve Jubilee College. It is the site of the Olde English Faire in June and the Harvestfest Days celebration in the autumn, both of which bring far more people to the site than Bishop Chase might have imagined. He lies beneath an immense fir tree in God's Acre Cemetery at Jubilee, the founder of a college that after nearly 150 years, has become a success after all. He was a man who was counted among the makers of the United States. During the formative period of the Middle West, he introduced culture, learning, and discipline into what had been an untamed wilderness. And here it remains.

THE OLD DINING HALL AT JUBILEE. THE SECOND FLOOR WAS USED AS AN APARTMENT FOR FACULTY MEMBERS.

226

THE HOROLOGY LABORATORY
AT BRADLEY. (F-STOP
SOCIETY).

LYDIA MOSS BRADLEY AT
HER HOME ON MOSS AVENUE.

228

TOBIAS BRADLEY. (PEORIA PUBLIC LIBRARY).

The fact that Lydia Moss Bradley's institute has had a greater effect on Peoria and the area than that of Philander Chase is almost an accident of time and circumstance. The Civil War, which dried up the financial sources from the South, contributed mightily to the demise of Jubilee College. Bradley Polytechnic Institute, which was chartered on November 16, 1896, and opened on its first Founders Day, October 8, 1897, coincided with the development of Peoria as a commercial, industrial, financial, and population center and its progress has been steadily upward.

Mrs. Bradley originally had no intention of founding what later became a university. She had been raised, if not in splendor, in surroundings that were certainly comfortable. Her father, the Reverend Zealy Moss, was a pioneer of some ability. He had been a captain in the Continental Army and was a Baptist preacher and farmer. He gave one of his farms near Vevay, Indiana, to Lydia, which she eventually sold for

$7000. That money purchased part of the land on which the university now stands. When she married Tobias Smith Bradley on May 11, 1837, her grandfather gave her a bag containing $1000 in gold.

The Bradleys moved to Peoria in 1846, when the town was hardly more than a village, and embarked on a profitable business career. Mrs. Bradley's brother, William S. Moss, was in the distilling business and was soon joined by the Bradleys. They also had a financial interest in a sawmill, in railroad building, and in the operation of a steamboat on the Illinois River. They bought farm land and developed real estate. Tobias was one of the organizers of the First National Bank of Peoria, for which Mrs. Bradley later served as director.

The Bradleys had six children. All died before growing up. Laura, for whom Bradley Park is named, lived the longest. She was fifteen when she died in 1864. But even these

THE BRADLEY GYMNASIUM UNDER CONSTRUCTION. THE BUILDING IS NOW THE HARTMANN CENTER FOR PERFORMING ARTS. (F-STOP SOCIETY).

WESTLAKE HALL AND BRADLEY HALL SHORTLY AFTER THE NEW COLLEGE OPENED.

230

BETTY GOLDSTEIN FRIEDAN
IN 1966. (COURTESY PEORIA
JOURNAL STAR).

repeated blows were not all that Mrs. Bradley endured. Three years after the death of Laura, Tobias was fatally injured in an accident involving a runaway horse and an overturned carriage. It was from such sorrow that the idea for Bradley Polytechnic Institute was to emerge.

Until the death of Tobias, the Bradleys had been planning an orphanage as a fitting memorial to their children. But after her husband's death, Mrs. Bradley began more and more to focus on the idea of a school, as the charter states, "...for the education of young people of both sexes in all the practical and useful arts, sciences, and learning usually taught in polytechnic schools, including a department of ethics in which instruction shall be given in the principles of morality and right living as exemplified in the life and teaching of Jesus Christ....but the chief aim of the Institute shall be to furnish its students with the means of living independent, industrious, and useful lives by the aid of a practical knowledge of the useful arts and sciences."

If the photographs of Mrs. Bradley, and the bust by Peoria's Fritz Triebel, portray a severe, dour, formidable, perhaps even fearsome woman, the impression might be softened by a consideration of the sorrows she must have suffered and by the lasting achievements of her long and remarkable life. What is now Bradley University was designated as a memorial "for Tobias and the children." The stones she erected on what was then a meadow remain. And so do the memories.

It seems almost redundant, even somewhat condescending, to point out that this university and this concept came from a woman who was a powerful figure in real estate, finance, banking, and education in an age when most women where supposedly regarded as second class citizens. Still, it was only a short step from the death of Lydia Moss Bradley on January 16, 1908, to the birth of Betty Goldstein (Friedan) just over a decade later.

Betty Goldstein was a member of the class of 1938 at Peoria High School, where she was known for her intellect amid a group that was to become famous for providing so much leadership to the city and the nation. She was one of six valedictorians of the class and went on to Smith College and a certain ineradicable fame as the founder of the Women's Movement with her book, THE FEMININE MYSTIQUE.

"It used to embarrass me even to admit that I came from Peoria," she wrote in 1978, when she returned here for her high school class fortieth reunion. "It was a vaudeville joke, the epitome of the hick town....I remembered only the pain of growing up in Peoria. I never would admit the sweet sure certainty of belonging in Peoria - that small, self-satisfied, deceptively simple, mysterious, complex heartland of America, which undeniably provided my roots, and therefore the roots of whatever vision of equality, passion for justice or sense of possibility that drove me to the Women's Movement in the world."

There is something almost bizarre in the sheer diversity of Peoria's more famous citizens, as if this were some kind of corporate version of Noah's Ark that has nurtured all manner of different breeds - bishops, explorers, radicals, freethinkers, poets, politicians, gangsters, comics, and visionaries. For some the city has been a breeding ground, a way station, a place to be from, a location that takes on that affectionate title of home.

BISHOP FULTON SHEEN. (COURTESY PEORIA JOURNAL STAR).

One of these was Fulton Sheen, born in El Paso, Illinois, but raised and educated in Peoria. He graduated from Spalding in 1919, studied for the priesthood at St. Viator's in Bourbonnais, and followed the footsteps of Peoria's first bishop to Louvain in Belgium. After his European studies, he returned to St. Patrick's on Peoria's near south side in 1926. It was to be his only parish assignment, for he was soon sent to teach at the Catholic University in Washington, D. C. - an institution which owes so much to Bishop Spalding. Fulton Sheen became the first preacher on the radio show "The Catholic Hour" in 1930 and went on to his famous television series, "Life Is Worth Living."

His penetrating gaze and almost Shakespearean delivery made him a mesmerizing speaker. He numbered among his converts such notable figures as Louis Budenz, Fritz Kreisler, Clare Booth Luce, Grace Moore, and Henry Ford II. He also was the author of a string of best-selling inspirational works and his fame, amplified by the medium of television, unquestionably exceeded that of Bishop Spalding. He was, however, not a politician and instead of becoming a major figure in his church - some had predicted he would become the first American pope - he was appointed Bishop of Rochester, an unhappy position he held for three years before retiring at the age of 74. He died ten years later, on December 9, 1979, after a long life during which he was known by many as "The Man from Peoria."

232

While the famous bishop made the world his stage, another important figure in the city's history played out his entire role here. He was Edward Nelson Woodruff, who served an unprecedented eleven terms as mayor of Peoria between 1903 and 1946, when he finished his last term and retired from political life.

These were steamy years for Peoria which, in the Woodruff era, gained the reputation of being a wide-open town.

Woodruff was hardly a reformer. One of his basic tenets was that some measure of vice is bound to exist in every community and that under municipal control and regulation, such activities should be required to help defray the cost of civic maintenance and improvement.

Despite the charges of scandal and machine politics that attended his long reign as Peoria's mayor, he compiled an enviable record of public improvements. Among these were the establishment of a public garbage collection department, the building of the Peoria Municipal Tuberculosis Sanitarium, the establishment of Eckwood Park, and the building of the Cedar Street Bridge. He also was head of the Woodruff Ice Company, treasurer and director of the Peoria Life Insurance Company, and a vice-president of the original Pere Marquette Building Company.

Much of Woodruff's political strategy was hammered out at a river cottage that had been converted from the hull of an old river boat. This somewhat shady rendezvous was widely known at "The Bum Boat." To most people of the time, the mayor was known simply as "Ed," or "E. N.," and while his reign might not have inspired universal admiration, his Peoria was safe, solvent, and operated with a certain pragmatic efficiency. Postwar reformers ended the city's dubious reputation as a center of gambling and prostitution; and by the time of Woodruff's death on December 22, 1947, the old Peoria that had been a wide-open, brawling river town was about to end as well.

Peoria Politicians

While the city of Peoria has never produced a president, vice-president, or governor, its role in national politics since the time of Abraham Lincoln has been a significant one. It was Lincoln's speech here, some historians claim, that launched him on the road to the presidency. This was the debate with Stephen Douglas on October 16, 1854, when he condemned slavery and said, "Stand with anybody that stands right. Stand with him while he is right and part with him when he goes wrong."

It was near here, in Pekin, that Senator Everett Dirksen, a powerful orator and minority leader, was born. Dirksen served in the United States Senate for nearly forty years until his death in 1969. In the Senate, he carried the standard of conservative Republicanism during a long era of liberal welfarism.

The current minority leader of the House of Representatives, Robert Michel, is a Peoria native and a graduate of Bradley University. Michel has served in the House since 1956 and has become a powerful ally of President Ronald Reagan.

Reagan, who was educated at nearby Eureka College, chose Peoria as the location to deliver his final nationwide campaign appeal on election eve of 1980, with an entourage that included entertainer Bob Hope.

Another Peorian, Roger Kelley, served as an assistant Secretary of Defense from 1969 to 1973.

An influential congressman from Peoria earlier in this century was William E. Hull, who was elected to the House of Representatives in 1922 and served for ten years. He had been manager of Clarke Brothers Distillery and was credited with bringing Hiram Walker and Sons, the world's largest distillery, to Peoria. In Congress, he succeeded in passing legislation that created the deep waterway from Lake Michigan to the Gulf of Mexico. He died May 31, 1942. And Richard Carver, Peoria mayor from 1977 to 1984 and one-time head of the United States Mayors' Association, was appointed an assistant Secretary of the Air Force in 1984 by President Reagan.

234

MEMBERS OF THE FAMOUS
SHELTON GANG. (PEORIA
PUBLIC LIBRARY)

Only one major chapter remained to be finished, and it closed the summer after Woodruff's death when Bernie Shelton, a member of the notorious Shelton Brothers gang, was shot and killed from ambush outside the Parkway Tavern on Farmington Road.

The Sheltons were not in the same league as gang-leaders Al Capone or Dutch Schultz, but their exploits had a legendary ring nevertheless. Back in the 1920's, the Sheltons and the Birgers had fought a five-year war in Southern Illinois using tanks, armored trucks, machine guns, and bombs. An estimated forty lives had been lost in the warfare. The Sheltons attracted wide attention during the Prohibition era. They muscled into Peoria shortly after Woodruff was reelected to his last term in 1941. They controlled gambling in the area until Mayor Carl O. Triebel, who succeeded Woodruff on a reform platform, closed down all gambling here.

The Sheltons originally came here as bodyguards and in their typical fashion, took over those relatively peaceable gamblers they had been hired to protect. Carl, the elder Shelton, headed their operation with a certain suaveness, but Bernie operated with considerably more roughness. He was, in fact, under indictment on charges of assault to kill as a result of a fight in his tavern on May 30, 1948, when he allegedly pistol-whipped an ex-Marine patron, James Murphy.

The end for the gang came with surprising quickness. Carl, head of the Shelton gang for years, was shot and killed from ambush near the family home at Fairfield in October, 1947. Bernie was killed by a single shot from a big game hunting rifle fired from a hilly area behind St. Joseph's Cemetery on the morning of July 26, 1948.

The killing set off a chain of reverberations that shook Peoria's official circles for months. Some of the revelations of graft and corruption were said to have helped propel Adlai Stevenson into the governer's chair at Springfield, and shortly after the Peoria killing, a United States Senate investigating committee, headed by Estes Kefauver, began its probe of the nation-wide operations of major gambling syndicates.

Peoria Police files, like those in any major city, are filled with unsolved crimes. But one of the most bizarre and sensational occurred on March 10, 1947, when George P. McNear, President of the T.P.&W. Railroad, was shot to death at 10:40 p.m. at the intersection of Moss and Sheridan.

His railroad at the time was undergoing a bitter strike. A year earlier, on February 6, 1946, five strikers had been shot by railroad guards in a confrontation at Gridley, Illinois. Two strikers died from their wounds.

The night he was killed, McNear was walking to his home at 202 Moss Avenue, following a Bradley Basketball game, played at the National Guard Armory at Hancock and Adams Streets. Bradley supposedly won the game, beating Colorado College 57-56; but the game was awarded to Colorado since the official timer's clock had stopped late in the game, enabling Bradley to score an illegal winning basket.

After leaving the game, McNear walked up Main to High Street, along High to Sheridan and north on Sheridan toward Moss. There he was struck by a single shotgun blast.

Ironically, in the shooting at Gridley, 12-gauge 00 buckshot had been used by the guards in the episode which killed Irwin Paschon and Arthur Browne of Peoria. McNear was killed with the same type shell which killed Paschon and Browne. Four months after McNear's death, the strike against his railroad was settled.

T.P.&W. RAILROAD PRESIDENT GEORGE P. McNEAR. (PEORIA PUBLIC LIBRARY).

236

Peoria in the 1950's entered an era of reform in government and growth in commerce and industry. The old, rip-roaring, wide-open, rivertown days ended and for most people, there were few regrets.

The city's reputation, tarnished though it may have been, was somewhat enhanced by a steady stream of performers who started here and went on to the big time.

Jim and Marian Jordan were native Peorians who met at a church choir practice when they were in their teens, got married in 1918, and began working the vaudeville circuit, finally getting into the new world of radio in 1925. They ultimately become "Fibber McGee and Molly" with a show of such nation-wide appeal that it remained on the air from 1935 until 1960.

Among the other Peorians who became famous in the entertainment business were Charles Correll, who was "Andy" of the long-running "Amos and Andy" show, movie actor Guy Kibbee, comic Richard Pryor, and composer and singer Dan Fogelberg.

FIBBER McGEE AND MOLLY.
(PEORIA JOURNAL STAR FILES).

GUY KIBBEE, MOVIE ACTOR.
(STUDIO PHOTO).

DAN FOGELBERG. (JOEL
BERNSTEIN PHOTO, COURTESY
PEORIA JOURNAL STAR).

RICHARD PRYOR WHILE
FILMING "JO JO DANCER" IN
PEORIA, MAY 1985. (RENEE
BYER PHOTO, COURTESY
PEORIA JOURNAL STAR).

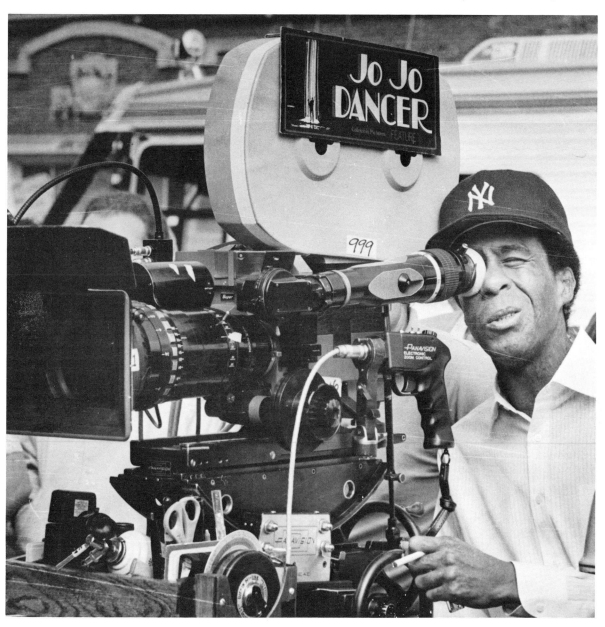

238

Louis B. Neumiller

During some of its greatest years, Caterpillar Tractor Co. had as its chief executive a kind, soft-spoken man who managed to keep the personal touch while running the world's biggest earthmoving business.

Louis B. Neumiller, who joined the firm as a clerk in 1915, retired from his full-time duties in 1962, having witnessed the growth of a small company, The Holt Manufacturing Company, with about 250 employees, to an international firm with over 35,000 employees.

Neumiller was already company president by the time the United States entered World War II. At that time the East Peoria plant produced transmissions and drive assemblies for tanks as well as howitzer carriages. Throughout the war it supplied the bulldozers and motor graders that scraped out airfields across the Pacific islands and helped win fame for the company and the reliability of its equipment.

When Neumiller moved into the chairman's position in 1954, he took the chief executive's responsibilities with him and Caterpillar continued to grow. When he retired in 1962, Caterpillar had doubled its plant space and tripled net assets since the war. During his twenty-one years as chief executive, sales and profits rose seven-fold, and so did wages paid.

There was, during the Neumiller years, a definite Caterpillar spirit, a pride in the product and a feeling among workers that this was the best place to work. Neumiller was a president and chairman who regarded his workers as humans, not numbers. "I managed to keep the personal touch," he once said. "You make friends one at a time. No great strokes or sweeps are going to occur. You win them one at a time, not in great bunches."

Peoria has its share of authors as well. Philip Jose Farmer, science fiction prize-winner, moved to the west coast after working in Peoria, but returned to do his best work here, including his "Riverworld" series. Thomas S. Klise, former broadcaster and religious writer, not only founded his own filmstrip company which originated religious, historical, and literary titles that have been sold throughout the nation, but wrote an epic novel, THE LAST WESTERN, which has attracted a steady and lasting audience. Other writers include Daniel Smythe, Bradley University's poet laureate; poet James Ballowe; essayist and critic Dennis McInerny; scholar and historian Romeo B. Garrett, Charles John Clancy; Jirac Disslerov; David Pichaske; and Jerry Klein.

All of these, along with Octave Chanute, Charles Duryea, and numerous captains of industry, educators, lawyers, preachers, doctors, musicians, and businessmen, are or were Peorians who lived and worked here, at least for a while. They left their stamp on the city and took some of its flavor with them.

If a city is like a family, every one of its members, famous or little known - it matters not - has helped to shape the whole. Peoria is what her people have made it, and will be tomorrow as well.

240

Peoria Churches and Synagogues founded before 1900. Some of these have since disbanded or merged with other congregations. Others have been renamed.

African Methodist Episcopal:
1846, Ward Chapel

Apostolic Christian:
1873, Sheridan Road

Baptist:
1836, First Baptist
1852, State Park
1879, Mt. Zion
1891, Bethany

Catholic:
1846, St. Mary's
1889, Cathedral dedicated
1853, St. Joseph's
1861, St. Patrick's
1878, Sacred Heart
1881, St. Boniface
1890, St. John's
1891, St. Mark's

Christian:
1845, Central

Christian Science:
1892, First

Congregational:
1834, First
1890, Union
1892, Averyville

Episcopal:
1834, St. John's
1848, St. Paul's
1874, Christ Reformed
1896, St. Andrew's
1898, St. Stephen's

Evangelical United Brethren:
1843, First
1896, Grace

Jewish:
1858, Anshai Emeth Temple
1886, Agudas Achim
*   Synagogue*

Lutheran, American:
1853, St. Paul's
1855, St. John's
1894, Zion

Lutheran, Augustana:
1883, Salem Swedish

Lutheran, Missouri Synod:
1857, Trinity

Methodist Episcopal:
1833, First
1852, German Methodist

Methodist:
1860, First Methodist,
*   East Peoria*
1868, Hale
1894, Averyville
1896, Grace

Methodist, Free:
1881, First Peoria Free
1882, First E. Peoria Free

Missions:
1888, Bacon

Presbyterian:
1834, First
1853, Second
1867, Calvary
1868, Grace
1887, Bethel
1896, Arcadia
1897, Westminster

Reformed:
1869, First

Universalist:
1843, First

PEORIA HISTORIC CHURCHES, FIRST BAPTIST (TOP LEFT), FIRST CONGREGATIONAL (TOP CENTER), ST. PAUL'S EPISCOPAL (TOP RIGHT) AND FIRST M.E. (BOTTOM LEFT), GERMAN EV. LUTHERAN (BOTTOM CENTER) AND FIRST PRESBYTERIAN (BOTTOM RIGHT).

WESTMINSTER PRESBYTERIAN CHURCH, 564 MOSS. THE BUILDING WAS DEDICATED IN 1899 AND BURNED ON JAN. 21, 1985.

THE AGUDAS ACHIM SYNAGOGUE AT THE END OF SHIPMAN, ABOUT 1950. (LEE ROTEN PHOTO).

ST. MARY'S CATHEDRAL DURING CONSTRUCTION.

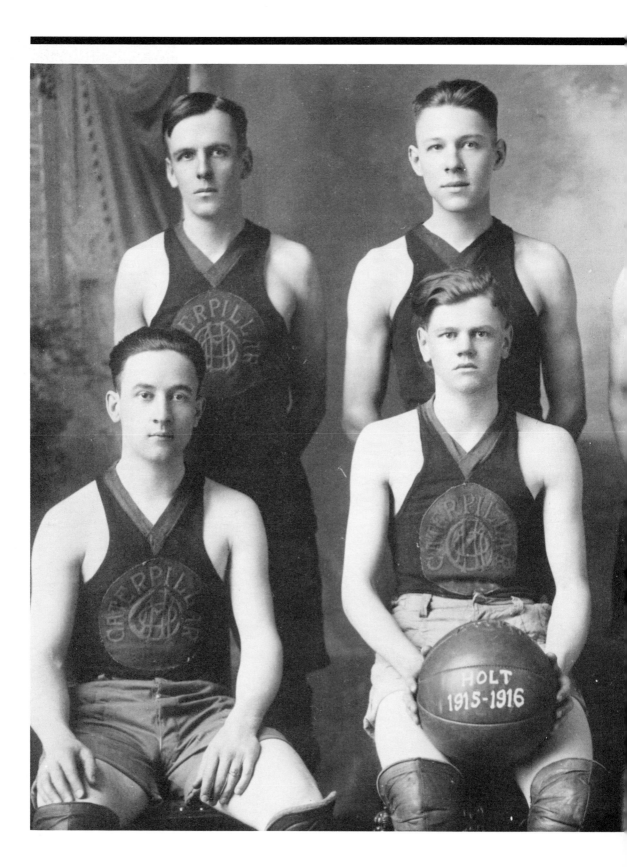

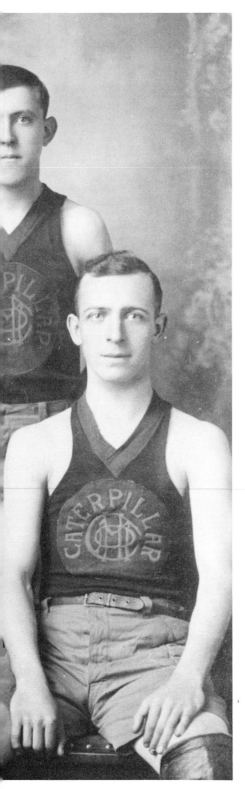

CHAPTER TEN

The early days of baseball. The famous
Five at Bradley to the 1949-50 basketball
scandal. Ups and downs of professional
sports. The situation today and the
opportunities for participation.

LOUIS B. NEUMILLER, (BACK
ROW, CENTER) LATER
CATERPILLAR PRESIDENT, AS
A MEMBER OF THE FIRM'S
1915-16 BASKETBALL TEAM.
(CATERPILLAR PHOTO).

244

KEN OLSON   CARL SCHUNK   DAR HUTCHINS   CH

In the DE GANNE MEMOIR, supposedly written by Tonti's cousin, the Sieur de Liette, there is an account of the Indian tribes around Peoria Lake participating in a violent game that was apparently a combination of jai alai and la crosse. If true, it would make sports one of the earliest recorded activities at the site of what was to become Peoria.

It was not until the middle of the nineteenth century, however, that organized athletics began to have an impact on the city. The early pioneers had neither the time nor the inclination for such activities. The first accounts of any serious athletic undertaking involved the German immigrants with their Turnverein societies, which generally emphasized personal fitness rather than competitive events.

TED PANISH   LES GETZ

The modern era of sports emphasis here undoubtedly began when a basketball team from an almost unknown Bradley Polytechnic Institute propelled the school and the city into national prominence. The team, known as "The Famous Five," compiled a 52-9 record from 1936 to 1939 and remained undefeated in conference competition. The team was invited to the first NIT tournament in New York in March, 1938, where it lost its opening game to Temple of Philadelphia. "The Famous Five" was invited back to the second NIT the following year, but instead accepted a bid to the first NCAA tournament, where it won 3rd place by defeating St. John's of New York.

BRADLEY'S FAMOUS FIVE—FROM LEFT, KEN OLSON, CARL SCHUNK, DAR HUTCHINS, CHUCK ORSBORN, TED PANISH AND LES GETZ. (PHOTO BY LEE ROTEN FROM A MURAL IN THE ROBERTSON FIELDHOUSE).

246

BRADLEY'S FAMOUS COACH, A.J. ROBERTSON. (COURTESY PEORIA JOURNAL STAR).

Head of the team was A. J. Robertson, who at one time also coached the football and baseball teams. "The Famous Five" actually consisted of more than five players. They were Ted Panish, Chuck Orsborn, Les Getz, Kenny Olson, Dar Hutchins, Carl Schunk, Bobby Theus, Paul Nunes, and Meyer Jacobs. Orsborn later became coach and athletic director at Bradley and the theatre in Bradley's Hartmann Center for the Performing Arts, converted from the gymnasium where the "Famous Five" once practiced, is named after Meyer Jacobs.

Bradley basketball has remained big time ever since. The famous 1949-1950 team finished second in both the NIT and NCAA tournaments, although its record was somewhat tarnished by charges of point-shaving. Bradley was ranked first in the final three Associated Press Polls that season, losing to City College of New York in both the NIT and NCAA championship games. It was the only time the same two teams competed in the two major tournaments in the same year.

Some of the University's better known players over the years include Paul Unruh, Gene Melchiorre, Billy Mann, Bobby Joe Mason, Chet Walker, and Roger Phegley.

Another Bradley standout was Billy Stone, who played for the university and the Chicago Bears, and was the school's last football coach when Bradley's seventy-year history in that sport ended at the close of the 1970 season.

A NEWSPAPER ACCOUNT OF THE FAMOUS FIVE BEATING WESLEYAN. (PEORIA JOURNAL STRANSCRIPT).

THE LEGENDARY PITCHER
"OLD HOSS" RADBOURN.
(PEORIA JOURNAL STAR).

"IRON MAN" McGINNITY.
(PEORIA JOURNAL STAR).

MEMBERS OF THE PEORIA
CHIEFS AT PLAY. (LINDA
HENSON PHOTO, PEORIA
JOURNAL STAR).

Baseball has an even longer history in the city. Among the famous early baseball players was Charlie "Old Hoss" Radbourn who was a pitcher for the Peoria Reds in 1878. He became known as "Daddy of All Pitchers." Radbourn supposedly had the ability to throw a ball alongside a wall and make it curve out of sight when it reached the corner.

Joe "Iron Man" McGinnity was another pitcher who had his beginnings here and ultimately was inducted into the Hall of Fame. He pitched for the Peoria Distillers in 1898. Later he moved into the major leagues and still holds the record for pitching the most double headers on one day - five - and for the most innings pitched in a season, 434.

Herb Jamieson, a native Peorian, competed in the first renewal of the Olympic Games at Athens in 1896, winning a first in the 400-meter semifinals and second in the finals, capturing a silver medal for his efforts.

Some of the most colorful and memorable games - baseball and football alike - occurred at Peoria's old Woodruff Field. Special streetcars carried fans to the games at this gem of a minor league field with its covered grandstand, fully equipped

248

WOODRUFF FIELD FROM THE AIR. NORTH ADAMS STREET IS IN THE BACKGROUND. (RAY BARCLAY PHOTO, LEE ROTEN COLLECTION).

Organized baseball in Peoria began about 1862 when the Olympic Baseball Club was organized. Two teams from this club played to a tie and the game was called after both had scored thirty-nine runs.

In July, 1878, the Peoria "Reds" defeated the Boston National League team. Charles Radbourn, who later became a National League pitcher, was on the Peoria team. Another member was Tom Loftus, who was to become the manager of the Cleveland Indians.

The Northwestern League was formed in 1882 and native Peorian George B. Pinkney was a member of the team. He later became a star third baseman of the Brooklyn Dodgers and played in 578 consecutive games from 1885 to 1890. Another member of the Peoria team was W.D. (Darby) O'Brien, who also became a Brooklyn player. They both had been members of the Peoria "Reds." Other professional players of the era who had their start here were Charles Bartson, pitcher, and Ed Dougdale, catcher.

In 1888, the Western League was formed. In a game played on July 26, 1898, Joe "Iron Man" McGinnity pitched twenty-one innings in a victory over St. Joseph. He later starred with the New York Giants.

The Three "I" League (Illinois, Indiana, Iowa) was formed in 1905. The Peoria team originally was known as the "Distillers" and later the "Tractors." In 1916, pitcher Paul Moore went twenty-two innings in a win over Clinton, Iowa. Games were played at Lake View Park, at the site of the present WABCO building, from the beginning of the century until 1923, when Woodruff Field was opened adajacent to it.

In July of 1930, the first game was played at Woodruff Field under lights. Some of the Three "I" Leaguers who graduated to the majors included Dick Egan, Bobby Veach, Charlie Dressen, Ossie Bluege, Walter Holtke, Tony Lazzeri, Tommy Sheehan, Pat Malone, Phil Cavaretta, Ben Coffryn, Bobby O'Farrell, and Liver Lebourveau.

In 1937, organized baseball in Peoria ceased temporarily because of the inroads of the depression.

dugouts and press box. It was located on Grant Street, just off Adams. It is now the site of a softball field. Three-I League and semi-pro football drew huge crowds and there are hundreds of older people today who got their first introduction to baseball as members of the "Knothole Club," which allowed them special ticket prices and other privileges. High school football games were played there as well until the Peoria Stadium was built toward the end of the depression.

However, except for Bradley basketball, which moved in 1949 from the Armory into the new fieldhouse with its 7000 seats and into the Civic Center in 1983 with its 10,000 seats, major sports in Peoria virtually vanished for a time. Semi-professional baseball collapsed around 1957 with the departure of the "Chiefs" and the demolition of Woodruff Field. While there were such popular sports practiced as bowling, golf, soccer, hockey, the Golden Gloves prize fighting competition and sailing on the Illinois River, most of these were done on a amateur level.

There were exceptions. A Peoria sailor, Ralph Bradley, captured third place in the world's championship of the Star Class on Long Island Sound in 1932 and won the Great Lakes championship in 1930, 1931, 1932, and 1937. Peoria was one of the first cities in the country to inaugurate a city golf competition for men in 1927, and it staged the Women's Western Tournament here in 1933 and the Men's Western in 1934. THE PEORIA STAR, under sports editor Fred Tuerk, started the first Brothers Bowling Tournament in the country. It remains to this day the largest of such competitions as well as the oldest.

Not until recent times, however, have major professional sports returned to Peoria. One of the first tenants at the new Civic Center Arena, now named after ex-Mayor Richard Carver, was the city's first professional hockey team, originally known as "The Prancers." The team was renamed "The Rivermen" in 1984, and is owned and operated by the Civic Center Authority.

250

NATIONAL SILVER GLOVES
MATCH, BRADLEY FIELDHOUSE,
JUNE, 1985. (JOURNAL STAR
PHOTO BY LINDA HENSON).

Until boxing was legalized in 1925, Illinois law provided severe penalties for principals and promoters of prize fights. Peoria was long known for its pugilistic exhibitions. In the early days, the bouts were held on a river barge or in some place most likely to escape police interference.

James Kenney, who wrote the history of Peoria boxing for a special edition of the Journal Transcript, *May 24, 1936, reviewed the careers of fighters, promoters, and boxing clubs for the previous half-century. Patsy Cardiff, a Peoria County coal miner, gained local renown as a heavyweight in 1884; and after a number of victories, was matched with Champion John L. Sullivan in an exhibition at Minneapolis in January, 1884. Cardiff took a lot of punishment but lasted the full six rounds and the match was called a draw.*

Kenny and Charlie Bartson were among the most active promoters at the turn of the century. Bouts were staged in Weast's Theater, Central Park, the Marquette Club, and Pfeiffer's Hall. State and local law-enforcing officers looked kindly upon the sport and although protests were made at intervals by reform elements, prize-fights were advertised publicly and drew large crowds. Peoria for many years was one of the few cities in the Middle West in which fights could be staged without interference from the law.

Young Kid Farmer (Harry Tibbets), a local lightweight, fought at Bartson's shows, won numerous bouts with quick knockouts, and might have been a champion. Billy Papke won several of his early matches in Peoria and went on to win the middleweight championship. Tommy Gibbons, Sammy Mandell, Johnny Coulon, Abe Attell, Packey McFarland, and other pugilistic stars fought at Weast's Theater.

—Ernest East,
  History of Peoria

While prize-winning teams are not unique here, a new chapter in sports history was written on May 24, 1985, when the Peoria "Rivermen," the city's International Hockey League team, beat the Muskegon "Lumberjacks" before a record hockey crowd of 9224 at the Carver Arena and won The League championship. This was the third year for professional hockey in Peoria. For two years, the Peoria team was known as the "Prancers." The "Rivermen's" franchise is owned by the Peoria Civic Center Authority.

THE PEORIA RIVERMEN'S RICK HENDRICKS HOLDS THE TURNER CUP ALOFT AFTER THE TEAM WON ITS PRIZE IN MAY, 1985. (AL HARKRADER PHOTO PEORIA JOURNAL STAR).

THE PEORIA RIVERMEN CELEBRATE WINNING THE TURNER CUP, MAY, 1985, PEORIA CIVIC CENTER. (CIVIC CENTER PHOTO BY CEDRIC THOMPSON).

252

JACK BRICKHOUSE OF WGN, FORMERLY OF WMBD, PEORIA. (PEORIA JOURNAL STAR).

Minor League baseball, as well, has returned to the city. Meinen Field, named for Bradley's Athletic Director from 1956 to 1964, John "Dutch" Meinen, has been extensively remodeled and enlarged. It originally accommodated a Los Angeles Angels farm team. The franchise is now owned by Peorian Pete Vonachen and the "Peoria Chiefs" are a part of the Chicago Cubs farm system.

The city's proximity to both Chicago and St. Louis has made this both "Cardinal" and "Cub" country. Jack Brickhouse, long the voice of the Chicago Cubs, got his start in Peoria where he broadcast sports for WMBD radio.

High school sports continue to draw enormous crowds of students and adults. Among Peoria's more famous coaches over the years are Salen Herke, John Nopenberger, Bill Robertson, Dawdy Hawkins, Tony Juska, and Harry Whittaker of Peoria High School; Bob Wilford, Paul Holliday, Bob Jauron, Ken Hinrichs, John Wilkinson, and Telfer Mead of Manual; Sport McGrath, Ron Patterson, Ed Murphy, Jim Smarjesse, Merv Haycock, and Ennio Arboit of Spalding; Byron Moore, Harvey Stamper, and Clarence Allison of East Peoria; Bob Baietto, Ty Franklin, Wayne Hammerton, and Tom Peeler of Richwoods; Don Mathews and Jim Heid of Bergan; Tom Correll, Virg Boucher, Roy Gummerson and Ray Wolf of Woodruff.

With its professional teams and Bradley basketball, there is sufficient opportunity in Peoria for spectators. Perhaps even more important are the opportunities for participants. With the Peoria Park District's far-reaching summer softball programs, the golf courses, tennis courts, bowling alleys, health clubs, swimming pools, hiking, and cross-country ski trails plus special events for runners and cyclists, there are possibilities for athletes of almost every age and proficiency level. The city offers the unique benefits of being able to watch the games played by professionals on their way to the Major Leagues, such as "Rivermen" hockey, "Chiefs" baseball, and Bradley basketball. Perhaps even more important is the fact that in a city such as Peoria, being able to play the game remains the most important opportunity.

BRADLEY'S BARNEY MINES, MEMBER OF THE BRADLEY 1982 NATIONAL INVITATIONAL TOURNAMENT CHAMPIONSHIP TEAM, IS SURROUNDED BY TWO TULSA PLAYERS DURING A GAME AT THE PEORIA CIVIC CENTER IN JANUARY, 1983. (JOURNAL STAR PHOTO BY LINDA HENSON)

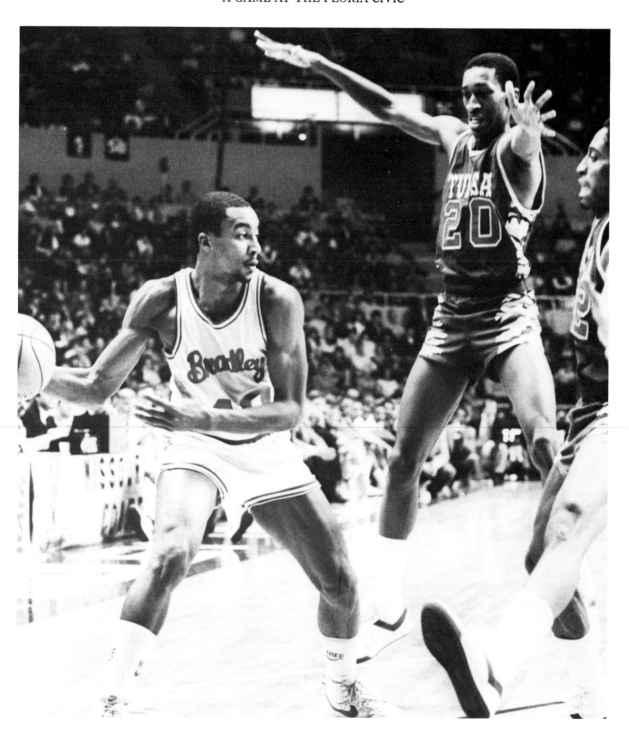

CHAPTER ELEVEN

PEORIA TODAY: A CITY WITH A PAST AND A PROMISE

The slow evolution of the city from blue collar to the present "Little Apple." Changing downtown. The exodus to the suburbs. What makes Peoria a good place to live. The cultural attractions. The new Peoria.

PEORIA'S SKYLINE AND RIVERFRONT REPRESENT A RICH HERITAGE AND A FIRM COMMITMENT TO THE FUTURE. (VISUAL COMMUNICATIONS PHOTO).

256

By the middle of the 1980's, Peoria's reputation as a pocket of prosperity, despite the prevailing nationwide recession, had begun to erode. Caterpillar, the city's major employer, was suffering from a series of reverses because of increasing foreign competition, a strong U. S. currency in the world market, and the reduced demand for earth-moving equipment felt by the industry. Unemployment was running between seven and ten per cent, and with each announcement of cutbacks and layoffs, the mood of pessimism deepened. The gloom at its lowest point was typified by the appearance of signs reading, "Will the last person to leave Peoria please turn out the lights." The city countered with its own campaign: "Keep the lights on. We're staying."

In the early 1960's, the downtown area had suffered much the same fate that had struck so many cities throughout the country. The rise of suburban shopping malls, the new freeways, and the increasing mobility of the American family had dramatically affected the downtown area, and one by one the retail stores left. Clarke's and Peoria Dry Goods went out of business, Block and Kuhl was bought by Carson, Pirie, Scott and Company and moved into Northwoods Mall, as did J. C. Penney and Montgomery Ward. The old five-and-ten-cent stores vanished and were replaced by huge discount stores that arose in the growing area to the northwest. Gift shops and specialty stores followed, buildings emptied out, and the proud old downtown began to deteriorate.

No longer did hordes of shoppers surge across Fulton Street between Block's and Bergner's at each change of the lights. Traffic, both vehicular and pedestrian, declined alarmingly. Patrons emerging from late movies at the Palace, Rialto, or Madison were likely to find a near-empty city.

But in the mid 1960's, moves were already being made to revitalize downtown. The first major effort grew from the formation of the Downtown Development Corporation, spearheaded by the Commercial National Bank. The initial results were spectacular. Caterpillar's impressive home office was built in the 100 block of South Adams, replacing rows of musty nineteenth century buildings. The old, baroque Peoria Courthouse was replaced by a new, efficient building, and its grounds, destined to become a blacktopped parking lot, were instead developed into an attractive garden and plaza, largely because of the determination of interested citizens. First Federal Savings and Loan erected its skyscraper, known as the Savings Tower, at the corner of Jefferson and Hamilton; the new Security Savings Building arose at Hamilton and Adams. Sears Roebuck and Company was persuaded to

THE FORMER CLARKE'S STORE AT MAIN AND ADAMS DURING DEMOLITION, 1980. (LEE ROTEN PHOTO).

258

DESIGN CONCEPT FOR A NEW
DOWNTOWN PEORIA BY
ANGELOS C. DEMETRIOU.

remain downtown and moved into its new building on
Washington Street and Bergner's remained as well with a
complete remodeling of its store at Fulton and Adams.

Although the exodus to the suburbs was not exactly reversed,
downtown had at least gained some breathing time. And as
Peoria moved into the 1970's and 1980's, its old business
district began to take on a new and inviting character. A
series of "Brown-Bag-It" events in the Courthouse Plaza
brought everything from string quartets and ballet to folk
music and the symphony into the heart of the city for
immensely popular noontime concerts. The grand old Pere
Marquette Hotel with its chandeliers and glittering splendor
became part of the Hilton chain and was modernized but
gradually declined. It was restored with most of its grandeur
intact and reopened in 1983.

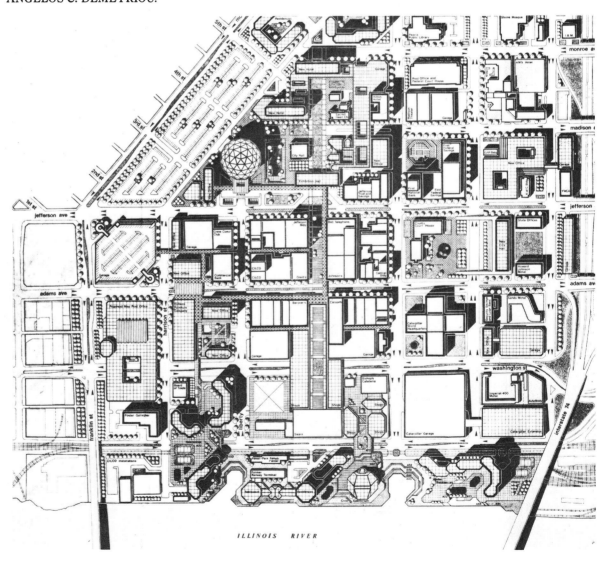

ILLINOIS RIVER

PART OF A NOONTIME CROWD
AT THE COURTHOUSE PLAZA
IN JUNE, 1985. (JERRY KLEIN
PHOTO).

260

THE NEW COURTHOUSE
PLAZA IN THE LATE 1960'S.
(LEE ROTEN PHOTO).

DOWNTOWN PEORIA, BEFORE
ITS REBIRTH IN THE 1960'S.

One of the early boosters of the city was a Peoria minister, the Rev. Asahel Augustus Stevens, pastor of the Main Street Congregational Church, which stood where the Madison Theatre is now located. During a Thanksgiving Day sermon delivered November 27, 1873, at the Fulton Street Presbyterian Church, he suggested the beautification of the city was not only a matter of public spirit but true benevolence.

"It is our duty also to seek the improvement of our city in its general appearance," he said. "We should aim to make it aesthetically what nature designed it to be, beautiful for situation, the joy of this whole region. God does not give such beautiful sites that we may deform them.

"Such variety, such diversity, with such sweet symmetry and beauty and fine facilities for enlargement and perfection, I do think, are no where else to be found. And I hope the people who dwell here will yet become worthy of their place and surrounding, so as to make them more nearly what they should be.

"Who can help feeling that this city is worth saving? Who would not like to see Peoria the thriving mart of trade, the center of boundless manufacturing, the place of beautiful residences, the city of rare intellectual taste and culture, the most delightful home of the great interior state, and the safest, most honest, most moral and principled city anywhere to be found? Then let us try to make it such. What a destiny awaits us if we can make the world feel that Peoria can be trusted! What a future we have before us if God our maker can be duly exalted here and His law be written on our hearts and carried out in our lives! Let the hope inspire us. And let the high aspirations cheer us on to noble endeavors, to act well our individual part in promoting such glad consummation."

262

In the meantime, downtown experienced both crushing reverses and startling new developments. The former Voyager Inn at Hamilton and Madison was purchased by a group headed by G. Raymond Becker and enlarged into a major hotel, the Continental Regency, with an adjacent office building and parking deck. A grandiose plan for downtown renewal, formulated by Washington, D. C. city planner Angelos Demetriou, seemed at the point of becoming another dream to be consigned to the files and forgotten. Downtown's progress remained largely esthetic. Not even the completion of the Fulton Mall with its bricks, trees, and fountains was sufficient to reverse the flow of people away from downtown. Ambitious plans for a new downtown shopping mall mushroomed and collapsed with depressing regularity. For every step forward, there was a price to be paid.

Even the decision to build the long-awaited Civic Center with its theatre, arena, and exhibition hall had its drawbacks, for it required that the old Jefferson Hotel be demolished, a spectacular event which was recorded as part of a now-forgotten Hollywood disaster movie. The busy and vital Rialto theatre, which had been the Hippodrome of the vaudeville era, also gave way to the Civic Center. Another old-time theatre, the Palace, was demolished to make way for G. Raymond Becker's Twin Towers, a downtown condominium project which is, for the first time, bringing a significant number of full-time residents into the heart of the city and which is now Peoria's tallest building with its twenty-nine stories.

THE ROCK ISLAND ROCKET AT THE DEPOT, FOOT OF FULTON STREET, IN THE 1930'S.

THE PEORIA CIVIC CENTER ARENA UNDER CONSTRUCTION, 1980. (LEE ROTEN PHOTO).

RONALD BLADEN'S SCULPTURE, "SONAR TIDE" IN FRONT OF THE PEORIA CIVIC CENTER THEATER. (LEE ROTEN PHOTO).

If the character of downtown has changed considerably from the time when it was the center of virtually all activity, there are some advantages that are almost immediately apparent. Appearance is one. In addition to the carefully landscaped attractions of the Courthouse Plaza and Fulton Mall, there are streets lined with trees and areas of greenery around the Civic Center and the restored City Hall. Sculpture downtown once was limited to Fritz Triebel's heroic Civil War Memorial at the courthouse. Now there are the WPA-era statues of "Peace" and "Harvest" at the courthouse as well, Triebel's "Love Knows No Caste" in the foyer of City Hall, Trova's "Gox" at the Peoria School of Medicine, and the enormous Ronald Bladen work, "Sonar Tide," at the Civic Center.

If there is a ripple effect from beautification, Peoria's downtown stands as a striking example. The restoration of the long-abandoned Rock Island Depot into an elegant and beautifully landscaped restaurant, The River Station, is one result. Another is the inclusion of an outdoor courtyard at Jim's Steakhouse, and the almost complete restoration of the block of Main Street across from the courthouse. The Christmas lights in the Courthouse Plaza have become a long-standing attraction and the trees and flowers that grace the Twin Towers complex add yet another touch of urban greenery to an area that once was all brick and sidewalk.

Much of the impetus for this has come from Peoria City Beautiful, which yearly awards "orchids" to firms and organizations which have made their premises more attractive, and "onions" to those distinguished rather for their ugliness and litter.

264

While it took newspaper editor Eugene Baldwin less than two years to get a Grand Opera House for Peoria in the early 1880's, the building of the Peoria Civic Center in the 1980's was a project that remained in the talking and planning stages for decades. Such a development was proposed as early as 1932. And over the next 50 years elaborate schemes were routinely unveiled and shelved.

Not until Washington architect and city planner Angelos Demetrious was engaged to design a plan for a revitalized downtown Peoria

THE PEORIA CIVIC CENTER HAS MADE IT POSSIBLE FOR EVENTS SUCH AS RINGLING BROS.—BARNUM AND BAILEY CIRCUS TO COME TO PEORIA.

did things finally begin to come together. His original drawings included a geodesic dome, or golfball, as the arena, and a turtle-shaped auditorium, the latter located on the riverfront.

His plans were later modified in a design by the Phillip Johnson - John Burgee firm to include the present unified complex. Even then, however, there remained considerable opposition to the inclusion of the theatre portion. Experts and consultants insisted it would be a money-loser. Nearly lost as well were one of the most distinguishing features of the complex, its linking, jewel-like glass arcades.

But the Civic Center has been a major factor in the revitalization of downtown

Peoria, not only from a cultural and entertainment standpoint, but from a commercial one as well. It has been estimated that the Civic Center, with its hockey, symphonies, opera, ice shows, rock concerts, circuses, conventions and theatre has been instrumental in over $100 million in private business dollars invested in downtown Peoria and surrounding areas, including Twin Towers, the Hotel Pere Marquette, the Continental Regency, restaurants and the like.

History is being repeated. What Baldwin's Grand Opera House did for Peoria a hundred years ago, the Civic Center is doing today.

The changing character of downtown, from a center of virtually all the city's activities to a focal point of commerce and entertainment, has not been completed. The possibilities for a downtown mall or a development of shops and restaurants along the riverfront remain alive. The old Madison Theatre, last of the great movie palaces, is scheduled to reopen as a dinner theatre with live professional entertainment, which would complete a cycle started in the great days of show business here.

The evolution of the city, which might be characterized by that which has occurred downtown, extends into areas far more important than renewal of the central city or cosmetic attractions, for Peoria, in its 300th year, has become a city in transition. The former hard-muscled, blue-collar factory town into which industry once imported thousands of laborers from the South has become something quiet different. The breweries and distilleries are gone; the reputation of the city as a wide-open, hard-drinking town with its red-light district, strip shows, and mobsters is no longer valid. Neither is that convenient characterization of Peorians as the most typical and provincial of all Americans.

It might be argued, on the contrary, that Peoria has become what might be called "The Little Apple;" that is, a moderate-sized city with many of the benefits of a major metropolis and with few of the disadvantages. The theatre, the visual arts, symphonic music, sports, opera, ballet, movies, and pop concerts are not only accessible here, but affordable, which is not often the case in Chicago or New York. And Peorians not only have the opportunity, but take it, to attend exhibitions, the Symphony, Peoria Players and Corn Stock, the "Chiefs" professional baseball team, the "Rivermen" professional hockey team, and Bradley University basketball.

Our attractions admittedly are not on a par with the Chicago Symphony or the St. Louis Cardinals, but they are here, they are affordable, and most are within a ten to fifteen minute drive. On a per capita basis, in fact, more Peorians participate in the city's cultural, athletic, and leisure activities than do the citizens of far larger cities.

Over half a million people a year, for example, attend concerts, art galleries, plays, and other similar events. Lakeview Museum alone draws 350,000 annually, and the symphony over 16,000. Another 420,000 participate in such events as the Heart of Illinois Fair, the Olde English Faire at Jubilee, Steamboat Days, and the Jubilee Harvestfest. The Peoria Park District encompasses some 8200 acres, which includes the almost primitive and untouched Forest Park off Galena Road. And Wildlife Prairie Park with its 1300 acres provides a rare opportunity to see native wildlife in its natural habitat.

JACK NICKLAUS AT PEORIA'S NEWMAN GOLF COURSE IN AUGUST, 1962 IN A SPECIAL EXHIBITION MATCH. (JOURNAL STAR PHOTO BY CARL MERCER).

THERE ARE FIVE PUBLIC GOLF COURSES AND FOUR PRIVATE ONES IN PEORIA, INCLUDING FIFTY PUBLIC TENNIS COURTS, FOUR OUTDOOR POOLS, FIVE INDOOR POOLS, AND TWO ARTIFICIAL ICE SKATING RINKS.

266

A NEW MOTHER GREETS
HER BABY IN ONE OF PEORIA'S
MODERN HOSPITALS.
(METHODIST MEDICAL
CENTER PHOTO).

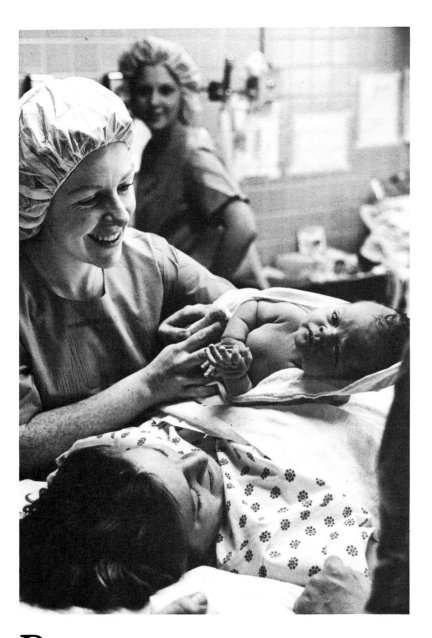

Peoria has emerged in recent times as a major center for health care with its three major hospitals, St. Francis, Methodist, and Proctor, and the University of Illinois School of Medicine. There are 1737 hospital beds and both Methodist and St. Francis have recently undergone or have in progress major expansion plans. Specialized health care facilities include the Institute for Physical Medicine and Rehabilitation at St. Francis, the St. Jude Children's Research Hospital Affiliate at Methodist, a veteran's outpatient clinic, the Allied Agencies Center, which provides special care for the handicapped, and the Zeller Zone Center.

The latter replaced the former Peoria State Hospital, where Doctor George Zeller instituted a series of sweeping reforms in the care of the mentally ill. His main focus was a considerably more humane treatment of the hospital's patients than was formerly practiced. He abolished virtually all forms of restraint, inaugurated an open-door policy except in the most violent cases, and generally brought to the institution the flavor of a sanitarium rather than that of a prison.

In its later years, the hospital site at Bartonville was utilized as an alcoholic treatment center. Several attempts have been made to convert the buildings and grounds to commercial and residential use but none have been successful. The only building still in operation is the theatre, which has been the location for several plays by the Campus Community Theatre. The remainder of the once park-like grounds is overgrown with weeds and abandoned.

In the past, the city also maintained the Peoria Tuberculosis Sanitarium off Forest Park Drive. It has been converted into an office and is home for an advertising firm.

The Northern Regional Research Laboratory of the United States Department of Agriculture contributed significantly to one of the major medical breakthroughs of the twentieth century when the method for the commercial production of penicillin was developed here.

General statistical data may have a dry and deadly flavor, but it is worth noting that there are almost twice as many churches as taverns in this formerly free-swinging river town. Peoria has 304 Protestant houses of worship, thirty-one Roman Catholic ones, two Jewish Synagogues, and Baha'i and Muslim Temples. And the city encompasses an area of forty-two square miles, making it almost exactly the same size as the city of Paris, excluding its suburbs.

The city has become known as well for the increasing quality and diversity of its restaurants. Dining out in Peoria once was routine and predictable, with half a dozen good places to go. Now there are scores of good restaurants of almost every ethnic variety and no longer is it necessary to venture to Chicago or St. Louis to experience either good or exotic restaurants. Despite what appears to be hard times, people are still experiencing this aspect of the good life here.

Neither the history of the city of Peoria nor its evolution are yet finished. From the erection of Fort Crevecoeur to 1985 is a timespan of 305 years, a relatively long time as American cities go, but a mere wink in the overall sweep of history.

268

ALMOST IN THE CENTER OF DOWNTOWN, TWIN TOWERS STRETCH 29 STORIES ABOVE FULTON MALL. (VISUAL COMMUNICATIONS PHOTO).

The changes in three centuries have been startling. From an outpost in the far-flung empire of Louis XIV, the Sun King, to a small French village with its tragic end, and on to an American frontier town, Peoria has passed through a remarkable evolution. It was a steamboat town, its wharves crowded with packets and excursion boats and a rail center so busy that the constant wail of whistles from arriving and departing trains was almost like a theme song. It was a coal-mining center, the world's most important whiskey city, the earth-moving capital of the universe, a sin city whose bars, strip houses, and red-light district attracted soldiers from Camp Ellis during World War II and thrill-seeking citizens from throughout the state. It was a major stop on the big-time vaudeville circuit, and more recently it has become an area-wide center for culture, entertainment, and recreation.

Some of Peoria's attractions, however, remain basically unchanged. It is still the only real city in Illinois outside of Chicago. The other major urban centers are either overgrown towns or shopping centers surrounded by endless suburbs. Peoria has a distinctive skyline, invariably a surprise to first-time visitors inward bound from the east on Interstate 74. It rises proudly at the foot of the hill, at the lower end of "Pimiteoui," the fat lake of the Indians, its tall buildings stabbing the sky at this old site that has been inhabited for over 250 years. Some claim it is the oldest continuous community west of the Alleghenies.

This is a city known throughout the world, partly because of its vaudeville reputation and the famous old song, "Oh How I Wish't I Was in Peoria," partly because of its rip-roaring, wide-open era, and partly because of the world-wide fame of Caterpillar Tractor Company, whose bulldozers helped scrape the way to victory in World War II.

This remains intact, this river and these bluffs, this rich and abundant land, the water, these hills and bluffs, these startling views. That happy combination of geology, nature, and man-made endeavor that have made the name "Peoria" one of the most enduring success stories in American history are still present and are still worth celebrating.

Peoria today has become a big-little city, economically besieged, perhaps, but a friendly, civil, cultured, appealing place to live. It is a city with an illustrious past and a future of boundless promise. It seems appropriate to call this place, and this book, Peoria!

270

BIBLIOGRAPHY

Chapters 1 through 4

Angle, Paul M., Editor and Compiler. Prairie State: Impressions of Illinois 1673-1967. Chicago, Illinois, University of Chicago Press, 1968.

Barrows, Harlan H. "Geography of the Middle Illinois Valley." Illinois State Geological Survey, Bulletin #15. Urbana, Illinois, State of Illinois, 1910.

Bateman, Newton. Editor. Historical Encyclopedia of Illinois, Volume 2. Chicago and Peoria, Illinois, Munsell Publishing Company, 1902.

Bess, F.B., Eine Populare Geschichte der Stadt Peoria. Peoria, 1906.

Custer, Milo. "Asiatic Cholera in Central Illinois from 1834-1873." Journal of the Illinois State Historical Society, Volume 23. Springfield, Illinois, Schnepp and Barnes, Printers, 1931.

Downing, Elliot Rowland. A Naturalist in the Great Lakes Region. Chicago, Illinois, The University of Chicago Press, 1922.

Drown, Simeon De Witt. The Peoria Directory for 1844. Peoria, Illinois, Printed for the Author, 1844.

Deuel, Thorne. "American Indian Ways of Life." Story of Illinois Series #9. Springfield, Illinois, Illinois State Museum, 1958.

Ellsworth, H.L. Illinois in 1837. Philadelphia, S.A. Mitchell Company, 1837.

Ellsworth, Spencer. Records of the Olden Times. Lacon, Illinois, Home Journal Steam Printing Establishment, 1880.

Farnham, Eliza W. Life in Prairie Land. New York, Harper and Brothers, 1846.

Gray, James. The Illinois. New York, Toronto, Farrar and Rinehart, Inc., 1940.

Hallwas, John E. Western Illinois Heritage. Macomb, Illinois, Illinois Heritage Press, 1983.

The History of Peoria County, Illinois. Chicago, Illinois, Johnson and Company, 1880.

Howard, Robert P. Illinois, A History of the Prairie State. Grand Rapids, Michigan, William B. Eerdmans Publishing Company, 1972.

Iliniwek, Volume #14, Nos. 1, 3, 4, January - December, 1976. East Peoria, Illinois, Richard M. Phillips, 1976.

The Illinois State Historical Society. Journal of the Illinois State Historical Society, Volumes 24, 30, and 46. Springfield, Illinois, State of Illinois, 1931, 1937, 1953.

Kofoid, Carrie Prudence. "Puritan Influences in the Formative Years of Illinois History." Transactions of the Illinois State Historical Society for the Year 1905. Illinois State Historical Library, Springfield, Illinois, Illinois State Journal Company, 1906.

Le Clercq, C. First Establishment of the Faith in New France, Volumes 1 and 2. New York, J.G. Shea, 1881.

Leighton, Morris M. "Pleistocene Studies." Report of Investigations, Bulletin 11. Urbana, Illinois, Illinois State Geological Survey, 1926.

Leverett, Frank. "The Illinois Glacial Lobe." United States Geological Survey, Vol. 38. Washington, D.C., United States Government Printing Office, 1899.

Livesay, Ann. The Past Speaks to You, The Story of Geology in Illinois. Springfield, Illinois, State of Illinois, 1951.

May, George W. Students' History of Peoria County, Illinois. Galesburg, Illinois, Wagoner Printing Company, 1968.

McDermott, John F. Editor. The French in the Mississippi Valley. Urbana, Illinois, University of Illinois Press, 1965.

McDermott, John F. Editor. Frenchmen and French Ways in the Mississippi Valley. Urbana, Illinois, University of Illinois Press, 1969.

McGoorty, Judge John P. "The Early Irish of Illinois." Papers in Illinois History and Transactions for the Year 1927, Illinois State Historical Library, Danville, Illinois, Illinois Printing Company, 1927.

Morison, Samuel E. Editor. The Parkman Reader from the Works of Francis Parkman. Boston, Massachusetts, Little, Brown and Company, 1955.

Nelson, Dr. C.S. "Medicine in the Illinois Country." Transactions of the Illinois State Historical Society for the Year 1925. Illinois State Historical Library, Springfield, Illinois, 1925.

Parkman, Francis. Jesuits in North America in the Seventeenth Century, Volumes 1 and 2. Boston, Massachusetts, Little, Brown and Company, 1867.

Parkman, Francis. LaSalle and the Discovery of the Great West. Boston, Massachusetts, Little, Brown and Company, 1907.

Ridgley, Douglas C. The Geography of Illinois. Chicago, Illinois, The University of Chicago Press, 1921.

St. Mary's of Lourdes. The Story of Our Parish. 1980.

Sauer, Carl Ortwin. "Geography of the Upper Illinois Valley and History of Development." Illinois State Geological Survey, Bulletin #27, Urbana, Illinois, University of Illinois, 1916.

Schlarman, J.H. From Quebec to New Orleans. Belleville, Illinois, Buechler Publishing Company, 1929.

Scott, James. The Illinois Nation, Part I. Streator, Illinois, Streator Historical Society, 1973.

Scott James. The Illinois Nation, Part II. Streator, Illinois, Streator Historical Society, 1976.

Shea, John Gilmary. Catholic Missions Among the Indian Tribes. New York, E. Dunigan and Brother, 1855.

Shea, John Gilmary. Discovery and Exploration of the Mississippi Valley. New York, Redfield, 1852.

Sheen, Dan R. Location of Fort Creve Coeur. Peoria, Illinois, Peoria Printing and Stationery Company, 1919.

Slane, Odillon B. Reminiscences of Early Peoria. Peoria, Illinois, Privately printed, 1933.

Smith, George W. History of Illinois and Her people, Volume I. Chicago and New York, The American Historical Society, Inc., 1927.

Snyder, John F. "Forgotten Statesmen of Illinois. Hon. Conrad Will." Transactions of the Illinois State Historical Society for the Year 1905. Illinois State Historical Library, Springfield, Illinois, Illinois State Journal Company, 1906.

Spooner, Harry L. Indians of Northern Illinois. Tiskilwa, Illinois, The Tiskilwa Chief, 1942.

Spooner, Harry L. The Site, Naming and Occupants of Fort Creve Coeur. Peoria, Illinois, typewritten manuscript, 1952.

Struever, Stuart and Holton, Felicia Antonelli. Koster: Americans in Search of Their Prehistoric Past. Garden City, New York, Anchor Press/Doubleday, 1979.

Temple, Wayne C. "Indian Villages of the Illinois Country." Illinois State Museum Scientific Papers, Volume II, Part 2. Springfield, Illinois, State of Illinois, 1966.

Thomas, Frank. Why Did They Come? Volumes 1, 2, and 3. Peoria, Illinois, WCBU Radio, 1983.

Thwaites, Reuben G. Editor. Jesuit Relations and Allied Documents, Volumes 59, 60, 64, 65, 66, 71. Cleveland, Ohio, The Burrows Brothers Company, 1896-1901.

Udden, J.A. "Geology and Mineral Resources of the Peoria Quadrangle, Illinois." United States Geological Survey, Bulletin 506. Washington, D.C., United States Government Printing Office, 1912.

White, Anne Terry. The American Indian. New York, Random House, 1963.

Wilson, Charles Banks. Compiler and Editor. Quapaw Agency Indians. 1947.

Chapters 5 through 7

Ackerman, William K. Early Illinois Railroads. Chicago, Illinois, Fergus Printing Company, 1884.

Alvord, Clarence W. Editor. Centennial History of Illinois. Springfield, Illinois, Illinois Centennial Commission, 1920.

Bateman, Newton. Editor. Historical Encyclopedia of Illinois, Volume 2. Chicago and Peoria, Illinois, Munsell Publishing Company, 1902.

The Brotherhood of American Yeoman. Peoria, Its Beauties and Advantages. Peoria, Illinois, 1923.

Brownson, Howard G. History of the Illinois Central Railroad. Urbana, Illinois, University of Illinois, 1915.

Buckingham, J.H. Edited by Harry E. Pratt. "Illinois as Lincoln Knew It." Papers in Illinois History and Transactions for the Year 1937. Springfield, Illinois, Illinois State Historical Society, 1938.

Business Directory of Peoria, Illinois. Place and publisher not given. 1909.

Caterpillar Tractor Company. Fifty Years on Tracks. Chicago, Illinois, Photopress, Inc., 1954.

City of Peoria City Clerk. The Heart of Illinois. Peoria, Illinois, City of Peoria, 1934.

Corliss, Carlton J. Trails to Rails. Chicago, Illinois, Illinois Central Railroad System, 1934.

Discover Illinois, Volume 1, no. 2, July, 1971, Salem, Illinois, Heritage Publications.

Donovan, Frank P., Jr. Mileposts on the Prairie. New York, Simmons-Boardman Publishing Corporation, 1950.

East, Ernest E. Scrapbook of articles on Peoria history clipped from newspapers.

Edwards, Harry. Compiler. Brown's Red Book and Classified Business Directory. Peoria, Illinois, B. Frank Brown, 1901.

272

Forsyth, Thomas. A True Account of the Expedition under Thomas E. Craig to Peoria, 1812. Madison, Wisconsin, Library of the Wisconsin Historical Society, 1812.

Franks, J.W. and Sons. Compiler. Michell Farm, Peoria, Illinois. Peoria, Illinois, J.W. Franks and Sons, undated.

Gardner, Ed. Rock Island Lines. Mountain Top, Pennsylvania, 1977.

Gates, Paul W. The Illinois Central Railroad. New York and London, Johnson Reprint Corporation, 1968.

Glenn, John M. "The Industrial Development of Illinois." Transactions of the Illinois State Historical Society, 1921. Springfield, Illinois, State of Illinois, 1921.

Goessl, Otto A. "The Street Railways of Peoria, Illinois." Electric Traction Quarterly. Wheaton, Illinois, Traction Orange Company, James D. Johnson, Publisher, 1963.

Grassels, Ernest. Scrapbooks of photographs. Transportation II and South Side III.

Greater Peoria Airport Authority. Air Growth. Peoria, Illinois, 1958.

Greater Peoria Airport Authority. Annual Report. Peoria, Illinois, 1952-1970.

Illinois in 1837. Published by S. Augustus Mitchell and Grigg and Elliot, Philadelphia, Pennsylvania, 1837.

Illinois Society of Engineers and Surveyors. Annual Report. Milwaukee, Wisconsin, S.E. Tate and Company, 1907.

Illinois State Historical Society. The Journal of the Illinois State Historical Society, Volume 8 (1915), Volume 17 (1924), Volume 24 (1931), Volume 29 (1936), Volume 45 (1952), Volume 51 (1958). Springfield, Illinois.

Inter-State Advertising and Excursion Company, Official Railway and Steamboat Timetables, 1896. Peoria, Illinois, 1896.

Jenkins, W.R. Publisher. Prosperous Peoria. 1924.

Johnson, Daniel M. and Veach, Rebecca M. Editors. The Middle-Size Cities of Illinois. Springfield, Illinois, Sangamon State University, 1980.

Kenyon, Theo Jean. Charter No. 176. Peoria, Illinois, The First National Bank of Peoria, 1963.

May, George W. Charles E. Duryea - Automaker. Ann Arbor, Michigan, Edwards Brothers, Inc., 1973.

McCulloch, David. "Early Days of Peoria and Chicago." An address read before the Chicago Historical Society. Chicago, Illinois, Chicago Historical Society, 1904.

McCulloch, David. "Old Peoria." Transactions of the Illinois State Historical Society, 1901. Springfield, Illinois, State of Illinois, 1901.

Mills, A.M., Andrew H. "1818-1918: A Hundred Years of Sunday School History in Illinois: A Mosaic." Transactions of the Illinois State Historical Society for the Year 1918. Springfield, Illinois, State of Illinois, 1918.

Morrow, Elise. "Peoria." Reprinted from the Saturday Evening Post, February 12, 1949, Philadelphia, The Curtis Publishing Company.

Nash, Francis D. City Clerk. City of Peoria Directory, 1937. Peoria, Illinois, 1937.

Oakford, Aaron W. The Aaron W. Oakford Collection, 34 volumes unpublished.

Peck, J.M. The Traveler's Directory for Illinois. New York, J.H. Colton, 1839.

Peoria and Pekin Union Railway Company. Peoria Gateway, 1980. Peoria, Illinois, Edward J. Smith Printers, 1980.

Peoria Area Chamber of Commerce. Directory of Manufacturers and Major Employers, Peoria Metropolitan Area. Peoria, Illinois, 1978 and 1980.

Peoria Association of Commerce. Golden Book. Peoria, Illinois, J.W. Franks and Sons, 1919.

Peoria Association of Commerce. Great Middle West. Peoria, Illinois, 1912.

Peoria Association of Commerce. Industrial Survey of Peoria, 1926. Peoria, Illinois, Schwab Print, 1926.

Peoria Civic Activities League, Newcomers Key to Peoria, 1952.

Peoria Civic Activities League. Newcomers Key to Peoria, Your Home Town. 1935.

Peoria Improvement Association. Peoria; Its Business, Its Resources, Its Attractions. Compiled by A.H. Rugg. Peoria, Illinois, H.S. Hill Printing Company, 1886.

Peoria, Illinois Air Trade Analysis. Fisher Associates, Inc., San Francisco, 1967.

Peoria Transcript. Peoria Illustrated 1893. Peoria, Illinois, 1893.

Peoria Journal Transcript. 1940-41 Classified Business and Professional Directory. Peoria, Illinois, 1940.

Rammelkamp, C.H. Editor. "The Memoirs of John Henry." The Journal of the Illinois State Historical Society, Volume 18, Part 1. Springfield, Illinois, Jefferson Printing Company, 1926.

Rennick, Percival G. "The Peoria and Galena Trail and Coach Road." The Journal of the Illinois State Historical Society, Volume 27, No. 4. Springfield, Illinois, 1935.

Roark, Leroy E. Industrial Peoria. Peoria, Illinois, J.W. Franks and Sons, 1924.

Smith, Arthur G. Peoria in the Eighties. Typed manuscript, 1944.

Soady, Fred P. "Time Was." A news release for Illinois Central College, 1974.

Stringham, Paul. Seventy-six Years of Peoria Street Cars. Chicago, Illinois, Electric Railway Historical Society, 1965.

Tri-County Regional Planning Commission. The Peoria Gateway. East Peoria, Illinois, 1977.

Wheeler, Estella M. The Geography of Peoria. A thesis for the degree of Master of Arts. Miami University, Oxford, Ohio, 1947.

Wooding, D.J. Publisher. State Manual and Pocket Business Guide of Peoria, Illinois. 1896.

Chapters 8 through 11

Amateur Musical Club. Seventy-Five Years of the Amateur Musical Club of Peoria. Peoria, Illinois, 1983.

Angle, Paul M. Bloody Williamson. New York, Alfred A. Knopf, 1952.

Bloom, Mariesta Dodge. The Song That Didn't Die. Peoria, Illinois, The Parthenon Press, 1959.

City Clerk of Peoria, Illinois. Historical Review of Peoria. Peoria, Illinois, 1975.

Cohen, Sol B. Years of Pilgrimage. Champaign, Illinois, The Mayfair Press, 1982.

Cooley, Adelaide N. A Biographical Dictionary of Peoria Artists. A typed manuscript, 1982.

Cooley, Adelaide N. The Monument Maker. Hicksville, New York, Exposition Press, 1978.

Cornstock Theatre 1954-1978, 25th Anniversary Book. Peoria, Illinois, Cornstock Theatre, 1978.

Fletcher, Alice C. Indian Games and Dances with Native Songs. Boston, C.C. Birchard and Company, 1915.

Garrett, Romeo B. The Negro in Peoria. A typed manuscript, 1973.

Illinois State Historical Society. The Journal of the Illinois State Historical Society, Volume 38 (1945) and Volume 47 (1954).

Kennerly, Carole F.R. A History of the Grand Opera House, Peoria, Illinois. A typed manuscript, 1978.

Lakeview Center for the Arts. Westward the Artist. Peoria, Illinois, 1968.

Lines, Louise S. A Short Study of Churches of All Faiths in Greater Peoria. A typed manuscript, 1956.

Marine, Don. A History of the Professional Stage Theatricals in Peoria, Illinois before the Civil War. A typed manuscript, 1972.

Miller, C.A. "Stretch." One Guy Called Me Stench. Bloomington, Illinois, Graphics, Inc., 1972.

Noonan, Rev. Daniel P. The Passion of Fulton Sheen. New York, Dodd, Mead and Company, 1972.

Peoria Area Jaycees. History of Peoria, Steamboat Days 1975. Peoria, Illinois, 1975.

Peoria Journal Star library files.

Peoria Journal Star Market Data.

Peoria Journal Star. "Illinois' Other Prime Market: Peoria." Peoria, Illinois, 1984.

Peoria Players. Peoria Players Theatre, 1919-1979. Peoria, Illinois, 1979.

Peoria Public Library. Newspaper clippings from subject files.

Peterson, Virgil W. Barbarians in Our Midst. Boston, Little, Brown, 1952.

Pollak, Bertha S. Evidences of Cultural Developments in Peoria, 1845-1963. Peoria, Illinois, Arts and Science Federation of Peoria, 1963.

Schapsmeier, Edward L. and Frederick H. Dirksen of Illinois. Urbana and Chicago, University of Illinois Press, 1985.

Sherman, Mrs. Nell. Peoria County Death Records 1837-1863. A typed manuscript, 1945.

Stevens, Asahel Augustus. The Future of Peoria in 1873 - A Sermon. Peoria, Illinois, Peoria Transcript Company, 1873.

Yates, Louis A.R. A Proud Heritage, Bradley's History. Peoria, Illinois, Observer Press, 1974.

273

Index